THE EUROPEAN NOBILITY IN THE
EIGHTEENTH CENTURY

European Culture and Society
General Editor: Jeremy Black

European Culture and Society Series
Series Standing Order
ISBN 0–333–74440–3
(*outside North America only*)

You can receive future titles in this series as they are published by placing a standing order. Please contact your bookseller or, in case of difficulty, write to us at the address below with your name and address, the title of the series and the ISBN quoted above.

Customer Services Department, Macmillan Distribution Ltd
Houndmills, Basingstoke, Hampshire RG21 6XS, England

THE EUROPEAN NOBILITY IN THE EIGHTEENTH CENTURY

Jerzy Lukowski

First published 2003 by
PALGRAVE MACMILLAN
Houndmills, Basingstoke, Hampshire RG21 6XS and
175 Fifth Avenue, New York, N.Y. 10010
Companies and representatives throughout the world

PALGRAVE MACMILLAN is the global academic imprint of the Palgrave Macmillan division of St. Martin's Press LLC and of Palgrave Macmillan Ltd. Macmillan® is a registered trademark in the United States, United Kingdom and other countries. Palgrave is a registered trademark in the European Union and other countries.

ISBN 0–333–65209–6 hardback
ISBN 0–333–65210–X paperback

This book is printed on paper suitable for recycling and made from fully managed and sustained forest sources.

A catalogue record for this book is available from the British Library.

Library of Congress Cataloging-in-Publication Data

Lukowski, Jerzy.
   The European nobility in the eighteenth century / Jerzy Lukowski.
      p. cm. – (European culture and society)
   Includes bibliographical references and index.
   ISBN 0–333–65209–6 – ISBN 0–333–65210–X (pbk.)
   1. Nobility–Europe–History–18th century. 2. Power (Social sciences)
   3. Europe–Economic conditions–18th century. 4. Europe–Social
   conditions–18th century. I. Title. II. Series.

HT653.E9L85 2003
305.5'223'09409033–dc21   2002044816

10   9   8   7   6   5   4   3   2   1
12   11   10   09   08   07   06   05   04   03

Typeset in Great Britain by
Aarontype Ltd, Easton, Bristol

Printed in China

CONTENTS

PREFACE

This book represents an attempt at a synthetic treatment of one of the most complex social phenomena of eighteenth-century Europe. While I have tried to provide as comprehensive a treatment as time and abilities allow, it does, as is almost inevitably the case with all such works, bear the particular stamp of its author's interests. These lie predominantly in the history of the Polish–Lithuanian Commonwealth. Anyone with any degree of familiarity with that recondite (to most Anglo-Saxon and western European readers) area of inquiry will be aware of the inescapable role and presence of its nobility, the *szlachta*. The peculiarities of this extraordinary group have long exercised Polish historians: virtually any historical textbook or monograph dealing with any aspect of early modern Polish history finds itself weighed down by their activities and attitudes. The moment a historian leaves Poland for other states and territories, the search for comparisons becomes inescapable. Hence the genesis of this book; I can only hope that readers do not feel that this author's hobby horse does not overwhelm his synthesising aspirations. If, on the other hand, it makes an exotic grouping more accessible and familiar, that can only give me cause for satisfaction.

In the aftermath of the Second World War, relatively little attention was given to the nobility of the eighteenth century by Anglo-Saxon scholars. Far more attention was paid to their inseparable companions, the peasantry. For a long time, the standard set of texts in English on the European nobilities were those in the compendium edited by Albert Goodwin, *The European nobility in the eighteenth century* (London: Black, 1953; 2nd edn, 1967). The majority of the essays in this wonderful volume have stood the test of time remarkably well and anyone with any interest in the subject can continue to profit from them. The trials, tribulations and triumphs, nuances and complexities of an extraordinarily long-lasting ruling group have inevitably attracted the attentions of

ever-widening groups of historians throughout Europe and America.
Since the 1960s and 1970s there has been a huge expansion of interest
and research into the subject, far too much for any single individual to
explore, even if the range of works under consideration were to be limited to those produced in English. To single out any one of the excellent
individual, local, regional or national studies for particular mention
from among the plethora of outstanding works by English-speaking historians (let alone their continental European confrères) would be foolish
and invidious. Nonetheless, surely few historians will begrudge drawing
particular attention to the outstanding two-volume collection edited by
Hamish Scott, *The European nobilities in the seventeenth and eighteenth centuries*
(Harlow: Longman, 1995), which brings together some first-rate international scholarship.

It is not my aim to compete with this. Nor is it my intention to go in
for any great degree of theorising. All efforts at a satisfactory, comprehensive typology of the nobility have failed to secure general approval
among historians; the only point of consensus seems to be an agreement
to differ. The nobility were too disparate, and often their activities too
much at variance with their proclaimed values and ethos, to permit any
easy schematisation. I have preferred to let the views (I hope) of (some)
contemporaries come through the text, for the purpose, nature and role
of the nobility was something that exercised them as much as it has any
historian. Contemporaries also had the inestimable advantage of knowing far more about themselves and their problems than any modern-day
scholar (though some might dispute this).[1]

This is a book aimed primarily at students, which seeks to bring out
some of the commonalities and differences of a non-democratic elite
grouping, most of whose members, despite their own view of themselves,
were very far from elite. Only the Balkans, under Ottoman rule, are
excluded, largely on pragmatic grounds: the author's own very limited
knowledge of the area, as well as a fear that dealing with a socio-political
structure and a cultural and religious context very different from that of
most of the rest of Europe would make the end product impossibly
unwieldy. Of course, a case for a significant 'otherness' can also be made
for any nobility. But most were united by a common culture of western
Latinity and similar institutional frameworks. The nobility of Russia
was something of an exception: but here there is no doubt that, over the
eighteenth century, more or less deliberate efforts were made by its
rulers and by many of its nobles to adopt a more 'European' persona.
That process is one of the most intriguing of the whole period.

The need to maintain their position and distinctiveness at a time when, at least in parts of western Europe, wealth and influence were becoming more accessible to ever-larger non-noble groups was an increasing problem for those already established within the nobility; it was particularly so for those who enjoyed the status, but lacked the means and resources. Nowhere was this more of a problem than in France, where some of the finest minds of the time grappled with what was to become of the *noblesse*. The agonisings of a Montesquieu or a Coyer were, in the end, swept aside by an unexpected revolution. For the first time since the nobility had emerged in the early Middle Ages, a question mark was placed over their very existence.

This book has built up over years of teaching students and conversing with colleagues. I trust that Peter Jones and Graeme Murdock will not object to being thanked for the help and stimulation that their company has provided me. I owe a great debt of gratitude to Jeremy Black for his kindness and support; and to my publishers, who have been more than generous in their patience. This kind of work is particularly open to error: I can only ask for readers' forbearance.

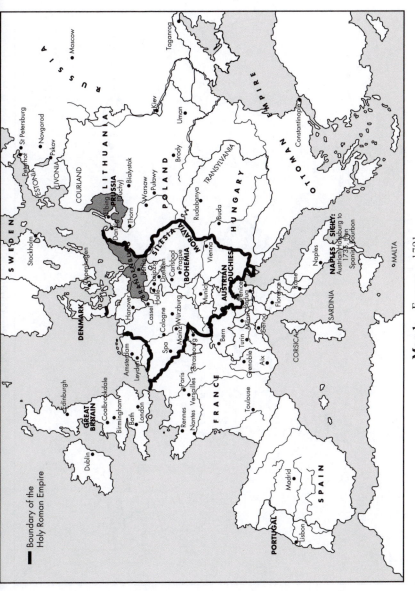

Map 1: Europe, *c.*1721

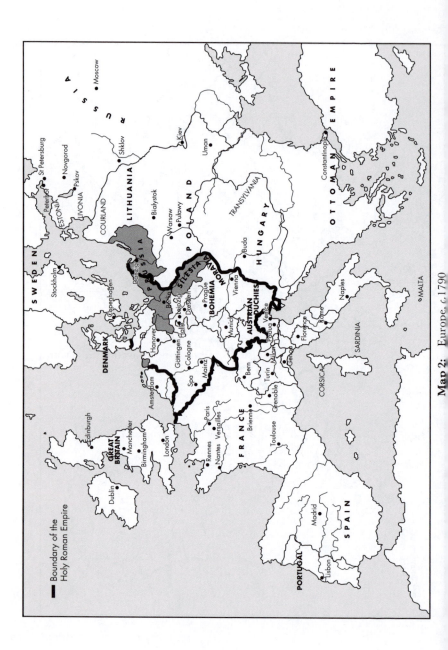

Map 2: Europe, c.1790

1

NOBILITY IN THE EIGHTEENTH CENTURY: AN INTRODUCTORY SURVEY

In 1765, an ennobled French lawyer was struggling to produce a comprehensive description of the terms *noble* and *noblesse* for that strange compendium of the informative and the subversive, Denis Diderot and Jean le Rond d'Alembert's *Encyclopédie*. The adjective *noble*, wrote Antoine-Gaspard Boucher d'Argis, was applicable to any person (or property) 'distinguished above the common, and graced with certain titles and privileges wherein resides the distinction of nobility'. A trifle vague, but at least it made the point that nobles stood above other men. Beyond that, the difficulties began to mount: in his pedantically heroic attempt to come to terms with an endlessly protean phenomenon, Boucher d'Argis listed at least 83 different categories of nobility to be found in France and neighbouring territories.[1] Almost a world away, as the eighteenth century began, Russia did not even have a native term for a nobility. Even in 1767 a grand commission of enquiry into Russia's laws admitted that it could not say what 'nobility' – *dvorianstvo* by then had become the usual term – comprised.[2]

With complexity and confusion came (and comes) terminological inexactitude. A 'gentleman', in a number of European languages, was synonymous with being a 'nobleman'. Or was he? The word 'gentleman', Dr Johnson pointed out, 'is used of any man however high' (that is, provided he was 'above the vulgar'). So it was equally applicable to gentry and peers – but to many others 'above the vulgar' besides. Those who were *gentiluomini* in Italy were merely owners of 'sufficient [landed] property to support themselves from its revenues'; by English standards,

1

they might be no more than yeomen or rich peasants.[3] In France, *gentil-homme* was matched by *noble* or *chevalier* or *seigneur*. In Germany, *Adel*, nobility, subdivided into *Herr* (lord), *Ritter* (knight) or *Junker* – the last largely applied to nobles of moderate means. In Poland, all nobles, *szlachta*, were *panowie*, a word which can be equally unsatisfactorily translated as 'gentlemen', 'rulers' or 'lords'; not unlike the German *Herren*, the term is so wide that it can be applied to territorial magnates or near-beggars who could carry off an appropriate front.

'Aristocracy' did not, strictly speaking, refer to a particular social group: it meant, literally, government by 'the best'. That indefatigable traveller and historian Archdeacon William Coxe could describe the Commonwealth of Poland–Lithuania as 'a state of perfect aristocracy' not because of its numerous nobility, but because of the near-untrammelled domination of that state by some two dozen great families. But he also spoke of the 'aristocratic licentiousness' that was destroying that state: aristocracy as a system was shading into a social grouping. For much of the eighteenth century, however, 'the best' meant the great landed nobility, who did indeed govern, and who would, at the very least, have been much put out to be informed that they were not 'the best'. The transformation was more than completed with the French Revolution, at least within France itself. Late in 1788, 'aristocrat' and 'aristocracy' established themselves as terms of opprobrium; and then, at the height of the Revolution, they could be used of all its enemies (real, imagined and contrived), not necessarily just nobles.[4]

Imprecision had long been to the fore in the concept of the three 'orders' or 'estates' of society – those who prayed, those who fought, those who laboured. If this notion of *oratores, bellatores et laboratores* was indeed first expounded by Aelfric of Eynsham in the tenth century, then it was an echo of an ancient formulation which reached back at least to Plato and Socrates in ancient Greece. But whether invoked by Athenian philosophers, medieval churchmen or French jurists, such taxonomy no more accurately described their societies than the convenient shorthand of 'lower', 'middle' or 'upper' class and similar designations in the nineteenth, twentieth or twenty-first centuries. The attempt by some Frenchmen during the Estates-General in 1789 to shoehorn reality into this ancient paradigm ended in spectacular disaster. No matter how much a hierarchical vision appealed to those who would rule, European society was too complex and too dynamic to be constrained by some predetermined mould. This has probably always been true. And in the eighteenth century, it was truer than ever before.

The absence of a clear legal distinction between the 'gentry' and their social inferiors might appear to have been a vagary of the British Isles, where distinctions were disguised (or distorted) by (landed) wealth qualifications: from 1711, county MPs had to own estates yielding rents of at least £600 per annum, borough MPs £300; game could not be shot by those owning land worth less than £100 a year, not even on their own farms. After 1732, Justices of the Peace had to have a landed income of £100 a year. All this at a time when over half the families in England were lucky to draw an annual income of £20–£30.[5] Disputes over whether gentry were or were not 'noble' in the 'European' sense are rather beside the point. Every European state had its own peculiarities. Most had a *de facto* or *de jure* division between a lesser, untitled nobility and an upper titled nobility of princes, dukes, counts or earls, marquises, barons and equivalents. In Britain this was represented by the peers, in France by the so-called *ducs et pairs*, in individual German states by the *Herrenstand* ('estate of lords') or *Hochadel* ('high nobility') as opposed to the *Ritterstand* ('the estate of knights') or the *Adel*, the ordinary, non-titled nobility. But since these lesser nobles sported what the French called the *particule*, a *de* or a *von* in their names, the way in which they styled themselves might still appear enormously impressive. Complex gradations, forming often bewildering sub-hierarchies, existed everywhere. Where representative or quasi-representative institutions, parliaments or 'estates' existed, the titled and non-titled nobility might, or might not, enjoy separate representation, in the manner of the Houses of Lords and Commons in England. The parliaments of Edinburgh (to 1707), Dublin or Westminster were simply a variation on the estate-style institutions found across much of Europe. By comparison with France or the territories of the Holy Roman Empire, they may have been unusual in operating at a national, rather than regional or local, level, but they were quite 'normal' by comparison with the *Riksdag* of Sweden, the *Sejm* of the Polish–Lithuanian Commonwealth, or the *Országgyűlés* of Hungary.

There was no lack of grey areas. Iberian *grandes* or *titulos* were generally wealthier and more powerful versions of *hidalgos* or *nobres* – but whether the former would really view many of the latter as the same social species is highly questionable. Russian *odnodvortsy*, owners of small farms and homesteads mainly resident in what had once been the southern marches of the Muscovite state, insisted that they were nobles; their status was never satisfactorily resolved. The same went for the 14,000 or so families of Hungarian *bocskoros* or 'sandalled nobles' (they could not afford shoes). An English 'gentleman' was clearly the equivalent of a continental 'nobleman' – if anything, in economic terms, probably his superior. On the European mainland, the differentials in wealth among those entitled to noble status tended to be more extreme since the legal status of noble was both widely diffused and, strictly speaking, independent of economic circumstances. An impoverished British provincial gentleman would slip into the ranks of yeomen or tenant farmers almost without fuss – gentility did not have a privileged legal status. But continental nobility mainly did, and those who possessed it were unwilling to lose it, no matter how dire their circumstances. *Krautjunker*, literally 'cabbage noble', gives some idea of the standing of those at the bottom of the heap in the territories of northern Germany and the Baltic lands of Estonia, Livonia and Courland. In Hungary and Poland, as in Spain and Portugal, in Russia and in much of Germany, thousands of families could genuinely call themselves noble, yet their economic circumstances were such as to leave them no better off, or even considerably worse off, than the local peasantry. Most European nobles were poor.

Truly wealthy nobles formed only a tiny minority. In late eighteenth-century England, 400 or so great landowning families, including the bulk of the 220 peers, enjoyed annual incomes of at least £5000. These were the 'poorest'. Around a dozen enjoyed incomes of between £40,000 and £50,000. Further down, incomes decreased inversely with numbers: around 700 families drew incomes of between £3000 and £4000 yearly, but between 3000 and 4000 lesser gentry made do with merely comfortable incomes of £1000–£3000; perhaps five times that number of families could still consider themselves gentry on less: those with incomes of between £300 and £700 shaded off into the better-off freeholders – some 25,000 of them, perhaps? In 1702, 32,000 land tax commissioners were appointed in England. Few, if any, would have been regarded as less than 'gentlemen'.[6] In the unusually prosperous Welsh county of Glamorgan, impoverished descendants of once substantial dynasties, clutching at rentals of £50 a year or so, might insist on styling themselves 'gentlemen', but contemporaries might equally regard them as yeomen, if that. The same individual might be described by both terms.[7]

A curious schizophrenia accompanied these differentials. At a theoretical level, most nobles in most countries affected to regard each other as, if not equals, then at least as good as one another. Few went as far as the Poles in openly proclaiming in law the equality of all nobles, but then, that legal equality was a practical fiction. Louis XVI of France and Gustavus III of Sweden regarded themselves as 'the first gentlemen' of their realms. George III played the role of the gentleman-farmer. Kings Stanisław Leszczyński and Stanisław Poniatowski of Poland were truly gentlemen in the sense that their noble equals had elected them kings of Poland. In reality, of course, rich nobles looked down on poor nobles. Yet rich nobles were ready to use the not-so-rich, or even court them, if their interests required; the latter reciprocated with suspicion and resentment, but also with collaboration, depending on the circumstances. The poorer the noble, the less able was he to assist in one of the principal roles of the nobility – ruling society. On the other hand, equality of noble legal status helped divide (and therefore rule) the economically inferior in general – for all its cracks and fissures, the great Chinese wall of status and distinction separated the poor and less well-off nobles from the great majority of poor and less well-off commoners.

The memory of glorious ancestral deeds, even if manufactured, engendered an additional dimension of solidarity among nobles in general. For all the arguments to the contrary, nobles preferred to see themselves as *bellatores*, if only in origin. Even those who, like Boucher d'Argis, tried to demonstrate that a civil, administrative and judicial nobility (as it was termed in France, a *robe* nobility) was as useful, if not more useful, to the state than that of the 'sword', had to concede that 'it is certain that this profession [of arms] was the first source of nobility'.[8] Accountants, barristers, notaries, clergymen – in France or elsewhere, such persons throughout most of Europe could find themselves in the ranks of the nobility, but, in the end, no profession, however worthy or necessary, was ever able to match that of arms for glamour. Even in England, with its established traditions of suspicion of large standing armies, the triumphs of the Seven Years War and the acquisition of empire were such that not even the humiliation of American independence could efface their impression. If, amid the successes against revolutionary and Napoleonic France, ordinary soldiers could not quite overcome the stigma of originating from the scum of the earth, the gentleman status of officers was assured. But the lustre of arms was a frothy one. Boucher d'Argis was right: the real importance of the nobility in the eighteenth century derived not from bearing arms but, as it long had done, from their role as partners to their rulers in government.

Most government was local government; and the dominance of the nobility in landownership meant that most governing was the responsibility of nobles, at least those of substance – though given the widespread presence of a poor nobility, not all nobles participated in the business of government. In Poland commoners had been forbidden to own land since 1469. This was extreme, unenforceable, but indicative of a general trend. A series of Prussian ordinances laid down that land owned by nobles (*Rittergüter*) could be sold to commoners only with the monarch's consent.[9] Swedish legislation sought to realise the same thing. Louis XIV's Ordinance of *Eaux et Forêts* of 1669 assumed as a matter of course that there could be 'no land without a *seigneur*' – that is, not only did land have to be owned, but its owner was invested with an array of public and judicial authority over it:[10] almost by definition, he partnered the state. Of course, in France not all seigneurs were noble. In most of western Europe, unlike so much of the east and centre, there was no ban on commoners, *roturiers*, purchasing land. Corporate ownership existed (the Church, municipalities, the state itself); commoners owned estates and exercised the jurisdictional panoply that went with them. But for a commoner to be a seigneur and landowner was also to have made a vital step towards the acquisition of noble status.

The monopoly on noble ownership or purchase of land, where it existed, was never enforceable. On the other hand, ownership of such land enabled the owner to 'live nobly', to facilitate his or his family's eventual legal recognition or *de facto* acceptance as nobles. As such, land-ownership only added to the security of the nobility. Even in England, where the feudal rights associated with landownership were more etiolated than almost anywhere else in Europe, ownership of a manor acted at least to enhance its owner's status as ruler of the local countryside. The manorial court (court baron, court leet – it had a variety of names) met in his name. Its jury might be elected by the village community, but it might also be picked by the lord of the manor or his representative. As one of the lowest rungs of judicial and administrative activity, the court not only ordered the work of the community, but it regulated village life in the lord's name, settled petty disputes, imposed and collected dues and fines on the lord's behalf.[11] Its continental equivalents exercised the same powers to a much greater degree, largely because feudal landlords were entitled to a wide range of dues and services from those who lived on the estate. It is small wonder that, given the amount of influence or jurisdiction at their disposal one way or another, the nobilities and landowners of England, or Poland, or Prussia were regularly described as 'little kings'.[12]

For most peasants in Poland and Russia, the right of appeal to higher authority beyond seigneurial jurisdiction did not exist; but where the state did begin to regulate and encroach on seigneurial powers, notably in the Austrian Habsburg lands, nobles still remained partners in government. The fruit of this partnership was the skewing of the institutional and political structures of Europe in favour of the nobility. The jurisdictional rights that so often went with landownership were only part of a huge panoply of privilege that raised nobles, in legal terms, above the common run of mankind. The defenders of privilege argued that it constituted a form of reward in return for services performed for the state, even if they had been rendered in the very dim past – the original concession had been for perpetuity and was thus a form of property, or contract. They maintained that privilege itself was a mechanism for ensuring the attachment of the social elite to the state and as such was essential to the preservation of government – that particular interpretation acquired its most elaborate and forceful expression in Montesquieu's European-wide best-seller, the *Spirit of the Laws*, in 1748.[13] Privilege was also a form of law – literally, private law. To undo it without the consent of the beneficiary, not least in a pre-revolutionary Europe where 'nothing had been abolished for over a thousand years', would be a form of illegality, even (depending on how hot under the collar an observer wished to become) a monstrous despotism – and would, of course, alienate the very persons on whom monarchs relied to govern.

There were two basic types of privilege: firstly, exemption from obligations that the rest of society had to bear; secondly, the conferral of positive benefits not accessible to others. The distinction between the two is somewhat artificial – the difference between a non-taxpayer's benefit and exemption might be rather lost on a taxpayer. Privilege, in whatever form, was rarely the preserve of the nobility alone. On the other hand, nobles were generally associated with privilege and were generally better placed to exploit it than commoners. The most important exemption privileges were fiscal, but even so, few nobles anywhere escaped being taxed altogether and, as the eighteenth century drew on, more and more of them found themselves at least notionally subjected to ever-increasing amounts of tax. It was very difficult to avoid indirect taxation. Governments resorted to it precisely in order to outflank exemptions from direct taxation. Even where provision for a degree of exemption from indirect taxation existed (Polish nobles were exempted from duties on imports for their personal or domestic use; French nobles could sell wine from their own home farms free of duties) it was rarely, if ever, a blanket exemption. What nobles could do, of course, was to utilise their position, connections and authority to abuse these concessions, going beyond the spirit and the letter of the law, or shifting the burden onto peasants and tenants, all in a manner of which the most enthusiastic twenty-first-century tax evaders and avoiders would whole-heartedly approve.

Certain taxes were deemed particularly odious. Thus, in France, the *taille*, the direct tax on land, was much resented, as a tax originally levied by landowners on their own peasantry – but many nobles were still obliged to pay it. English landowners grumbled at the land tax, but at least they, or their own kind, had voted for it in parliament, and their own kind collected it and generally ensured that its burden was not as heavy as it should have been. The further the landowners were from London, the less reliable (and lighter) the assessments to which they were subjected. The Polish nobility grumbled at the *pogłówne*, the head or poll tax, as 'unbecoming to the noble estate', but they too had voted for it. By contrast, the French nobility accepted their poll tax, the *capitation*, even though it came by royal fiat, but then they managed to get it watered down. Russian nobles could not pay the *podushnaia podat'*, the soul tax, for it was literally a fiscal mark of servitude. It was paid instead by those who performed *tiaglo*, heavy-duty labour services on the land or service obligations in towns.

On the other hand, distinctive privilege was difficult to restrict to the nobility, if only because it was aped by so many non-nobles. In most continental states, only nobles had the right openly to carry a sword – yet they almost universally complained that this was being copied by the bourgeoisie. Such imitation, of course, was an implicit tribute to the nobility, a guarantee of social stability, betokening a wish to join them. Sumptuary laws, supposedly in force since the Middle Ages, aiming to regulate dress, apparel and accoutrements appropriate to particular social groups were largely a waste of time. Commoners who wished to pass themselves off as nobles had no scruples in manufacturing fictitious pedigrees and coats of arms, another supposed noble preserve (not that nobles were any less guilty in this respect). In England, the right of peers and gentry to display their coats of arms may have signalled who or what they were, but this honorific distinction was, in itself, little regarded. There were, after all, 9458 such families in Britain in 1798 – but the Office of Arms had given up any serious efforts to check up on entitlements to display heraldic crests as long ago as 1686.[14]

Positive privilege found concrete expression in corporate bodies and organisations specifically reserved for nobles. They were most common in Catholic countries, where the Reformation had failed to sweep away foundations and benefices erected for the nobility. Only nobles could become bishops and prelates in Poland, save for a few cathedral canonries. Likewise, in Germany, places in cathedral chapters were specifically reserved for nobles. Where such formal prohibitions did not exist, they could be enforced almost as effectively informally. Of 240 appointments to French bishoprics made between 1700 and 1774, only 9 were commoners; of 192 appointments between 1774 and 1790, only 2 went to commoners − no commoners held bishoprics at all in 1789.[15] A lucratively endowed ecclesiastical apparatus was a godsend for grappling with that most vexatious of problems, supernumerary sons and daughters. The survival of women's monastic orders in Catholic states enormously facilitated the honourable (and cheap) disposal of excess females.

Protestant landowners frequently retained the right of presentation to livings. Entry into the ranks of the parish clergy, an acceptable career for younger sons in England (where just under half of parishes lay in the gift of country landowners), was less so on the Protestant continent (or, for that matter, in Wales and Scotland), where the generally impoverished incomes attached to parish livings hardly carried the same cachet as well-endowed Catholic cathedral canonries. In Sweden, though many sons of bishops became ennobled, the nobility did not reciprocate by being attracted into the bishoprics on any scale.[16] Had the Swedish church not suffered from massive sequestrations of land under the early Vasa kings, the situation may well have been different − nobles usually found a rationale for tapping into wealth-generating resources.

The greatest privilege was exclusivity − something enjoyed by as few people as possible. This was above all the domain of the English nobility: clearly defined and clearly limited, everyone knew who the peers were. True, it was easier to become an English peer than to become a Venetian patrician, but it was still far more exclusive than the Venetian Republic's Maggior Consiglio, simply because the House of Lords had a much smaller membership. There were 163 peers in 1700, 267 by 1800. By contrast, the Maggior Consiglio, whose membership was open only to the patriciate, had 1710 members in 1718 and 1090 in 1797. The House of Lords may have been expanding, the Great Council contracting, but there was no doubt which had the greater prestige, even before France and Austria killed off Venetian independence at the peace of Campo Formio in October 1797.[17] Apart from their numerical exclusivity, the members of the English or British peerage derived comparatively few privileges from their legal status. If they were entitled to trial by a jury of their peers in criminal cases, so were most Englishmen (whereas, on the continent, juries were rarely found). They were exempt from arrest in civil proceedings, especially debt (after 1711, their servants lost exemption from arrest for debt); they were entitled to punitive damages if slandered (though this privilege of *scandalum magnatum* had fallen into disuse); they were entitled to direct access to the king. They enjoyed the automatic right to participate in the councils and judicial processes of the realm, inasmuch as these were represented by membership of the House of Lords (admittedly, Catholic peers did not take up their seats). They were not only few, but they were constitutionally locked into the processes of government. Likewise, if peers enjoyed residual jurisdictional rights over their properties, then that was something they shared with thousands of non-peers – the gentry. By the standards of the twenty-first century, such perquisites seem intolerable; by the standards of the eighteenth, they were insignificant.

With the conjunction of wealth, land and authority went lineage – real or manufactured. For lineage brought continuity and continuity betokened, no matter how illogically, respectability, an attachment to the land, a place in the natural order of things. In fact, comparatively few eighteenth-century nobles could genuinely claim noble origins from before 1600, but those who could do so, or whose nobility was accepted as ancient even if no formal proofs were available, might well be entitled to privileges and perquisites not open to the 'reproach' (Boucher d'Argis) of more recent ennoblement; and access to such privileges only reinforced the prestige of these ancient, even immemorial, pedigrees. What counted for these people was not so much the family as family, but the family as the 'House', a veritably dynastic enterprise, Edmund Burke's 'partnership not only between those who are living, but between those who are living, those who are dead, and those who are yet to be born'.[18] This hierarchical ordering of society could only begin to change when society as a whole came to be convinced that a largely hereditary hierarchy was not the natural order of things. And when, eventually, the revolutionary new French state overturned such a hierarchy, for many it served only to confirm that without hierarchy, civilised life was impossible.

The indefeasible right to rule others, even if the extent of that right increasingly existed more in the mind than in law, naturally bred feelings of superiority, most deeply expressed in the elusive notion of noble honour. Honour might cover everything from the punctilious discharge of one's social and political obligations (which is how Diderot attempted to describe it, with disturbing inadequacy, in his article 'Honneur' in the *Encyclopédie*)[19] to a mindless contempt for others, going beyond mere snobbery. Its ultimate manifestation was private violence. Personal courage and the readiness to lay down one's life or suffer wounding, the primal *raison d'être* of nobility, was demonstrated in the individual combat of the duel. Duels, fought in defiance of legislation banning them, which had been enacted and repeated since the middle years of the seventeenth century, were a signal manifestation of private noble jurisdiction and independence. One should be cautious in following this line of argument. It may have a sociological or psychological rationale, but ultimately it was the recourse of persons who felt themselves to be above the law. Of course, duels were for equals only, a lesson that Voltaire learned the hard way in 1726. Guy-Auguste, chevalier de Rohan-Chabot, scion of one of the greatest of French families, much resented the esteem the upstart writer enjoyed, not least at the royal court. After a mutual name-calling session (provoked by Rohan) at the opera and the theatre, the chevalier had Voltaire beaten up by thugs while he looked on from his coach. No-one, not least his few social equals, much liked the thoroughly unpleasant Rohan and it was gener-ally agreed that he had gone further than he should have. But Voltaire earned little sympathy – given his station in life, he should have swal-lowed Rohan's rarefied insults without meeting like with like. There could be no question of judicial proceedings against the chevalier. No-one condemned Rohan for his contemptuous rejection of a challenge to a duel from his aggrieved inferior ('the man's only a poet' expostu-lated Marshal Villars). It was Voltaire, the victim, who was clapped in the Bastille in preventive arrest (rumour had it he was intending to commit the appalling social solecism of hiring his own thugs to beat up Rohan), from which he was released only on the understanding that he would remove himself to England.[20]

The Voltaire–Rohan encounter was an exception, a *cause célèbre*, but it underscored the unpleasant reality of a society of orders, in which one order felt itself by its very nature above the rest. A Prussian writer com-plained in 1791 that officers (almost exclusively noble), in dispute with civilians, were far more likely to give them a good thrashing than go to law.[21] Polish magnates were not above beating up town councillors in public. In 1759, the empress Elizabeth of Russia felt impelled to order the imprisonment of Darya Saltikova, who had distinguished herself by torturing to death over 100 female peasants on her estate.[22] Saltykova was obviously psychotic, but the leaders of a hierarchical Europe preferred not to take sanctions against the misdemeanours of their own kind, save in the most extreme circumstances. Even in Eng-land, the execution of Laurence Shirley, fourth earl of Ferrers, in 1760 for the sadistic murder of his steward stemmed more from an appreciation by his peers that they had to show an occasional example than from any real desire to visit his just deserts on him. The determination to uphold the image of aristocratic justice extended even to refusing Ferrers an aristocratic death by beheading: instead, the noble lord was treated like a common criminal and hanged (though he had the honour to be the first to have been executed by the new 'drop' method). Ferrers's death was literally a class act: he had himself driven to his place of execution at Tyburn in a landau and six. But Ferrers was very much the exception. In the British Isles as much as in continental Europe, 'the arrogant attitude to the law taken by the sons and daughters of the elite demonstrated that they were in no doubt that they were above it'.[23] Since the law so often discriminated in their favour, tacitly or openly, such arrogance was hardly surprising.

While those who stood above others liked to think of themselves, by definition, as superior and liked to think of themselves in caste-like terms, consciously closed off from the rest of the population, the deliberate, systematic exclusion of outsiders was infrequent. It was most notably found in parts of Italy – Genoa, Lucca or Venice. Where nobles were very few in number, such exclusivity normally came at a heavy demographic price. Genoa, which boasted 289 noble families in 1621, was down to 128 in 1797; Lucca's nobility fell from 249 to 88 families over roughly the same period. Denmark's nobility, down to around 80 families in 1720 from some 180 families in 1600, were saved by fresh creations by the monarchy, bringing the number of Danish noble families up to 215 by 1800.[24] By the end of the eighteenth century, the nobility of the Dutch Republic were on the verge of biological extinction (the new, nineteenth-century monarchy was created in time to ward off such an ignoble fate).[25]

Nobles were both few and numerous. In 1789, the abbé Emmanuel Joseph Sieyès's estimate of 110,000 in a French population of 28 million, or one noble for every 255 inhabitants, is regarded by many historians as an acceptable figure. It was, however, in the interests of the blistering anti-noble polemic contained in his *Qu'est-ce le Tiers État?* (*What is the Third Estate?*) to minimise the number. Yet even if Sieyès's figure is doubled or quadrupled, as it plausibly can be, the French nobility remain a tiny minority. Similar, if not more extreme, ratios existed in Prussia, Russia, the Italian states. On the other hand, in Hungary, Portugal, Spain and Poland nobles accounted for at least 6 per cent of the population – according to some estimates in Poland, as high as one

in ten. The eighteenth century had its censuses, but nobles were generally exempt from them (they tended to be aimed at certain tax-paying
sectors of the population). The figures are almost always irritatingly in
dispute, and the disputes are much more than sterile debates over numbers. An estimate of 120,000 nobles for France (say, 25,000 families)
(Guy Chaussinand-Nogaret's – roughly the same as Sieyès's) posits a
nobility that is very different to that implied by alternative estimates of
315,000 (Jean Meyer) or 400,000 (Vivian Gruder, Rohan Butler). The
first estimate is used by its author to portray a dynamic, rapidly expanding, relatively 'open' nobility, the latter, larger estimates to paint an
altogether more conservative picture. Both figures can, of course, be
interpreted in other, even diametrically opposite, ways.[26] But whatever
territory is chosen, whatever their absolute numbers, nobles almost
invariably formed a small, even tiny, minority (Spain's Basque provinces were an exception). And where nobles were in relative terms
numerous, the great bulk of them were poor, open to the contempt of
their wealthy confrères. In 1803, the count of São Lourenço grumbled
that within the space of a few years, Portugal's 3 million inhabitants
'have become three million nobles; to-day, the greatest distinction that
can exist is that of not being a noble . . .'. In fact, the *nobreza* numbered
'only' some 6 or 7 per cent of the population – still far too high for a
titled grandee.[27]

It can be a misleading shorthand to pin nobles down in terms of
'national' categories during a century which only began to invent nation-
alism towards its end. For those in a position to make use of it, there
was European-wide scope for geographical mobility. The Order of the
Knights of St John of Jerusalem (more usually known as the Knights of
Malta) existed to fight Turkish and Barbary infidels at sea and provide
Catholic younger sons of whatever nation, but of proven ancient aristocratic lineage, with the opportunity to gain prestige and escape from the
doldrums of being younger sons. It was, of course, unnecessary to belong
to a formal international body. The ability to speak French, to a lesser
extent German or Italian or Latin, virtually guaranteed those with such
mastery entry into a cosmopolitan world. After all, to nobles like
Montesquieu, 'Europe is a state made up of several provinces'.[28]

Dear Boy
You will now, in the course of a few months, have been rubbed at three
of the considerable Courts of Europe – Berlin, Dresden and Vienna;
so that I hope you will arrive at Turin tolerably smooth, and fit for

the last polish ... I send you ... a letter of recommendation to Monsieur Capello, at Venice ... a letter of recommendation to the Duke of Nivernois, the French Ambassador at Rome ... Monsieur and Madame Fogliani will, I am sure, show you all the politeness of Courts ...[29]

To the youthful Philip Stanhope in 1749, all the best doors in Europe were open – not just because his father, the earl of Chesterfield, knew so many of the best people, but because he was a grandee. In 1754, as exotic a personage as Stanisław Poniatowski found a welcome in the greatest houses in England, thanks to the recommendations of Sir Charles Hanbury Williams, Britain's ambassador to the king of Poland.[30] Prussia and Russia were exceptional in banning their nobles from foreign travel save by express permission of the ruler. In Russia, this restriction was informally lifted after 1762, formally in 1785. In Prussia, it was tacitly dropped only in 1794. Nobles living in Alsace (French-ruled) might find it just as convenient, if not more so, to serve German princes or the Habsburgs, or take advantage of lucrative German *in commendam* abbacies or canonries in Basel, Würzburg, Eichstädt and other ecclesiastical centres.[31] Analogous situations had long been found in many border zones, often encouraged by family ties. The composite structure of dynastic agglomerations encouraged service between territories, in the case of the Austrian Habsburgs producing a quite distinctive Bohemian–German–Hungarian elite. But similar hybrids emerged wherever very different territories came together under common rule: Saxony and Poland under the Wettin elector kings, the Spanish and Austrian Habsburg ties to Italy. The British–Hanoverian connection was something of an exception, for there was very little social or even political mixing of its ruling circles. Britain may not have called much on the elites of Hanover, but, in the first half of the eighteenth century, French Huguenot refugees enriched its commercial, financial and military activities. And England certainly made use of the elites of Scotland and Ireland. Even so, Britain was probably a net loser: talented Jacobite expellees, younger sons and hard-up adventurers found their way to leading positions in Spain, France, Russia, Prussia, Austria.

Assimilation might take two or three generations, but noble migrants played a visible role across Europe. Within the Holy Roman Empire, there was a constant circulation of nobles and notionally autonomous Imperial Knights between states. Assimilation often took the form of adopting the ruling religion – Catholic states, headed by the Habsburgs, were by and large the beneficiaries. Of the 157 field marshals in Austrian Habsburg service in the eighteenth century, 77 came from beyond the Habsburg lands.[32] The Russian, Scandinavian and Polish lands around the Baltic offered a plethora of opportunities to ambitious Germans. And others, of course . . . How long would Italians cravenly grovel after service with German rulers, Frederick the Great wished to know of the Italian Girolamo, marquis of Lucchesini, in 1780? 'For as long as the Germans are stupid enough to employ them', came the answer. Hired on the spot, Lucchesini went on to become Prussia's premier diplomat. The more modest contribution of the Irish Lynch family, furnishing magistrates to the *parlement* of Bordeaux (even if their 'nobility' was somewhat dubious),[33] was more typical of such diasporas, but there were few territories in Europe that did not benefit in a very visible way from such arrivals and adventurers. Not being of noble birth was not necessarily an obstacle to such geographic mobility; but noble origins and family connections facilitated introductions and opened doors.

For most of the century, insofar as there was an obvious threat to the nobility, it was limited and more likely to come from above than below, from monarchs who wished to constrain their nobles, not abolish them. In 1660, in an event almost forgotten outside Scandinavia but which caused an immense impression on contemporaries, King Frederick III of Denmark had overturned the ruling noble oligarchy to assume almost untrammelled royal powers (insofar as it was possible for royal powers to be untrammelled): yes, he had the support of the clergy and of commoners; yes, he greatly restricted noble privileges; but no, he did not abolish the nobility. And so it was elsewhere. Governments could spectacularly assert themselves against errant nobles. Philip V of Spain, mistrusting the grandees for their apathy or support of his defeated Habsburg rival, Charles 'III', inaugurated a policy of excluding them from the central councils of government and keeping them on their estates and bypassing their local influence through directly appointed royal bureaucrats.[34] After 1746, in the wake of Bonnie Prince Charlie's doomed rebellion, the British parliament pushed through the suppression of private jurisdictions and heritable sheriffdoms in Scotland. On 13 January 1759, Portugal's duke of Aveiro and the marquis of Tavora Velho were publicly broken on the wheel, before their mangled and still sentient remains were burned alive and the ashes thrown into the sea – but then, they had been found guilty of hatching an assassination plot against King Joseph I (other members of their families received marginally less savage executions).[35] These measures against nobles, rebellious or just recalcitrant, were, of course, often endorsed and backed by nobles in power and acquiesced in by the rest. It was the duty of the nobility to support the state and the monarchy, not to rebel or intrigue against it. None of these measures amounted to an outright assault on the nobility as such. Even in the Scottish case − an eradication of privilege of an intensity rarely seen in Europe − nobles and gentry were being brought into line with their English counterparts. It was essentially regional liberties and privileges in Catalonia, Aragon and Valencia that were cut back by Philip V after the War of the Spanish Succession, rather than those associated directly with nobles.[36]

At a more mundane level, however, real tensions between nobles and monarchs or ministers existed and were on the increase in many European states. It was not only Polish or Hungarian nobles who fretted that strong monarchy was a foe to liberty. Montesquieu's great articulation in 1748, in his *Spirit of the Laws*, of nobility as a necessary restraint on monarchy found a ready echo in France, where clashes between the crown and the judicial nobility were long established and grew in intensity as the century progressed. Joseph II's radical social and political experiments so alienated his nobles that, at his death in 1790, the Austrian Habsburg monarchy was on the verge of revolt, perhaps even disintegration. For as rulers sought to make their governments more efficient, as they pursued the goal of 'the well-ordered police state', they found themselves entangled in a contradiction: on the one hand they needed their nobles to help them govern; on the other, the extent of noble privilege all too often got in the way of good government.

Slow, gradual extinction, rather than violent eradication, seemed more of a long-term problem in some states, but it was nothing that an infusion of fresh blood could not remedy. Around 1780, most nobles probably thought their position as a ruling order seemed as secure as ever. Only perhaps in Sweden, where a combination of demographic crisis among the nobility (so many males had been killed in Charles XII's war against Russia) and the existence of a highly professionalised bureaucracy which conveyed status without ennoblement helped diminish the attractions of noble status by the end of the century.[37] Even where local elites were non-noble, they enjoyed a quasi-noble status. In the more heavily urbanised provinces of the Dutch Republic, in the larger cities of the Holy Roman Empire or of Switzerland, burgher elites functioned as a kind of nobility (in terms of wealth and influence) that did not require formal ennoblement (this was, of course, how many Italian urban patriciates had become 'ennobled' − by regarding themselves as nobles and being accepted as such). A Europe without nobles was inconceivable, if only because so many of those who were not nobles, or as the abbé Sieyès might have put it, so many of those who were 'NOTHING', wished to join those who were 'SOMETHING' – the nobility. But the question of survival only became critical after the unexpected explosion of the French Revolution. To the nobles themselves, the main issues of the century found reflection in the extended pedantry of a Boucher d'Argis and his numerous kind: Were some nobles better than others? How and why could one become ennobled? And if one was a noble, how best could one maintain that status?

2

ENNOBLEMENT

'It is well-known that a thing loses its value as soon as wide use is made of it. Could gentry dignity retain the fullness of its lustre when its inherent authority is spread among so many?'[1] This same rhetorical question, posed during discussions inside Catherine the Great's Legislative Commission in 1767, could just as easily have been asked (and often was) almost anywhere in Europe. The infusion of new blood may have been helpful in keeping the nobility in existence; but that did not mean that nobles were at all welcoming towards newcomers. In Britain, the creation by Queen Anne of 12 new peers in December 1711 provoked a general outcry. The royal physician, Sir David Hamilton, was moved to remonstrate with her at such unbecoming largesse.[2] William Pitt the Younger caused similar consternation when he persuaded George III in 1784 to create 11 new peerages, almost at one fell swoop. One of the most distasteful aspects (to Scots at any rate) of the aftermath of the 1707 Act of Union with Scotland was the ruling, in December 1711, barring Scots peers who also held English peerages from using those English peerages to sit in the House of Lords. The so-called 'Hamilton judgement' was not to be reversed until June 1782. On the other hand, the attempt by a majority of the Lords in 1719 to place formal restrictions on the size of their number (it would have been fixed at its then size of 209) was furiously rejected by the Commons, who feared 'the shutting the door upon [their] family ever coming into the House of Lords'.[3]

One of the strongest attractions of nobility was psychological – the sense of exclusivity, of being not as others; and the more 'others' that were admitted into noble ranks, the more that feeling of exclusivity was threatened. In an age during which governments looked increasingly to paperwork, and, for the nobility, to documentary evidence of their status, this touched some very raw nerves. For while nobles might glory in their claims to ancient pedigree or title, and imagine their forbears among ancient Trojans, Etruscans, Romans, Goths, Alemans, Sarmatians and others, documentary proofs of original noble status were harder to come by. Of course, it was mainly poor nobles whose paperwork was lacking or unconvincing who were degraded to commoner status during Louis XIV's 'reformations' of the French nobility.

Nobility was as much a mental construct as a legal one, often more so. Most lesser nobles and many great ones owed their status as much to tradition as to any specific original act of elevation. Sweden's nobility up to and for much of the sixteenth century largely consisted of those who could afford to perform cavalry service in wartime: formal patents of ennoblement only began to be issued from the 1520s. Thousands of Polish petty nobles were originally peasants ennobled not by individual patents but by blanket grants by Polish kings during the fifteenth and sixteenth centuries, in order to smooth the reincorporation of old fiefs into Polish territory. In the Pomeranian provinces of Prussia, many, perhaps most, of the numerous 'Cabbage-nobles' were descended from peasants who had simply assumed the surname of their ancient seigneurs. Whole provinces in northern Spain were ennobled, or their inhabitants claimed they had been ennobled, during the course of the medieval Reconquista. All over the continent, petty 'nobles' owed their status to such fortuitous circumstances.

Poverty did not deter such nobles from resisting dilution by social 'inferiors'. Many of the indigent *hidalgos* who peopled Spain's Basque provinces had to resort to manual trades to keep body and soul together. When, in 1692, Charles II's government settled Flemish workers there to boost arms and munitions production in the workshops of the region, the newcomers found themselves subjected to massive harassment and discrimination from the local *hidalguia*. In 1712, Philip V tried to confer protection on the Flemings by equalising their rights and privileges with those of the local majority: he conferred *hidalgo* status on them all. The quarrels became even more inflamed, rumbling on for at least another 50 years, with the 'old' *hidalgos* denying the right of the crown to confer noble status on those not entitled to it by blood and the crown resorting to fines and imprisonments to keep the old nobles in place. It was often impossible to know (let alone 'prove') who was noble, who was not. As far as the crown was concerned, the status of *hidalgo* was so widespread that it might as well have been equated with that of commoners.[4]

Bickering over status erupted almost wherever large concentrations of petty nobles were found – their 'status', usually ignored or despised by their own governments, was all that differentiated them from the peasantry, who might well in economic terms be their equals or even superiors. But who was qualified to ennoble? In most cases it was the ruling head, but not always. Key corporate institutions might do so. This was the case in individual Italian territories, particularly where there was a strong republican or communal tradition, even if republican rule was a distant memory. In Milan, Genoa, Lucca and Venice a range of diverse municipal and oligarchic institutions, dominated by nobles, regulated entry into the noble patriciates, though the nobility of many of these owed their origin more to repute than to any formal creation. Just to be on the safe side, nobles living in Italian states under Spanish or Austrian rule often preferred to secure formal confirmation of their status from their royal masters. Throughout much of Italy the situation was made fiendishly complex by the existence of urban and non-urban, metropolitan and non-metropolitan nobilities side by side in the same state (Venice, Tuscany, the Papal State). Thus, after 1775, would-be newcomers to the Venetian nobility had to have not only an annual income of 10,000 ducats, but also to show four generations of noble descent.[5] In Milan, entry into the exclusively noble patriciate was regulated by the Collegio dei Conservatori degli Ordini (though after 1768 the nobilities of Milan and Mantua came under closer Habsburg scrutiny via the new Office of Heralds).[6]

Such formal, corporate endorsement was found elsewhere. In the vast agrarian republic that was the Commonwealth of Poland–Lithuania, from 1601 only Poland's parliament, the *Sejm*, could ennoble. There was, however, an arresting exception: since 1588, Jews who converted to Christianity in the Grand Duchy of Lithuania received automatic ennoblement, provided they lived a noble lifestyle. They did not need to refer to the *Sejm*. In practice, the custom extended to Poland proper, although it is impossible to say how many Jewish families were thus elevated. When the measure was finally repealed in 1764, the *Sejm* promptly went on to confirm conferral of nobility on 50 converted Lithuanian Jews.[7] In the more regular course of events in Poland, between 1601 and 1764, 366 commoners were ennobled, plus 183 foreigners (many of whom had claims to foreign nobility anyway). At least 420 parliamentary ennoblements followed between 1768 and 1775 (though many of these involved confirmations of supposedly long-established noble status and most took place in the extraordinary confusion and coercion attendant on the first Polish Partition). In three extraordinary weeks during November 1790, the Polish parliament sanctioned about another 400 ennoblements, half of them military (otherwise, the bulk of those made between 1764 and 1775 were civilian elevations). In practice, most of these ennoblements, except perhaps those of 1790, were mainly inspired by the monarch. In Sweden, another 'republic of noblemen' during its *frihitsted*, its 'Age of Liberty' between 1720 and the monarchist coup of 1772, the king was allowed to make only a few token ennoblements at his coronation: otherwise, ennoblement had to be approved by the executive state council and the parliament, the *Riksdag* (though here, as in Poland, parliament normally went along with the king's recommendations).

Of the more important European states, only the Dutch Republic lacked a noble-creating mechanism, possibly because of the chronic mistrust that existed between the towns and the premier noble family of Orange. That rivalry apart, had the 'regents' who governed Dutch towns wished, they could doubtless have set up the same sort of noble-creating machinery that some of the Italian city states had done. By the later eighteenth century, a kind of informal ennoblement (again, reminiscent of much of Italy) was under way among many of the republic's patrician-regents.[8]

Nowhere, perhaps, was formal ennoblement harder to come by than in Venice. In 1718, the nobility of the Venetian patriciate counted 1710 males over the age of 25: only these were qualified to sit in the Maggior Consiglio and hold public office. But the decline in the number of Venetian nobles had long caused concern about filling public offices: the notorious reluctance of older-established Venetian families to allow newcomers access to the most crucial 30 or so posts within the government and administration acted as a deterrent to potential incomers. The 1775 decision to recruit more members to the noble patriciate secured only 11 new recruits (at least 40 had been hoped for) before the overthrow of the republic by French forces in 1797. Ironically, many eligible mainland families with four generations of nobility in their own right would not consider putting themselves forward for consideration, not just because they had no doubts as to their own nobility, but because they looked down on many of those 'new' nobles who had managed to squeeze into the Venetian patriciate after 1646, when a fresh tranche of ennoblements, the first since 1381, had been agreed. Between then and 1775, approved newcomers did not have to show noble ancestry, but they did have to put up an entry fee of 100,000 ducats. In 1789, Lodovico Manin was elected doge. He was the richest man in Venice with a personal annual income of at least 80,000 ducats. He belonged to the first 'new', post-1646 family ever to hold the office. His forbears were counts from Friuli admitted to the Venetian patriciate 'only' in 1651. A disappointed rival of less impeachable pedigree grumbled, 'They have made a Friulian doge: the Republic is dead.'[9] The snobbery and complexes that went with nobility almost inevitably provoked such absurdities, but what the Venetian patriciate was doing was not so unusual. If long-established nobles felt themselves threatened by influxes of newcomers, they reacted by endowing in their own minds their own, longer-established nobility with 'superior', more numinous qualities. There were many nobles, but some were better than others.

Many monarchs were prepared to use ennoblement with little discrimination, as a cheap, convenient psychological device to reward loyal service and, indeed, to help give significant numbers among the economically poor a psychological stake in the maintenance and preservation of the social hierarchy. Those who complained at the scale of ennoblements may have feared the etiolation of their order, but to perceptive, or cynical, monarchs it was a way of buttressing social norms, not weakening them. In Spain, Charles II or Philip V were quite ready to confer and confirm mass grants of ordinary nobility; but those whom they truly wished to honour received grants of titled nobility. Philip V created over 200 of these to reward his bureaucrats and ministers.[10]

It was perfectly possible to 'acquire' nobility by fraud (or, closely related, by repute – much of the eighteenth-century nobility of Italy was noble because it had long been reputed such) – it was even normal. No-one can really say how widespread the practice was in France or Poland or Spain, where some of the loudest complaints were heard. Even in Prussia, two outstanding noble military reformers of the Napoleonic era, Hans David Ludwig von Yorck and August Wilhelm Neidhardt von Gneisenau, had such dubious antecedents. If such usurpation could happen in Prussia, then it could probably happen anywhere. And even in Prussia, the General Law Code, the *Allgemeines Landrecht* promulgated in 1794, accepted the inevitable when it stated that 44 years of unchallenged living as a noble did indeed confer 'an express or implicit recognition by the state' of noble status.[11] Such infiltration was impossible to stop, unless either there were very few nobles (as in the Dutch Republic) or there was a clear and visible register of nobles, as in those Italian cities that boasted their 'Golden Books' of nobility.

Britain fell into both categories, since its peerages (English, Scottish or Irish) were both highly visible and so small as to be documented almost by definition. On the other hand, the process whereby successful merchants and professionals could buy a small landed property and begin their ascent through the informal gradations of the gentry corresponded pretty closely to the processes of usurpation on the continent, though without the attendant judicial and bureaucratic irritations. The lack of formal legal distinction between gentry and non-gentry removed one major hurdle to such advancement. It normally took 'three generations to make a gentleman'. In Castile, it was accepted that the exercise of noble *rights*, as opposed to possession of noble *status*, over three generations did indeed finally confer the status itself. In Spain, France and, after 1785, Russia, the state itself used the prospect of the eventual acquisition of nobility – by permitting merchants and entrepreneurs to exercise the trappings of nobility, such as the right to bear a sword, or exemption from certain taxes or militia services – as a means to impart a new lustre on commerce: but this separation of rights and status inevitably made usurpation easier. In the end, the most important single component of the ennoblement process was acceptance by others, and that required, above all, time.

The social entrepreneur had to possess the wealth, the land and the connections to carry off the sleight of hand that would enable him to 'live nobly'. Granted those, then such 'usurpation' (or 'acquisition') went through smoothly enough. In Poland and Spain it was almost a regular legal procedure. The prospective noble would arrange for an associate or debtor, or even a noble who made a living out of the ennoblement process, to launch a legal challenge to the noble status of the pretender. A number of similarly disposed nobles would be found to testify to the status of the defendant's family and antecedents, the court would find in his favour and rule that he did indeed possess noble status: ennoblement, accompanied by appropriate paperwork, would take effect. This could lead to the odd situation where an ambitious sibling might secure nobility, but a less pushy sibling remain a commoner. Calculating the numbers involved in such transactions is impossible, but even back in the late Middle Ages, it made traditionalists' teeth grate.

Nobility was of course associated with ownership of land. Where there was no legal obstacle, or at least, no enforceable legal obstacle to the acquisition of land by commoners, then land purchase offered an alternative route to informal ennoblement. Where land was officially classified as a 'fief', that is, 'noble', its acquisition by commoners was a sure boost to their elevation. Indeed, in France, until 1579, a family that held a noble fief for three generations was considered ennobled.[12] The practice survived informally. True, commoners were supposed to pay *franc-fief* for the privilege of owning such land – or, in most of France, one year's income from that estate, payable at the beginning of every 20-year period and at the succession to the estate of every non-noble heir. The law of 9 March 1700 reiterated the obligation. But, as was universal in anything relating to the *Ancien Régime*, the process was riddled with anomalies. The bourgeois of Paris and Périgueux were exempt. So too, on the lower Loire, were the regions of Chartres, Orléans and Angers, and Perche in Normandy. At the behest of a cash-strapped Louis XIV, the Dauphiné purchased blanket exemption from *franc-fief* in 1693. Possession of more important local offices often exempted from *franc-fief*. All such exemptions were abolished in 1771, too late to have any significant effect. In any case, enforcement was always problematic. If an accommodating *intendant* could be persuaded to turn a blind eye to non-payment of *franc-fief*, the non-noble seigneur would be transformed into a noble. This was all the more so after 1718, the last time a 'reformation' enquiry into noble claims was held. And since many of the *intendants*' principal assistants, the *subdélégués*, were commoners themselves seeking ennoblement, such ennoblement by default was easily arranged. Those so situated were in 1789 categorised as 'bourgeois living nobly off their revenues' – 'bourgeois', of course, in the accepted eighteenth-century sense of propertied town-dwellers, often enjoying their own array of privileges and exemptions. Thus could 'silent ennoblement', *anoblissement taisible*, take effect.[13] The ability of nobles to get commoner land that they acquired reclassified as noble land (as was the case in Provence after 1556) added complications which commoner purchasers could further exploit.[14] According to Henri Carré, more nobles were created by such usurpations in France than by any other means – a suggestion as plausible as it is unquantifiable. Nor did an individual have consciously to try to become ennobled in order to be reputed noble. Two of the French Revolution's most enthusiastic exponents, Louis Saint-Just and Bertrand Barère, were widely thought to be nobles, though neither man was.[15]

Wealth helped: one might only have to live an appropriate lifestyle and wait. Wealth could purchase nobility legally. It was indeed the French monarchy that showed the most mercenary approach to ennoblement: in the sixteenth century, it had pioneered the systematic sale of offices in order to raise cash. Outright sale of nobility was less common, usually occurring when governments were desperately pressed for cash in wartime. In March 1696, Louis XIV sold 500 titles of nobility in order to raise cash to help finance the debilitating Nine Years War. In 1704, 200 letters of ennoblement were sold, this time to finance the War of the Spanish Succession.[16] But sales on such a scale were exceptional.

Paperwork attesting to nobility was not strictly speaking necessary, but it was certainly helpful. In France, up to 1718, the crown periodically conducted investigations (*réformations*) into 'false' nobles – investigations which could, and did, mean that *bona fide* nobles, especially if they were poor but lacked convincing paperwork, were relegated to the ranks of the commoners. Even those who had purchased patents of nobility might be affected – the crown could revoke such grants, although in such cases it normally reimbursed the purchase price (though it would take its time about it). The crown could, of course, confer nobility outright and increasingly did so. In the Habsburg lands, Maria Theresa and Joseph II of Austria sold ennoblements, though never on the scale that Louis XIV did.

Ralph Giesey and Guy Chaussinand-Nogaret both posit that in order to enable an individual to support in France the costs of what the eighteenth century considered a noble lifestyle, a capital of some 1 million *livres* was necessary – not excessive by English standards: at the exchange rate that prevailed for most of the eighteenth century (22 *livres* to the pound sterling), 1 million *livres* came to £4545 – or into the bracket of reasonably well-to-do (English) gentry. There was no lack of those who could make the necessary funds by either commercial or financial activities, or by the patient accumulation of land and office over several generations. For this was an era in which those who sought social advancement thought not just in terms of personal careers but in terms of dynastic strategies. What linked such social ascent was almost invariably money. The overwhelming mass of offices that ennobled cost money; and since the crown was in a position to manipulate the financial terms of these offices, at least before the final conferment of hereditary nobility, it saw in such office a device for the extraction of what were, in effect, forced loans. Or rather, forced contributions: the offices carried a salary, the *gages*, which was supposed to represent an interest rate on the original purchase price. But it might be paid very irregularly; and, occasionally, the crown would generously decree an *augmentation des gages*, an increase in the interest – but the hapless office-holder was required to pay a supplementary lump sum in order to receive the augmentation: failure to stump up would lead to the loss of office. And this was just one of a huge range of financial wheezes to which office-holders were subjected: confirmation of status, of rights of inheritance, of freedom from exactions, confirmations of confirmations – not to mention outright impositions.

It is easy to scoff. 'As soon as the Crown creates an office, God creates a fool willing to buy it', one of Louis XIV's controllers-general of finances supposedly said – but the social and political, to some extent even the fiscal, advantages of being a noble were such that it would have been foolish not to have bought such office if it were on offer. Hardly anyone defended the practice of venality; not one of the *cahiers de doléances* of 1789 stood up for it; those that mentioned it were all hostile. Yet individuals in a position to take advantage of venality did so. The number of venal offices cannot be measured with any certainty – it could have been around 51,000, it may have approached 80,000.[17] Only a tiny minority of these offices conferred any form of ennoblement – around 4000, perhaps; and a minority of these ennobling offices were always held by persons already noble. With all these qualifications, nowhere was ennoblement more readily accessible by formal legal channels than in France. A vast range of professions, mainly connected with the law and finance, simply could not be legally practised without venal office. But all offices were connected: for those who could not afford the purchase of the generally more expensive ennobling offices, non-ennobling office at least permitted a gradual distancing, even over several generations, from one's 'base' origins. By 1771, the Guillaume de Chavaudon family boasted a dossier of documents going back to 1370 (admittedly, those papers and parchments that predated 1558 were forgeries), in order to demonstrate four centuries of office-holding in provincial, municipal and judicial administration. The incremental acquisition of office, a compliant *intendant* in Troyes who confirmed noble status in 1696 and dropped the *franc-fief* charge, meant that by the 1740s, the family's noble status had been cleansed of the taint of sixteenth-century commercial activity.[18]

But social ascent in France could be much quicker. It could be secured within one, two, or three generations, perfectly legitimately, by purchase of some form of office whose conferral of ennoblement was (at least as far as the crown was concerned) unimpeachable. The most common pattern was via an office which conferred full ennoblement after a tenure of between 2 and (more usually) 20 years. All such offices conferred immediate nobility on the purchaser, but only for his lifetime. Twenty-eight tax and fiscal offices (*bureaux de finances*) carried at least 769 ennobling posts, which ennobled mainly over two generations; 16 *parlements* and their equivalent *conseils supérieurs* boasted some 1250 ennobling offices, though given the high prestige of these institutions, the overwhelming majority of these posts were held by existing nobles. By the 1780s, those in Brittany, Lorraine, Toulouse, Grenoble, Bordeaux and Aix barred commoners altogether from the most important judicial councillorships, although they contained a few lesser ennobling offices, while most of France's other sovereign courts were increasingly reluctant to admit commoners. Some 80 per cent of those taking up *parlementaire* office were already nobles. Between 1710 and 1790, *parlementaire* magistracies produced only some 150 ennoblements. The less prestigious financial tribunals, the *chambres des comptes, cours des aides, cours de monnaies* (15 in all), contained 980 ennobling offices, of which 359 conferred first-generation nobility, the rest second-generation. *Noblesse graduelle* would eventually become *noblesse parfaite*. As less prestigious offices, they were responsible for a much higher rate of ennoblement, setting well over 400 individuals on the path to ennoblement between 1774 and 1789. Some of these companies had been instituted in the seventeenth century precisely to raise money for the crown from the venality of their offices; almost all had been expanded for the same reason. Creation, much of it involving the forced purchase of office by unhappy holders, always peaked in wartime. 'Even an approximate calculation of the number of new offices created . . . between 1689 and 1715 [the Nine Years War and the War of the Spanish Succession] is quite impossible.'[19]

Death was a great accelerator. The prevailing 20-year tenure rule did not apply if the holder died in office: where office conferred first-generation ennoblement, the next generation was automatically fully ennobled. Since most offices which ennobled did so over two generations, it was only in the third that full ennoblement took hold, buffered from plebeian origins by the intermediate stages of ascent. Since the age limits on the acquisition of public office (judicial office was supposedly unavailable to those under 25) were easily circumvented (not least by the purchase of exemptions), it was perfectly possible for sons or grandsons of the originator of the process to join the ranks of the grandiosely styled *noblesse d'ancienne extraction* during his lifetime. Senior municipal offices (around 100 offices in all) in 16 towns ennobled – as *nobles de cloche* ('nobles of the bell-tower'). The same process of three generations of ascent and acceptance operated elsewhere. William Denison, an immensely wealthy cloth merchant from Leeds, was told in no uncertain terms by the neighbours of his Ossington estate in Nottinghamshire that he was 'no gentleman' – he objected to their hunting foxes across his tenants' cornfields – but such a charge was unsustainable against his many grandsons, who included one speaker of the House of Commons, a governor-general of Australia and a bishop of Salisbury (and therefore an ecclesiastical peer).[20] In the Polish–Lithuanian Commonwealth, the device of the *skartabellat* complemented the three generations of full acceptance by explicitly barring newly ennobled families from offices reserved to nobles until the fourth generation – although its enforcement was highly problematic.

The plum office of ennoblement in France was that of royal secretary – *secrétaire du roi*. It conferred full and immediate ennoblement on the holder (and his wife); after 20 years in office or on the holder's death (whichever came sooner), all his offspring were also ennobled, in heredity. If the holder held a second ennobling office, then the length of tenure could be shortened by counting twice.[21] This was the prized (and expensive) *savonnette à vilain* – the 'soap for scum' that washed away vile origins. The office was originally attached to royal chancelleries located in Paris and the provinces, for the despatch of royal, though often mundane, administrative business. In reality, such work was done by clerks. The *secrétaires du roi* proper (530 in 1698, 857 in 1785) were mainly sinecurists who had purchased their office in order to procure swift, guaranteed ennoblement for themselves and their descendants. To David Bien, the chancelleries to which the post was attached were nothing less than an 'assembly line' for the manufacture of nobles.[22]

The result was a staggering rate of ennoblements in France over the eighteenth century. Between 1715 and 1771, some 6000 families were ennobled; over the eighteenth century as a whole, it may have approached 10,000 ennoblements by office-holding alone. By the 1780s, it may well have amounted to between 500 and 700 ennoblements per year, or around two per day (by contrast, the Polish rate up to 1764 was about 3.37 ennoblements per annum). Such figures would of course appear even more impressive if one could calculate the number of *descendants* of all *anoblis* since 1700.[23] The claims of Guillaume Chaussinand-Nogaret, that 'a noble was now nothing but a commoner who had made it', take on a disconcerting plausibility, although the issue is far from resolved. There were those who thought so at the time: 'In truth, not every noble is rich, but every rich man is a noble', observed the *philosophe* and minister Chrétien-Guillaume de Lamoignon de Malesherbes.[24]

Such venal ennoblement reduced 'nobility' to little more than a commercial commodity – and quite deliberately so on the part of the French crown. Office, ennobling or not, was sold to raise money. As with any market place, it was of course possible to go too far. In December 1708, at the height of the fiscal crisis of the War of the Spanish Succession, Louis XIV's government created 600 *secrétaires du roi*, but when credit was extremely tight it could sell only 150 of them, even at a rock-bottom price of 4000 *livres*.[25] Once sold to its holder, an office became his to dispose of – he (or she – women were allowed to own office, but not to exercise it) could even lease its tenure to others – although the second-hand purchaser of such office would have to pay a range of registration and other fees to confirm the legality of his tenure. Venality was widely condemned in France but accepted as a necessary evil simply because everyone appreciated that the monarchy lacked the resources to buy out the huge amount of money invested in the incalculable number of ennobling and non-ennobling offices.

Increasingly, however, the crown ennobled directly via letters patent of nobility for merit, though never on the scale it sold ennobling office. The recipients of such letters had to pay various registration and chancery fees, but they did not purchase the actual letters of ennoblement. The military disasters of the Seven Years War spurred on reform. Commentators increasingly stressed that nobility, even old-established nobility, should go hand in hand with service and therefore merit. By the same token, genuine merit among those who did not possess nobility should be recognised by the conferment of nobility. The real problem was the definition of merit, or, as the eighteenth century put it, 'services' or 'utility'. How were these desirable qualities to be recognised or defined? It was all very well to say, with the Spanish reformer Benito Feijóo, that 'Each person should be esteemed for his own works, not those of his ancestors',[26] but to which 'works' should esteem be accorded? A massive debate followed the publication in 1756 of the abbé Coyer's *La noblesse commerçante*, which over the next decade was translated in turn into German, Spanish, Italian and Russian. Coyer's opponents, headed by Philippe-Auguste de Sainte-Foy, chevalier d'Arcq, invoking the authority of no less a figure than Montesquieu, warned that the principal *raison d'être* of the nobility was military – hence the title of d'Arcq's treatise, *La noblesse militaire*. To encourage it to participate in commerce or industry would be to dilute and undermine it. The French judicial nobility, the *robe*, likewise argued that commerce diverted nobles from their true task of dispensing justice – indeed, the sovereign courts banned their officials from participation in commercial ventures.

But under a French crown that increasingly did want nobles to participate in active commerce, the purchase of an ennobling office, even of the notorious *secrétaire du roi*, could be seen as a means of rewarding merit in the very fields of commerce or industry or banking that the holder may have practised. The *arrêt du conseil* of 30 October 1767 made specific provision for the ennoblement of two wholesale merchants every year by royal letters patent: that tiny number, of course, did little to enhance the prestige of a business route into the nobility. Men of 'talent', real and imaginary, fared a little better: 31 doctors and surgeons (admittedly, mainly those who ministered to the royal family) were ennobled between 1750 and 1785, as were 25 artists, sculptors and architects – and one musician, Jean-Philippe Rameau (in his case, the talent was real). There was undoubtedly a new recognition on the part of the monarchy of the need to recognise and honour talent by grants of ennoblement, but it grew from a pitifully small base. But even these ennoblements seem to have arisen mainly through connections with the court and powerful patrons. The almost total failure to honour lawyers and writers was to do the monarchy little favour during the French Revolution.[27]

In France, then, purchase remained the prime route to ennoblement. It could be argued that the purchase of nobility was a hybrid form of reward, since it was often associated with some form of real service, not least in the judiciary or administration. The 32 merchants of the Breton port of Nantes who bought the office of *secrétaire du roi* during the century would doubtless have claimed that they merited ennoblement as a result of the economic benefits brought to France by their trading and slaving activities.[28] Be that as it may, the raw purchase of ennoblement turned the process into a sordid financial transaction, one, moreover, that stoked tensions and cleavages within the body of the nobility itself. France was not exceptional in the venality of offices, nor even in its scale: legal (though not judicial), fiscal and, to a lesser extent, municipal offices were sold and inherited widely in Spain, but there, as in other states where it was sold, office as such never ennobled: at best, its acquisition might help pave the way to future ennoblement.[29]

Where did this commercial trafficking leave those who maintained that nobility should be, above all, the reward for valour in the field? Whatever arguments could be put forward in favour of a supposed parity of esteem between the old fighting nobility, the *noblesse d'épée*, and the judicial nobility, the *noblesse de robe*, it was always the *épée* that enjoyed that extra whiff of prestige.[30] Venality did indeed extend into the French army (as it did into most other armies): most commissioned officerships were bought and sold from one holder to another. In November 1750, in recognition of the services of non-noble officers during the War of the Austrian Succession, a new species of nobility, *noblesse militaire*, was created. But it was a much harsher road than civil ennoblement. Between 14 and 30 years' service was required of commoner officers before the process of ennoblement (*commencement de la noblesse*) could even begin, with exemption granted from the land tax, the *taille*; full hereditary nobility arrived, as normal, only in the third generation and after the minimum stipulated lengths of service (only death in service, or retirement through wounds sustained in action, reduced the term for the serving officer). Only those appointed to general rank obtained outright hereditary nobility.

Moreover, all commissioned office, unless by exceptional royal favour, still had to be bought. The cheapest infantry captaincy might cost 6000 *livres*. The 'cheapest' colonelcies cost between 25,000 and 50,000 *livres*. A colonelcy in a dragoon regiment cost around 120,000 *livres*, a humble sub-lieutenancy in an elite gendarmerie unit around 200,000 *livres*. A generalship could cost near on a million. For most, three consecutive generations of military service represented a far more demanding process than the purchase of ennobling office in the civilian world (though understanding colonels, rather like understanding *intendants*, could provide long-service certification). Probably fewer than 300 individuals were ennobled under the terms of the November 1750 edict, plus a further 100 or so directly elevated by royal letters patent – this during a period when the army numbered between 6000 and 8000 officers.[31] Yet, after 1750, four or five times as many nobles were created by the venal post of *secrétaire du roi* alone. No wonder there was growing animosity between old-established nobles of modest means who believed that their ancient pedigrees and family histories entitled them to a place of honour and consideration, yet saw themselves squeezed out by *nouveau riche* interlopers – not only were they eclipsed within the body of the *noblesse* as a whole, but even within the *noblesse militaire* or *d'épée* they were being elbowed out by those who could afford to pay higher prices for commissions.

Almost everywhere, it was easier (and safer) to secure ennoblement by non-military means, even though ennoblement was recognised as a fitting reward for bravery in the field – provided, of course, that the beneficiaries did not originate too far down the social scale. It was vastly simpler to secure a patent of nobility under Charles VI of Austria (1711–40) for a civil official (327 ennoblements) than for a military man (29 ennoblements) – although the balance swung the other way under his two successors, Maria Theresa (1740–80) and Joseph II (1780–90) (478 civil as opposed to 548 military ennoblements), as they desperately sought to galvanise their disparate territories into a fit state to take on Frederick the Great's Prussia.[32] In Sweden, between 1680 and 1700, 500 individuals (with their families – on average, 20 families per annum) were ennobled, chiefly through the civil service. All commoners in the Swedish army who reached the rank of major were normally ennobled, although at this and higher ranks, established nobles predominated. In 1699, of the 21 (out of a total of 77) commoners who had reached this elevated slot, none had managed to progress beyond a colonelcy. Two-thirds of all officers in 1719 were commoners (2267 of 3419), but only one-quarter (78 of 301) of senior ranks were – for most of the rest of the eighteenth century, levels of commoner entrants remained well below these. Commoner officers, however, predominated in the less prestigious navy, where, except in the 1750s and 1760s, over half of all officerships went to them. Some 75 per cent of entrants into the Swedish civil service were commoners in 1680. By 1700, 44 per cent of all Swedish civil servants had become ennobled in service. There was a sharp drop in bureaucratic ennoblements after 1727 and the influx of commoners was mainly confined to the lower ranks – partly because the noble-dominated parliament did not wish to increase ennoblement, partly because the Swedish nobility's manifest pursuit of self-advantage reached such proportions that other social groups increasingly became indifferent to the cachet of noble status, a process much enhanced when Gustavus III began to turn against the nobility after 1789.[33] In Spain, the bulk of titled creations (as opposed to mere elevation into *hidalguia*) specifically granted by the crown went to civil servants – a process described by one authority as 'a renovation of the aristocracy by the aristocratization of the bureaucracy'.[34]

Among the major states of Europe, only in Prussia did a clear predominance of official ennoblement by military means exist. On 20 March 1763, Frederick the Great decreed that henceforth only distinguished, especially distinguished military service, could ennoble. He underlined the point by dismissing *en masse* officers of commoner background appointed during the exigencies of the just-finished Seven Years War. Formal ennoblement in Prussia, by royal letters patent, was extraordinarily difficult. Reliable figures before the years 1790–1806 are hard to find. But 1790–1806 witnessed 212 creations: 89 for officers, 68 for officials, 10 for owners of landed properties classed as 'noble' and 15 for manufacturers, industrialists and others. Frederick the Great may have made around a fifth of this number, overwhelmingly for military achievement; this was twice as many as under his father, Frederick William I, although the majority of his appointments went to ministers and bureaucrats in his service (Frederick II ennobled only one minister). Given that there were around 20,000 noble families in Prussia, most of whom looked to state service rather than just their own resources for a decent standard of living, there was never any shortage of noble candidates for office.[35]

Only one state, Russia, had a systematic mechanism for the elevation of non-nobles to noble status. Under Peter the Great's Table of Ranks, promulgated in February 1722, all key military, naval and civilian-administrative positions were grouped into 14 categories: *klassy* or *rangi*. According to article 11:

> For all Russian or foreign servitors [of the state] who find ... themselves in the first [i.e. top] eight ranks: they, their legitimate offspring and posterity for all time are to be considered equal to the better, older nobility [*luchshemu, starshemu dvorianstvu*] in all dignities and benefits, even if they be of humble birth, and have never been advanced to noble dignity by crowned heads nor endowed with coats of arms ...

Article 15 specified that this parity with the older nobility applied to all commissioned military officers (that is, from rank 14).[36] The Table of Ranks certainly served as an important social escalator. Up to one-third of officers in wartime might have risen from a non-*dvorianin* background. In 1755, of approximately 10,500 civilian officials, 2051 figured on the Table of Ranks, 497 of them at ranks 6–8. Of these, 113, or 22 per cent, were of non-*dvorianin* origin; and even among the top five ranks, the so-called *Generalitet*, 10 out of 110 (9 per cent) were also non-*dvoriane*. The bureaucracy continued to grow rapidly, increasing to 16,500 officials in 1763 and 38,000 officials by 1800. Though posts on the Table of Ranks remained in a minority, the opportunities for commoners to rise in status continued to expand, much to the alarm of established nobles. The purpose behind the Table had always been to lock the nobility into the service of the state, rather than to further social mobility. A number of measures were taken to act against this. In 1724, Peter banned the appointment of non-*dvoriane* as secretaries (ranks 13 and 14), who handled much of the paperwork in the chancelleries. In 1727, peasants were formally excluded, though their chances of getting into the service were in any case extremely slim. The influxes continued, so much so that in the nineteenth century, civilian ennobling rank was raised from 8th to 5th in 1845 and to 4th in 1856.[37]

Like it or not, established families, often themselves of comparatively recent background, had to endure a greater or lesser influx of new recruits. In theory, this ought to have been a healthy sign from the viewpoint of the nobilities themselves: it demonstrated that noble status was desirable, that aspiring elements within societies wanted to join the nobility, not to overthrow it. Nobility was seen as part of the natural order of things. In recognition of social aspirations, and seeking to impose some kind of order on them, governments and rulers encouraged the development of a kind of half-way house noble status, which conferred at least some of the rights and trappings of nobility. This was precisely one of the objects of the French *arrêt du conseil* of 30 October 1767, which not only allowed for the ennoblement of two *négociants* (wholesale merchants) a year, but conferred collective distinctions on such wholesale merchants: they were assured of precedence in all assemblies of the Third Estate, exemption from militia service, the right to carry a sword.[38] In Spain, from 1773, wholesale merchants enrolled in *consulados* (mercantile companies) were exempted from militia service. Membership of a *consulado* was generally reckoned a staging post on the road to full ennoblement.[39] Catherine the Great's reforms of 1775 and 1785 accorded exemption from the soul tax to merchants with over 500 roubles' capital; and after 1785, merchants with over 1000 roubles' capital, together with so-called 'honorary citizens' – bankers, artists, scholars, elected officials, wealthier traders and entrepreneurs – were also exempted from corporal punishment: thus, in two key respects they were treated as nobles.[40]

The creation of special categories of near-nobles went furthest in Prussia, in 1794, when the *Allgemeines Landrecht* recognised the existence of 'servants of the state' (*Diener des Staats*): military (*Militairbediente* – who included civilians attached to the army administration) and civil officials proper (*Civilbeamte*). Those who, among them, held any positions of responsibility were classified as *Eximierten* ('Exempt persons'), subject only to higher state courts, liable to less severe legal penalties, freed from compulsory military service; they could freely intermarry with the nobility.[41] Teachers in secondary schools and universities, as well as 'senior officers of burgher origin', also counted as *Eximierte*. The sociopolitical taxonomy of the *Allgemeines Landrecht* represented the most elaborate formal attempt to come to terms with the need to accommodate new or socially aspiring professional groups within the framework of a traditional hierarchical order. But it was also a recognition of the tension between that traditional order and the evolution of social forces that were making old hierarchic frameworks increasingly strained.

In most cases, it was natural that those near the top of the bourgeois pinnacle would seek to make the transition to what was generally regarded as a superior hierarchy. Only where cities existed as a more influential force in their own right, and where their elites regarded themselves as equal, or even superior, to those of non-urban-dwelling nobles, did that transition appear to be unnecessary: in the Dutch Republic, even in parts of Polish Prussia, where the townsmen of Danzig, Thorn and Elbing enjoyed an exceptional regional importance; and in the confusion of many Italian city states. The evolution of the English gentry, commoners but not quite nobles, was simply a variation on a theme within a wider European process.

The *Ancien Régime* could not conceive of a society in which there was no nobility. In 1750, the French state had grudgingly accepted that commoners, *roturiers*, might indeed be capable of demonstrating the same martial and leadership qualities traditionally ascribed to the nobility – hence the creation of a *noblesse militaire*. The catastrophes of the Seven Years War threw all this into question. Ancient, immemorial, feudal nobility received a new lease of life. For the diagnosis made in senior French military circles was that there was indeed such a thing as a noble military ethos, that it was cultivated in the families of ancient provincial nobles, worthy, virtuous, brave, but often impoverished. Such excellent officer material, however, was utilised far too rarely: officer posts were for sale, and too many were bought either by wealthy commoners or by recently created nobles who owed their social status not to virtue but to wealth. Types such as these cared little for their men, for discipline or even for courage. They bought commissions not because they wished to give genuine service in the armies, but because they wished to cut a figure and enhance their lowly origins with the prestige of military rank which owed nothing to their positive qualities, everything to their money. There is no real evidence to suggest that officers of commoner or recently ennobled background were any more or less incompetent than their old-established counterparts; the British and Prussian armies that thrashed them were as shot through with venality as the French military. Yet this is the analysis that was made. To give them their due, the French did set about dismantling the system of officer venality. 'Venality in military appointments is surely the most destructive and prejudicial thing for the good of the service. Money confers neither talent nor merit; and the military calling demands a great deal of both.' So wrote the comte de Saint-Germain in 1779, on a topic on which he had been fulminating for the past two decades. In 1763, the duc de Choiseul secured the abolition of venal captaincies in infantry line regiments. After 1776, under the war ministry of the comte de Saint-Germain, all other commissions (except in the court-dominated regiments of the royal household) were to be abolished, with the reduction in the price of any commission by one-quarter each time it was sold on. The process took time, but it was sufficiently effective for it to be considered for extension into the civil sphere.[42]

But there was another way of dealing with the problem – directly restricting the access of commoners and *anoblis* to officerships altogether. In 1781, under the Ségur war ministry, a law was passed denying officerships to those who could not show four generations of nobility on the paternal side: new officers had to be fifth-generation nobles (sons of those ennobled under the 1750 ordinance creating a *noblesse militaire* were exempted). Tens of thousands of nobles could not meet these criteria.[43] Worse still, the desire to exclude was increasingly establishing itself in other spheres. In 1759, newly ennobled persons and members of the *robe* nobility (except ministers or nobles not actually ennobled through *robe* service) were barred from access to the court.[44] A number of *parlements* insisted with Rennes (Brittany) after 1732 that any new entrants should already possess full nobility – though in the Rennes case, the principle had already been in operation for a good century; after 1750, Nancy (Lorraine), Toulouse (Languedoc), Aix (Provence), Grenoble (Dauphiné) all insisted on similar requirements – the Ségur law was indeed partly inspired by *parlementaire* precedent at Aix, Grenoble and Toulouse.[45] Perhaps the final insult came in 1789, when *anoblis* were barred from participation in the drafting of nobles' assemblies' *cahiers de doléances*.[46] These fissions and rivalries in the key order of the most dynamic society in Europe rendered it impossible for the nobility to maintain anything like a solid front against the revolutionary turmoil that so unexpectedly overwhelmed the French monarchy after 1789.

3

THE NOBILITY AND THE STATE

'It is an incontrovertible maxim in politicks that dominion ought to follow the property', wrote Andrew Fletcher of Saltoun in 1703.[1] He meant, of course, landed property. True, it was not only noble landlords who benefited from the greater or lesser panoply of rights that arose from ownership of the soil. But their ownership was on such a scale as to make them the most significant factor in local government. Peers and well-to-do gentry owned around a quarter of all the cultivated acreage of England. The nobility of France may have owned around a quarter of all the land in France outright. Polish nobles owned about two-thirds of all the land in Poland, Prussian nobles over half in the Hohenzollern lands. Fewer than 300 noble families owned almost half of all landed property in Lombardy. In Spain, it was said that four great families owned one-third of all the cultivated land. At least half of the serf population of Russia at any one time belonged to the nobility. Not only did nobles exercise extensive jurisdiction within their estates, they were the natural choice for exercising seigneurial or governmental authority beyond it. As lords-lieutenant or Justices of the Peace peers and gentry ruled most of England. The nobility of France exercised jurisdictional rights over most of the one-third or so of France in peasant 'ownership'. Even where a corporate body such as the Catholic Church enjoyed ownership or exercised jurisdictional rights, it tended to be dominated by nobles. There was thus a basic community of interest and understanding between state and nobility.

Direct access to the centre of power was vital to great nobles and magnates if they were to remain great. Except in the case of purely republican states such as Venice or the United Provinces, this meant access to the monarch, or at least to the monarch's ministers and the court. Physical entry was simple: it was normally enough to be respectably dressed. An appropriate tip to a doorman or concierge, or a bribe to a nobleman already well ensconced in the court circle, would help. Access to the royal person and the eliciting of some form of recognition, even if it were only a royal nod of acknowledgement, was another matter altogether. The court was certainly not for all and sundry, even among the nobility. In France in the 1780s, there may have been some 25,000 noble families, or there may have been some 100,000 such families. Either way, only around 4000 had been officially presented at court. Between 1715 and 1790, a mere 492 families were presented. From 1774, Louis XV insisted on vetting all applications for presentation, which had to be submitted in writing to the first gentleman of the bedchamber. Much to the disgust of other nobles, those so favoured regarded themselves as a 'high' nobility, or *haute noblesse* – the *présentés* as opposed to the *non-présentés*. Of the 882 noble families that adorned the province of Provence, only 34 (3.8 per cent) received the 'honours of the court'. After 1760, those *honneurs de la cour* could only be granted to those who could show proofs of nobility going back to at least 1400. Members of the *robe* nobility and newly ennobled persons were specifically excluded.[2]

As ever in the *Ancien Régime*, such restrictions were riddled with loopholes. Ministers and their families, even of comparatively recent nobility (like the Colberts), were automatically given full access to the *honneurs de la cour*; royal favour could always dispense with the usual requirements (spectacularly so in the case of Louis XV's mistresses); and the court genealogists, the Chérins, father and son, could always be relied on to furnish appropriate pedigrees for the favoured few, usually upstarts from the world of finance. Only a small number of the *présenté* families could actually have been said to constitute a proper 'aulic', or court, nobility, since the costs of living at Versailles, plus the indispensable necessity of an appropriate town house in Paris, were prohibitive.

Proximity to the royal person enhanced the local or regional standing of great territorial magnates, which in turn enabled monarch and ministers more easily to conduct what official business needed to be discharged, even if it was only the collection or negotiation of taxation or the gathering of recruits. It also oiled the wheels of central finance: governments relied on loans, grants and gifts from great nobles, which they would concede in part because it was difficult to resist such pressures, but even more so because they expected to be rewarded in the longer term: with monopolies, concessions, commissions, money or land grants, titles, heiresses or favours for their own protégés. The heavily indebted Henri-Charles de Tavanes used his influence and connections in Burgundy (from 1721 he acted as stand-in for the governor, the rather grander prince de Condé) to help the running of the king's business in the province. While it was patronage and influence that greased the wheels of *Ancien Régime* governments, it was the court that was the central exchange trading in these commodities. Access to these invisibles did not free Henri-Charles de Tavanes of his debts, but it permitted him to stay afloat and maintain a lifestyle he could not possibly have afforded without access to Versailles.[3]

Versailles was, of course, an exceptionally lavish court, but those of Vienna or St Petersburg approached it in splendour. And the same sorts of great aristocrats frequented them for the same reasons. The very few banks that were set up in Russia in the 1750s and 1760s functioned, in practice, as open-ended lenders to influential, high-spending courtiers; and imperial favour ensured periodically that these debts did not have to be paid or that the debtors were immune from recovery proceedings. But even at the more modest courts of Warsaw and Dresden, aristocrats would dance attendance for similar reasons: either to secure royal favours, offices and crown estates, or, even if they were not particularly well in with the monarch, to remind him that they should not be overlooked, if they were not to start being troublesome in their localities. Monarchs could demonstrate a sensitive understanding of what proximity to their person meant. Maria Theresa, conscious of the low regard in which professional soldiers were so often held in the Habsburg lands, a low regard which in turn was reflected in poor military performance, gave entry to the court to all commissioned officers in uniform for the first time in 1751.[4] Her son, Joseph II, wore military uniform at court, in emulation of Frederick II of Prussia – and these well-meaning efforts to improve the quality of the Habsburg officer corps by association with the court did indeed achieve some real success, though not as much as the dynasty would have liked.

Nobles, to be useful to themselves and to their rulers, needed influence. A whole network of institutions dominated by them existed through which that influence could be exercised in a formal manner. It was important to be a landowner; but if landownership could be exercised in conjunction with some form of public office, then the two – office and land – could be used to reinforce each other's authority. Everywhere outside Russia and the Balkans there existed the *Ständestaat*, the 'Estate-state', that is, the state composed of different corporate orders and institutions. These ranged from central parliamentary bodies such as the Houses of Lords and Commons in Britain, the *Riksdag* in Sweden or the *Sejm* in Poland, down to the level of municipal and parish councils and trade and craft guilds, with a protean mass of analogous institutions in between. Quasi-parliamentary institutions of a more or less representative character were among the most widespread manifestations of the *Ständestaat*.

The contrast with Russia is instructive, for it tells us much about the relationships between nobles and the state. When Peter the Great's Table of Ranks referred in 1722 to a 'better, older nobility', it was indicating a core of a few dozen families of princely descent, or those that had served the tsars in a close capacity for generations. Their status depended not on institutional or legal underpinning but on tradition, court connection and favour. Below these, in the seventeenth century, came several tens of thousands of 'serving people', *sluzhilye liudi*: 'serving' in the sense that they owed the tsar direct service primarily in a military capacity. It is this (extremely disparate) group that is usually identified as Russia's 'nobility' or 'gentry'. This identification can be made, provided the consequences of the absence of formal privilege or of forums of self-expression or self-government are borne in mind. *Sluzhilye liudi* included *pomeshchiki*, holders of land assigned to them by the tsar in return for service. Calculating the numbers of these fluid groups, whose actual role was defined by the state according to its needs and circumstances, is almost impossible. One estimate places the tentative number of males who might be defined as nobles in 1681 at some 19,000 – presumably these were the more substantial among them, holding land and serfs. But 15 years later, Peter the Great forcibly resettled around 20,000 lesser *pomeshchiki* in the vicinity of Azov, as forced labour on the construction of the new harbour works at Taganrog. Presumably this involved a combination of persons taken into 'service' on an ad hoc basis and masses of petty servitors with little or no land assigned to them. A bewildering variety of names and overlapping concepts indicated that in the seventeenth century, the state accorded status to those it deemed expedient, often on a temporary basis. Peter's Table of Ranks rationalised all this up to a point: those holding any of the 262 offices originally specified within the framework of the table formed an inchoate new nobility. Some somehow clung on as a kind of nobility bereft of office: many are known to have served in the army and in the Imperial Guard. Others became *raznochintsy*, 'persons of varying condition', a term which significantly came into use at about the same time that the Table of Ranks was formulated. They did not neatly fit into the structures of the Russian state but provided a useful store of ad hoc manpower and skills, particularly amid petty officialdom. Masses of petty *pomeshchiki* and *sluzhilye liudi* dropped back into the peasantry with a greater or lesser degree of resistance. Among these were the *odnodvortsy*, descendants of petty servitors settled mainly in the southern frontier zones, who persisted in protesting noble status throughout the eighteenth century, while the government was never quite able to decide what to do about them. Only between 1782 and 1819 did the government finally settle for recognition of the noble status of those who gained the appropriate rank or could offer formal proofs of nobility.[5] Those members of the old service groups who held *pomestya* and serfs were the most likely to survive as *dvoriane* or *shliakhtiche*, 'nobles'. In 1744, they numbered some 37,000 males, in 1764, 53,000.[6]

Outside Russia, however, the nobility almost invariably dominated the institutions of the *Ständestaat*. Especially in Catholic countries, they might be seconded by the clergy and were often closely linked by family ties to them. The sole major exception was the Dutch Republic, whose government was dominated by the regents, the patrician oligarchs who ran town governments. The prominence of commerce and industry and the extensive urban ownership of land combined to restrict nobles' influence in the United Provinces. The nobility had only one vote on the parliamentary estates of the two most important provinces, Holland and Zeeland, and were easily outnumbered by the towns (which held 18 and 6 votes respectively). But even in the Dutch Republic the nobles were much more important in the poorer, landward provinces. The aristocratic house of Orange acted as a kind of surrogate royal family which could be called on in times of crisis to head the government. In 1787, with Prussian military help, William V of Orange forcibly took over the running of the state as a whole. The biggest problem facing the nobility of the republic was not so much exclusion from political power as the threat of extinction, brought about by the non-replenishment of their ranks by newcomers.[7]

By contrast, the Polish–Lithuanian Commonwealth contained a systematic plethora of parliamentary-style institutions designed both to protect and to assert noble rights and to assure the nobility's monopolistic grip on their state. Only nobles had full political rights – which meant that only they were eligible to sit in the *Sejm*, the central, biennial parliament. They were elected by local *sejmiki*, 'mini-parliaments', which all nobles were free to attend: the bans imposed by many *sejmiki* on active participation by landless nobles were widely ignored. Attendance could vary from a handful to five or six thousand. These institutions not only elected MPs: in differing guises and meeting at different times during the year, they elected local officials, voted local taxes, made appointments to the local and national judiciary, made decisions on local administration. They were, in effect, local administrative bodies with a range of powers comparable to, indeed more extensive than, those of the quarter-sessions in that gentleman's commonwealth, England.

However, in Poland, the stalemate of political forces in the seventeenth century, which continued into the eighteenth, had produced a device for the disruption of both central and local parliamentary bodies in the shape of the liberum veto, the right of participating individuals to terminate and disrupt proceedings. Notwithstanding this, the power of the nobility/gentry to dominate society through key institutions was as entrenched in Poland as in England – and, if anything, tending to become stronger. Thus, Polish nobles were in law forbidden to involve themselves in the government of royal towns – but this was widely ignored. Except in the major towns of Polish Prussia, whose prosperity made them a major political force in their own right, members of the nobility regularly sat on town councils. The reformed constitution of 1791, which supposedly gave wider political rights to townsmen, actually made it easier for nobles to dominate the towns by legally throwing open civic office to them. Polish towns could, at best, only petition national and local parliamentary assemblies. As for England, it is all too easy to regard the gentry as the 'landed' interest (which, of course, is how most chose to project themselves). But the insistence on landed income even for non-shire, borough MPs and Justices of the Peace, the role of local notables and men of influence in the selection of sheriffs, land and window tax commissioners, and parish officials, and not least the fact that legal jurisdiction over some of the most dynamic, non-chartered urban centres such as Birmingham or Manchester continued to be vested in feudal courts and/or commissions of the peace, meant that this 'landed interest' had an immensely strong hold over the functioning of the entire country. For most of the eighteenth century, only Hungary had a comparable network of noble-run local institutions to those found in England and Poland, although its central diet was much more vulnerable to the whims of Habsburg rulers. It was not called at all between 1729 and 1741, or between 1764 and 1790.

Comparable elective or semi-elective institutions were prevalent in most major European states. There were pockets, such as parts of north-west Germany, where there were no nobles to speak of and even peasants dominated such local assemblies. Sweden was, by any standards, remarkable in having parliamentary representation in its *Riksdag* not only for towns and clergy, but even for peasants. However, these lesser social groupings had to send elected or co-opted representatives: every Swedish noble family was entitled to sit in the *Riksdag*. The only limitations the nobility recognised were self-imposed: in 1756, concerned by the threat of new royal ennoblements, the *riddarhus*, the *Riksdag*'s house of nobles, voted to close itself to all newcomers until its current numbers, standing at some 1200, fell to below 800. Considering the nobility also dominated the key positions in the army and the civil service, its overall grip on the state seemed unshakeable. This was, in its own way, a 'republic of noblemen'[8] to rank alongside Poland or Venice.

Estates could still be useful, even where they had little real power. Frederick II of Hesse-Cassel was in a position to rule his principality without them: most nobles and aspiring nobles found employment either in his paternalistic bureaucracy or abroad. He had enough income not to rely on the estates' generosity – indeed, in the damaging aftermath of the Seven Years War, he refrained even from claiming traditional grants in the interests of economic reconstruction. But the estates were valuable in other ways. They served as a channel of communication, as occasions for reasserting the authority of the nobility and the just nature of the social hierarchy, as a point at which ruler and the ruling establishment could renew their ties. If they met infrequently (in Hesse-Cassel, usually only once every six years), they usually kept in being a residual *Ausschuss*, or standing committee, to represent themselves. Even in the Hohenzollern lands, where the estates had even less of a presence than in Hesse-Cassel, the committees and the lesser district assembles (the *Kreistage*) survived, both as useful, if symbolic, reminders to the nobility of their collective past and privileges, and as a link between the ruler and his local establishments. Indeed, after the Seven Years War, as Frederick the Great encouraged the nobility of his provinces to take collective steps towards economic reconstruction, new assemblies and institutions, the *Landschaften* emerged as a forum in which nobles might air their problems.[9] The seven separate local assemblies of the electorate of Hanover (where, incidentally, commoners were entitled to sit in the noble estate provided they owned land classified as noble) also had a useful role in maintaining links between the ruler, his ministers and the collectivity of nobles.[10] True, the power that these quasi-parliamentary bodies had once wielded, and the authority that the nobility had enjoyed through them, had been largely decanted (as in Prussia) into the permanent bureaucracies and officer corps which the nobility dominated; but there was no point in abolishing the estates. They helped raise taxes, loans and recruits and to elect individual noblemen to participate in the work of local administration. To dispense with them would be to alienate them; to alienate them could be very dangerous. This was the harsh lesson learned by Joseph II of Austria. Unlike his mother, Maria Theresa, he failed to appreciate that one of the very purposes for which he was ruler was to preserve such institutions. His efforts to do without them led only to their spontaneous coming together in 1790 and the near-collapse of the state; it was left to his more tactful successor and younger brother, Leopold II, to reaffirm the privileges of the estates.

No-one came to appreciate the value of estates more than Joseph's contemporary and ally Catherine II of Russia, though she was determined to ensure they could never get above themselves. Russia, as we have seen, was almost entirely bereft of the autonomous and semi-autonomous institutions that were the hallmark of the *Ständestaat*. Only on the peripheries, principally in the non-Russian Baltic provinces, did these survive. Otherwise there were no parliaments, *parlements*, *Landtage* or *Kreistage*; there were no autonomous municipal corporations. Russian rulers did not even take a coronation oath, for to do so would have implied some contractual obligation towards at least some of their subjects. Estate-style institutions existed, or had existed, in Russian territories: in Pskov and Novgorod, where they had been suppressed when these city republics had been conquered by Moscow in the late fifteenth century; in the eastern Ukraine, which had been annexed from Poland in the mid-seventeenth century; and in the Baltic lands, annexed from Sweden by Peter the Great. But in these newly acquired areas, especially in the Ukraine, such institutions were ever more being depressed by the central state, until they became moribund. The attempt by the Ukrainian nobility to revive them in 1763 was met by the imposition of 36 death sentences by Catherine the Great (though all were subsequently commuted to life imprisonment in Siberia).[11]

Traditionally, the tsars ruled through the unmediated power of centrally appointed governors. Insofar as politics spilt out beyond the court to engage with the wider nobility, it remained largely limited to the Imperial Guard, created by Peter the Great. This still under-researched body, although including some commoners, may, at different points during the eighteenth century, have accommodated almost one in five of active Russian male nobles. Enjoying a comparatively privileged position – higher pay, laxer discipline, accelerated promotion, greater prestige – the Guard regiments had a vested interest in the preservation of the autocracy. In 1730, following the unexpected death of the young tsar, Peter II, on his wedding night, and with no immediately apparent successor in sight, the unusually numerous concourse of nobles assembled for the wedding celebrations demonstrated some ability to sign up to programmes which would, in some measure, regulate imperial power and do something to establish and protect nascent rights for the nobility themselves. Whether or not the various proposals mooted in January–February 1730 for governmental reform had any realistic hope of success is beside the point: the lack of any tradition or machinery of joint consultation and co-ordination among the nobility meant that even if they had been adopted, the proposals for government reform, aimed at producing a wider political involvement among the nobility, were doomed to failure. The vacuum was filled by the Imperial Guard and their commanders and manipulators who opted decisively for a preservation of the status quo. Moreover, when a ruler proved disagreeable to enough of these elements, then the Guard could be used to overthrow them, as happened in 1741 and 1762.[12]

The post mortem that followed the revolt of Pugachev of 1773–4 made much of the absence of responsive local institutions and of effective local government throughout Russia. Catherine's reaction was to embark on the creation of a Russian version of the *Ständestaat* (as a cultured, well-educated German and admirer of Montesquieu, the great lauder of 'intermediary bodies', she was fully acquainted with the theoretical implications). During the 'reforming decade' of 1775–85, she embarked on a programme of controlled decentralisation, encouraging or ordering the establishment of regular noble and town assemblies with limited rights of self-administration. The exercise aimed to foster an *esprit de corps* among the nobility in particular by extensive, and hitherto non-existent, grants of rights, privileges and freedoms. She was the first monarch to set up a network of elective, local courts, distinct from the outgrowths of the centralised administrative structures of the state. Her confirmation in 1785 of the nobles' emancipation from compulsory state service (an emancipation first granted in 1762 by the husband she subsequently deposed and had murdered) was meant to convert the nobility from conscripted and dragooned servants of the state to willing ones, on the pattern of other European states. That these devolved institutions never really took root is another matter. The traditions and the habits of mind, the infrastructures that helped condition them, were, elsewhere, built up over centuries. Nevertheless, they were seen by Catherine as essential to Russia's future well-being. She could only make a start. But the rewards of serving the central state directly (reinforced by Peter's Table of Ranks) were so strong that provincial and local service had virtually no prestige. Catherine's creation of devolved institutions was seen (and projected) as a favour handed down from the ruler. After 1797, her son Paul, in the interests of what he regarded as efficient government, set about dismantling Catherine's local reforms, assemblies and institutions. There was hardly a murmur of protest. Once again, an uncongenial (and possibly insane) tsar had to be constrained by extraordinary means: in a plot reminiscent of Agatha Christie at her more improbable, Paul was assassinated by elite nobles and officers. His son, Alexander, it is true, restored his grandmother's reforms, but this chronic reinvention of devolution from the centre did nothing to reassure the nobility of the value of these institutions. If Russian nobles were to be associated in government, it was through staffing centrally controlled bureaucratic and military organisations, not through organs of genuine self-government.

Where formal estates had disappeared or become weakened, the nobility could generally find alternative local and regional institutions through which to exercise their power. In the poorer, landward provinces of the Dutch Republic, a range of municipal offices continued to be reserved for the numerically declining nobility. In Spain, with the decline of the *Cortes*, the old regional parliamentary assemblies, and with the preference there among many nobles for urban-based residence, control of town councils was either wholly or partly in their hands. In Cordoba, Madrid and, after 1739, Granada, only noblemen could be *regidores* (town councillors). An informal noble monopoly was exercised in many other towns of note. This 'monopoly', however, followed the Italian pattern: a local nobility developed simply by virtue of well-established local elites, not necessarily noble as such, behaving as if they were noble or regarding themselves as noble. That was good enough, one way or another, to bolster noble predominance. If the crown sought more money, it was with these noble-dominated municipal bodies that it had to negotiate – usually at the cost of ceding ever wider jurisdictional rights to them. By 1787, some 50 per cent of the villages and population of Castile had been devolved under the jurisdiction of nobles and towns. But the Spanish crown was always sufficiently strong to reserve the right to intervene in their affairs and to hear appeals against them.[13]

In much of France, estate-style institutions had lapsed by the eighteenth century, though they survived as important forces in the more outlying provinces, the so-called *pays d'états*. The nobility, or would-be nobles, compensated by consolidating their position in the great law courts, the regional *parlements*; and, in the battle between a centralising crown on the one hand and the defence of local rights on the other (which so often included the privileges and immunities of the nobility), it was, of course, the *parlements* that were in the van. After 1750, the *parlement* of Paris came, sporadically if ever more frequently almost by default, to act as a forum for the discussion and criticism of at least some royal measures – although as a primarily judicial institution, it was neither able nor willing to act in the co-ordinated, constructive manner of the British parliament. In practice, this limited role meant that instead of constructive treatment of royal policies, all too often questions of principle on the extent of royal power and its relationship to custom and law were debated in a way which served only to discredit the monarchy (and, in the end, the *parlement* itself).

Venice provides an object lesson both in how effectively nobles could monopolise the levers of power but also in how much of a drawback excessive exclusivity could be. A bewildering array of councils and committees, many of whose workings remain unfathomable today, offered a governing nexus of some 800 posts. Of the roughly 200 families making up the patriciate, 40 dominated the 60 key posts which together made the real decisions in the republic, spread across the so-called Council of Ten, the Lesser Council and the 'Great Wise Men' (*Savi Grandi*) of the College of Twenty-Five. The control was too effective: so reluctant were the patriciate to admit newcomers that, even during the seventeenth century, doubts were emerging as to whether these limited numbers of nobles were sufficient to staff (and more importantly, to staff effectively) all the positions available. In 1775, Alvise Zen warned the nobility that in another 20 years the machinery of government would cease to function.[14]

Of course, nobles who staffed, ran and influenced these bodies tried to do so for their own profit. The pursuit of such sectional advantage reached its highest pitch in Poland. If the laws tying peasants to the land, forbidding townsmen from buying landed property, banning guilds, controlling prices remained unenforceable, that did not alter the fact that they served as a sign of noble aspirations. All over Europe, local elites in general were determined to maintain and protect their social ascendancy. Yet what made the Poles different was the lack of an effective central government to keep such aspirations within bounds. It was, after all, noble ministers in France who aided and abetted policies that nobles outside the government saw as opposed to their interests. And, provided they were not pushed too far, or were aware of the necessities of the situation, nobles were prepared not only to participate in government but to bear the burdens of it. It was all very well for French revolutionary propaganda to portray them as parasites who contributed nothing to the state while the common people groaned under the burden of taxation, and undoubtedly there were those whose reality fitted the caricatures. But it was, of necessity, a hopelessly simplified picture.

That there was widespread exemption of nobles from taxes is true. But it was never wholesale. The extent to which nobles were taxed varied not only from state to state, but from area to area and from locality to locality. On the other hand, there is little doubt that those who were in a position to do so minimised, avoided and evaded taxation as best they could. Commenting on the *Kontribution*, the land tax voted by the estates of Bohemia, Moravia and the Austrian duchies of the Habsburg monarchy in 1765, the British ambassador, Lord Stormont, observed that it was raised 'according to a fixed and pretty equitable proportion, with no Exemption for any man that has property. The Nobles pay their full share ...'.[15] Doubtless Stormont would have said that the *Kontribution*'s equivalent in Britain, the land tax, was a fair one. He might even have complained that in wartime the 'landed interest' was made to pay a disproportionate amount of taxation (certainly the 'landed interest' grumbled loudly about this during the War of the Spanish Succession) at a rate of four shillings in every pound (20 per cent) of landed revenue. But the English land tax was, or at least came to be, a classic example of tax avoidance and manipulation by the gentry and aristocracy, precisely because they controlled its administration and collection at local level. Local bigwigs in the shape of MPs, lords-lieutenant, Justices of the Peace, appointed collectors, receivers and assessors; they sat on the commissions that allocated the tax on a parish-by-parish basis and ran the appeals boards. The initial assessments on which the land tax was based could easily date back to the early seventeenth century or the Middle Ages and were rarely, if ever, uprated on anything other than an individual basis. The further away from London, the less reliable the assessments, although glaringly disproportionate assessments could be found within any region. In Westmorland or Yorkshire, the actual incidence of the tax in wartime was more likely to be closer to two shillings than to four shillings in the pound. In individual cases, it could be much lower still. In real terms, the overall burden sank over the eighteenth century.

Since the land tax was rarely levied at its full amount in real terms, the much more efficiently collected (by trained, professional, fully salaried civil servants) indirect taxes, the excises on individual consumer items, were heavier than they need have been. Indirect taxation hit the poor disproportionately hard. But ministers in London were prepared to tolerate underpayment and late returns in the land tax, and even private financial ventures using tax revenues, precisely because they were conducted by the county establishments and their clients – in other words, by the very people who had to be kept sweet if England was to be effectively administered.[16] It would be astonishing if these practices were not replicated in lands where similar taxes were voted, or where local lords were made responsible for the collection of such taxes.

It was certainly the case in France, where, especially during wartime, the monarchy did attempt to impose extraordinary taxes on nobles. The case of the *capitation*, or poll tax, introduced in January 1695 at the height of the Nine Years War, is instructive. Payable by all families except those of the very poor (those paying less than 40 *sous*, or 2 *livres*, in *taille*), in its first incarnation it stipulated an annual payment, ranging from 1 *livre* (payable by soldiers and day labourers) rising through 22 gradations to 2000 *livres*, payable by the Dauphin, princes of the blood and the farmers-general of the Tax Farm. Wound up in 1698, the tax was reimposed in 1701 on what proved to be a permanent footing. But instead of being imposed on an individual or family basis, it was levied as a set sum allocated among the *généralités*, the principal regional fiscal units. To those who already paid *taille*, it became a supplement to that tax; the level at which the privileged non-*taillables* paid was supposed to be determined by the *intendants*, in consultation with local notables. Many were reluctant to co-operate, while the *intendants*, themselves noble, chose not to be too scrupulous in their assessments. In the eighteenth century, many *intendants* developed strong local ties, and needed to keep the local nobility sweet for their administration to be effective. Special arrangements were made for payment by members of corporations, such as the *parlements* (the *capitation* was deducted directly from their salaries, or *gages*). In the *pays d'états*, the estates divided up the tax as they thought best. The French clergy initially compounded for a lump sum (4 million *livres* per annum in 1695), only to buy themselves permanent exemption for a one-off payment of 24 million *livres* in 1710. The effect of all these modifications was to turn a tax that had never been particularly heavy for those who already enjoyed fiscal privilege into a largely symbolic payment. In 1789, the economist Dupont de Nemours reckoned that, on average, the *capitation* took up one-eleventh of the income of those who already paid *taille*, principally commoners; for those exempt from *taille*, he put the average *capitation* payment at one-seventieth of their overall incomes! [17]

Much the same fate befell other extraordinary taxes which the French government periodically introduced. Under the enormous pressures of the War of the Spanish Succession, on 14 October 1710 Louis XIV introduced a *dixième*, a 10 per cent tax on all forms of income in any way connected with property, in the widest sense of the word: houses, industry, incomes from office, royal salaries and pensions, even profits from indirect taxation (which in France, unlike England, was largely privatised). Such was the resentment against the intrusion at all levels of propertied society and such the evasion and blatant under-assessment that the tax was dropped in 1717.[18] Though subsequently reintroduced during the Wars of the Polish and Austrian Successions (1733–6, 1741–9), it was peppered with exemptions; the same applied to its successor, the *vingt-ième* (a notional 5 per cent tax) introduced in 1749. Once again, taxation, compounding, influence and connections kicked in. Thus, in 1784, when the *vingtième* was being supposedly collected at a threefold rate, that is, at 15 per cent, Charles-François-Casimir de Saulx, comte de Tavanes, with an income from his landed estates alone of 95,000 *livres*, was paying his *vingtièmes* at a total rate of 7 per cent, less than half of what he ought to have been paying. The triple-rated *vingtième* levied between 1782 and 1786 returned some 23 million *livres* annually: it should have returned almost eleven times as much. On this reckoning, the comte de Tavanes was actually paying more than his fair share!

None the less, the extent of such underpayments needs to be kept in perspective. The rate at which direct taxes on income such as the *dixièmes* and *vingtièmes* were imposed on individuals was ultimately determined by the local *intendant*. Powerful nobles such as Saulx-Tavanes were not the sort an ambitious *intendant* could afford to alienate. Assessments could be adjusted appropriately. Philippe, duc d'Orléans, admitted as much in 1787: 'I do a deal with the intendants and pay more or less what I please.' The end of such deals would bring a tax hike of 300,000 *livres*.[19] Lesser nobles, lesser opportunities. The evidence from at least some areas of France in the last two decades of the *Ancien Régime* suggests that although nobles continued to pay less than their fair share, they were being made to pay uncomfortably more: the real levels of *vingtièmes* in Normandy were close to what they should have been, while the energetic and intrusive assessment methods of the royal administration came as a real shock.[20] The same fate hit petty nobles elsewhere. In Hungary, the so-called 'taxed ones', the *taxalistae*, accounted for around 90 per cent of all nobles. Owning tiny scraps of land, usually with no serfs on them (some *taxalistae* even sought employment with serfs), they had to pay the land taxes from which they were technically exempt but which were still owed from their properties.[21]

Up-to-date cadasters (that is, assessments of land, its yields and returns) were extremely complex and difficult to conduct, still more difficult to keep up to date, and depended as much on local attestations as on professional, independent surveys. Overall levels of underassessment in France, it has been calculated, ran at anything between 45 and 75 per cent. Some more public-spirited nobles declared up to 80 per cent of their incomes, others virtually nothing.[22] The French government was so impressed by the scale of the potential problems that it would contemplate, at best, only local and regional surveys, very thorough though some of these were, particularly after 1772. Colbert had planned a national cadaster in 1679, but such was the opposition from nobility and clergy that he dropped the plan. The most far-reaching survey inaugurated under the *Ancien Régime*, that instigated for Corsica in 1769, was completed in 1796 (only two years behind the original schedule). The Milan cadaster, widely regarded as a model of its kind, begun by the duchy's Habsburg rulers in 1720, was only completed in 1759. The much less exacting 'Theresian' cadaster for the Austrian and Bohemian lands (on the basis of which Stormont praised their equitable tax burden), begun in 1749, was only completed by 1784, and over a third of the productive land in these provinces may not have been surveyed at all.[23] The great Castilian cadaster begun in 1750 was complete by 1760; subsequent re-evaluations occupied a further four years (1760-4) only for practical and political problems to frustrate the financial reforms it was supposed to support.[24]

Tax exemption could be taken a stage further: nobles were better placed than most to block fiscal measures detrimental to their interests. The 1764 Hungarian Diet refused to accept either increased taxation or government proposals for much closer monitoring of peasant obligations to landlord and state. In 1784, coal-owning gentry and magnates in England were able to use their parliamentary clout to scupper William Pitt's plans for a tax on coal. Paul I's efforts to convert noble indebtedness in Russia into obligations to the state, to be redeemed by the payment of punitive rates of interest, not merely failed but contributed to an atmosphere in which his removal by assassination in 1801 was ecstatically welcomed by the Russian nobility.

Many European states were dynastic agglomerates: taxation depended more on ad hoc and historical circumstances than on anything resembling rational planning. In France, the chief land tax, the *taille*, was so closely associated with commoner status that to obtain exemption from it was to place oneself well on the road to outright ennoblement. But there were two kinds of *taille* – 'personal' and 'real'. *Taille personnelle* was owed by the individual, although poor nobles who worked their land directly were exempted, unlike their Hungarian counterparts. Even so, if the land in question was worked directly for the benefit of the nobleman (as opposed to being leased out to tenants or sharecroppers), there was a limit to how much exemption he could claim for it: up to 'four ploughs' (the actual extent varied from one area to another, but some 400 acres can serve as a guide) would return no *taille*, but anything above that would. In truth, this was hardly a burden, since direct farming was comparatively rare in France, and most lands were indeed worked through tenants, who were subject to the *taille*. On the other hand, the south in particular was the home of *taille réelle*, tied directly to the land itself. Since at least the fifteenth century, properties had been classified as 'noble' or 'commoner'. 'Noble' lands were exempt from *taille*, commoner ones were not. But if nobles purchased commoner lands, then they were liable to pay *taille* on them; in turn, commoners, *roturiers*, purchasing noble land were exempt from the *taille*.

Nobles were liable to indirect taxes – but again the system was skewed in their favour. They could normally sell at least some of the produce of their estates free of tax and customs and buy in items for their personal consumption free of tax (in France, this applied above all to estate-produced wines).[25] The response of a government that needed ever greater sums was to place more weight on indirect taxation, rather than to burden the commoner taxpayer disproportionately. Indeed, one of the reasons why Necker in 1780 agreed that increases in the *taille* should, unprecedentedly, be subjected to registration by the *parlements* lay in his confidence that those bodies were extremely unlikely to agree to register them: the government would then have no choice but to look to other, more inclusive forms of taxation.[26] It has to be remembered that evasions, avoidance and exemptions in all areas were not confined to the nobility.

There is another side, however, to noble reluctance to take on fresh taxation (of course, this reluctance was peculiar neither to the nobility nor to the eighteenth century). Whatever benefits the nobility enjoyed, they derived at least notionally from the duties and services expected of

them. Public or state service could, at the individual level, be very onerous indeed for the nobles and gentry of Europe. In general, in wartime
the nobility did accept higher rates of tax – the English land tax doubled
from two to four shillings in the pound; the French objection to the *vingt-
ième* stemmed not so much from the tax itself as that it was being levied in
peacetime; even in Poland, confronted with the threat of massive Russian invasion in 1791, the *Sejm* voted unprecedented taxation which, it
was accepted, would fall in the first instance on noble landlords. Those
who did evade could take the line that they were, after all, expected to
perform a whole host of unremunerated, or poorly remunerated, vital
tasks for the state. Central governments, in effect, used landowners,
noble, ecclesiastical and commoner, as an informal, largely unpaid network of local administrators. The offices of sheriff or Justice of the Peace
could be very onerous, but they went unremunerated. French *parlementaires* and other sovereign court officials had complex and difficult judicial and administrative tasks to discharge, yet their official pay, their
gages, was not only meagre, irregular and frequently in arrears, but vulnerable to continuous and arbitrary demands for payments confirming
the rights of such *officiers* to hold office, to pass it on to their sons, or for
confirmations of their noble or ennobling status. When *gages* were paid,
tax deductions at source, mainly for *vingtièmes* and *capitations*, bit deeply
into them, in some cases leaving the hapless official with nothing at all.[27]
The unsalaried nature of most high-ranking Venetian offices and the
often burdensome duties and expenditures associated with them contributed significantly to the reluctance of Venetian nobles to hold office
or of outsiders to seek Venetian noble status. Diplomats, almost invariably noble, of all countries were routinely expected to depend on their
own resources not only to finance themselves, but to pay for clerks, assistants and secretaries. Polish and Hungarian magnates offered the services of armed followings, even of private armies, to the state in times of
need. The combined private armies of Polish magnates probably
exceeded the strength of the national army (admittedly, around a pitiful
12,000 men for most of the century), and if they were useless against
invaders, they at least performed something of a police role in the wild
Ukrainian marches. In 1741, Paul Anton Esterházy fitted out a regiment of 200 hussars at his own expense for the defence of the Austrian
monarchy. In 1797, Thomas Mansell-Talbot of Glamorgan offered to
raise a private army of 1000 men for the defence of the Welsh coastline
against revolutionary French invasion.[28] Gentlemen-officers were
expected, in wartime, to dig deep into their own pockets to provide for

their men while they themselves were unpaid, or ran up debts in the discharge of their duties for which (in Britain certainly) they were liable to be legally pursued. Frederick William I of Prussia was quite prepared to treat the nobility like serfs, tearing 12-year-olds away from home and conscripting them into military academies and the army. At the end of the Seven Years War, hundreds of Prussian nobles were in dire economic straits, not just as a result of the devastation wreaked by the fighting, but as a result of debts incurred in the course of active service.[29]

Under the framework of Peter the Great's 1722 Table of Ranks, Russian nobles simply had no official standing in society unless they held some form of efficient, executive office, military, naval or civil (though this was to be modified, in favour of the rich, by Catherine II in 1785). From 1711, all noble male youths aged ten had to register in the local government chancelleries, to attend schools (many of which did not exist), and enter active military service at the age of 15. Such service would be for life, or until disablement. A decree of 1736 reduced the term to 25 years, with the proviso that the state could waive the concession as it found fitting. True, noble officers were allowed extensive furlough in peacetime, but there was not a decade in the eighteenth century when Russia was not engaged in major warfare. For most nobles, Peter III's 'emancipation' from service obligations in 1762 (confirmed by Catherine in 1785) was a fiction: leaving aside the small print of these decrees, the vast majority of nobles simply could not afford not to serve the state. Poorer nobles might find themselves treated like serfs. Among the demands of the nobility presented during the 1730 crisis were pleas for an end to forcing nobles to serve as sailors and even artisans.[30] Grandees might expect compensation in the form of honours and offices, but these benefits were rarely available at the level of captain or lieutenant. The numerous local officials elected by Polish local assemblies might, or might not, be salaried – certainly the Poles continually harped on about the need to rely on men of 'virtue' rather than officials drawing salaries (and it did keep the taxes down).

Nobles, then, found that their status not only brought them benefits, but enabled the state to exploit them. Kings and their ministers had always relied on nobles, especially landowning nobles, to help them rule. But in the eighteenth century, the range of obligations expanded, partly because governments began to be more active in promoting the shape of the state, in gathering information, in the expansion of their armed forces. The tasks were often onerous, tedious and unpaid. To be a gentleman living off one's rents was ceasing to be the desirable ideal it had once been: the ideal noble had to serve, and preferably serve the state and the community. Individual nobles would have put their own particular interpretation on what Philippe-Auguste de Sainte Foy, chevalier d'Arcq, the doughty defender of traditional noble values and of a distinct nobility, had to say in 1751, but few would have dared disagree with the sentiments:

> Since the state nourishes its members, all its members should serve the state. The idle and therefore useless citizen comports himself like a criminal towards his own country, depriving it of all he consumes. A gentleman is a citizen before being a noble and the only privilege which nobility confers on him, is in the choice of important services which the state can and should expect from him. The moment in which he ceases to think in this way is the moment in which he ceases to be a noble.[31]

Twenty years later, perhaps more ominously, a French minister, Joseph Terray, the controller-general of finances, made the same point:

> Nobility should only be the reward of service rendered to the State ... It seems therefore that when ennobled persons or their descendants give the State no service and are content to be noble so as to enjoy the privileges and prerogatives attached to nobility the State has a right to demand that they serve in their own way and particularly by contributing to its needs ... they can only be regarded as simple privileged persons, equally onerous to the nobility whose labours they do not share, and to the people whose burdens they do not bear.[32]

This kind of rhetoric left many questions unanswered. During the seventeenth century as never before, the state had begun to impress the need for political obedience on its great nobles, and this process continued, with a greater or lesser degree of success, into the eighteenth. But the eighteenth also saw a new development: as the demands of the state grew (and within the term 'state', of course, are comprehended numerous noble ministers and administrators), not only were more and more regulated duties imposed on nobles, but so, too, did the state seek to impose greater economic and fiscal subordination on its nobility. Even in states run by the nobility and gentry themselves this was accepted. The demands of war, the desire for a healthy, productive and disciplined (and, therefore, not dangerous) population, meant that the excessive exploitation of the peasantry by their seigneurial masters became increasingly less acceptable to central governments. Few nobles could genuinely boast such an impeccable ancient pedigree as the Austro-Bohemian Kaunitz family. Yet it was that family's most illustrious representative, the chancellor Wenzel Anton, who wrote to Maria Theresa on 1 May 1763 that 'our sovereigns increasingly seek to curb the nobility, because the true strength of the state consists of the greatest number of its people, namely the common man. It is he who deserves priority of consideration.'[33]

Eighteenth-century governments increasingly faced a dilemma, and the nobility were at its centre. On the one hand, governments were aware of the need to become more effective, and the nobility were recognised as being both the principal obstacle to that (though in Catholic states, they might come a close second to the Church in this respect); on the other, the nobility were necessary precisely to help discharge the business of government. Frederick the Great of Prussia resolved the matter by issuing patents against serf exploitation which he well knew would be ineffective; Joseph II's much more energetic efforts to regulate serf relations so alienated his nobles that they brought the Habsburg monarchy to the edge of collapse. Either way, if the nobility and the governments with which they maintained a love–hate relationship were to survive, even before the French Revolution erupted it was becoming clear that the relationship between them as it had stood for most of the eighteenth century would have to be recast in the nineteenth.

4

EDUCATION

What sort of education, if any, did the nobility, the born, natural leaders of society, need to acquit themselves well in their station in life? Educational accomplishment meant different things in different places. In Russia, where the huge mass of society was overwhelmingly illiterate, the fact that this illiteracy was shared as late as the 1760s by around one in six nobles was less embarrassing than it would have been for the aristocracy and gentry of England and France, among whom literacy was pretty well universal. In the 1730s and 1740s, the heir to the greatest fortune (and debts) in Lithuania, Karol Radziwiłł, was taught his letters by having them set up as shooting targets in the palace courtyard. He learned little else, but he acquired all the sottish primitive social skills that allowed him to mix freely with the local petty (and frequently illiterate) nobility. To Charles de Rohan, prince de Soubise, his woefully inadequate education was of no account compared to his ancient pedigree, immense wealth and personal courage; but even among his kind, educational shortcomings were, at the very least, a growing embarrassment. Rohan's case was compounded by the humiliating defeat inflicted on the army he commanded at Rossbach, on 5 November 1757, at the hands of someone from the same social sphere but one of the best-educated men of his time, Frederick the Great of Prussia. The spate of critical pamphlets that followed the disaster in France, the 'Soubisades', did nothing to hide the unfortunate ignoramus's intellectual shortcomings.[1]

The pressure for nobles to attain a decent standard of education was nothing new. 'Do your lessons! There is nothing more ridiculous for a gentleman than stupidity', grumbled a Lithuanian magnate, Karol Chodkiewicz, at his son in 1611. He would have been horrified by the young Karol Radziwiłł. In the eighteenth century, as learning, literacy and the commercialisation of the intellect became more widespread than ever, that pressure was growing, the Radziwiłłs and Rohans of the world notwithstanding. Most education had to be paid for: those nobles who were poor and unlearned were among those most conscious of their deficiencies and most anxious for them to be corrected. Without education, they would simply stagnate, perhaps even fall back into the body of commoners. Non-noble parvenus would overtake them. For almost as soon as anything new entered the educational curricula, commoners proved as adept at aping it as they did in the areas of dress or fashion. In France, in Russia, in Poland, impoverished nobles increasingly clamoured for improved access to a new education.

Until the state began to take a grip on education at a national level after the French Revolution, education in most countries, not least for the nobility, was based largely on a mix of provision by unregulated private and ecclesiastical enterprise. However, something like a core curriculum existed for the European nobility at least since the humanist educational programmes of the Renaissance. This was the study of classical learning, that is, an acquaintance with the Latin language and the history and philosophy of ancient Rome and Greece. Greek remained a minority interest; it was more common to read the Greek classics in Latin translation. It is hard, in the twenty-first century, to appreciate the importance of the classical world to the cultivated eighteenth-century mind. The point was well made by Voltaire: 'It is the history of the Roman Empire which most merits our attention, for it is the Romans who have been our masters and legislators.' Commenting on the Greek and Athenian victories over the Persians, he noted that 'This superiority of a small, but generous and free people, over all of enslaved Asia, is perhaps the most glorious feature of human history.'[2] Although John Locke was one of many who complained that rather too much classical learning was drummed into young noblemen (noblewomen who benefited from such a classical education were very much the exception), he nevertheless conceded that '*Latin*, I look upon as absolutely necessary to a Gentleman'.[3]

Greece and Rome furnished the paradigms of political, social and intellectual success. They set models of patriotism and self-sacrifice (particularly neatly conveyed in the many Latin translations of Plutarch's *Lives*) which virtuous statesmen were expected to emulate. The memory of the virtuous men of antiquity carried the assurance that the memory of the virtuous men of the eighteenth century would be preserved. The military stratagems of the Greeks and Romans remained a living model for the educated soldier. Through study of the ancients' language, laws and literature, any ruling class would be able to hone its own skills in political discourse, maintain standards of elegant rhetoric, adorn its conversation with emblems and allusions only dimly perceptible to the common herd. The *parlement* of Paris was proud to compare itself to the Senate of ancient Rome, the English were absurdly pleased to be told by Montesquieu that their political system was superior to that of ancient Rome (perhaps not too many reached that point in the *Esprit des Lois* where he admitted he was not quite serious), the Polish nobility needed no-one to tell them that they had improved on the institutions of ancient Rome (they did not make the mistake of sharing liberty with commoners), and the assassins of Tsar Paul I compared themselves to republicans freeing Rome of its tyrants. They even set the original date of their deed for the Ides of March – the 15th – 1801, until events obliged them to bring it forward. (The same self-images, of course, also gripped the revolutionaries in France.) The two seminal historical works of the eighteenth century, Montesquieu's *Considerations on the causes of the grandeur and decline of the Romans* (1734), and Gibbon's *Decline and fall of the Roman Empire* (1776–88) reflected the eighteenth century's obsession with the topic. Yes, Rome had declined – but it had lasted a very long time and had conquered most of the world worth conquering. Most cultivated gentlemen in most European countries were probably better informed on classical antiquity than on their own histories. And Latin remained practically useful as a vehicle of communication: Dr Johnson, visiting Paris in 1775, got by perfectly well on Latin alone.[4]

   The basics of reading, writing and religion were above all to be inculcated at home, possibly by a governor or governess, but more likely by a member of the family: the mother or some spinster aunt, or by a local clergyman (who might well be family). For the majority of those nobles who could afford it and were prepared to send their sons to school, formal structured education and immersion in the worlds of classical antiquity began at around the age of 11 or 12, in a *Gymnasium* or grammar school, college, academy or private pension. Grammar schools were, above all, precisely that: they offered a six- or seven-year course primarily in Latin, starting from a very elementary level, working through texts on literature, history, philosophy, rhetoric and culminating in works such as Cicero's *On duties*, laying out in detail the virtues expected of a gentleman. The classical curriculum was probably found at its fullest, most far-reaching and persistent in the schools and colleges of Poland–Lithuania and Hungary. Both countries obstinately sought to preserve, even petrify, their existing governmental institutions, and an unchanging education was the way to secure that. But even here, innovation began to make some headway from mid-century.

If the nobility were to remain culturally distinct, their educational establishments had to be set apart. As early as the mid-sixteenth century, some secondary schools in the Austrian Habsburg lands were reserved purely for nobles. Amid the chaos of the French wars of religion, when noble violence and brutality seemed to plumb new depths, there were those, such as the Huguenot François de la Noue, who dreamed of a new, fitting education for the nobility that would both permit them to exercise self-mastery and bring out their supposedly innate moral superiority. The upshot was the establishment, first in Germany and Italy, later in France, of 'academies' for gentlemen. After spending perhaps two or three years in grammar schools or coming directly from some form of domestic education, nobles would attend these to receive instruction in subjects more appropriate to their status: riding, dancing, fencing and weapons-training, drawing and mathematics (enough to master the theoretical basics of military architecture), in addition to modern languages and whatever else might become fashionable. The earliest Italian academy, established at Verona in 1565, was a glorified riding-school, and the academies founded in Saxony and Baden in 1540 and 1587 or at Siegen in 1617 were little better. But the subjects offered were essential to the cultivated nobleman. He had to be able to manage a horse in a 'noble' fashion, more gracefully and more effortlessly than his social inferiors. Fencing was a necessity: the nobles' near-universal right to bear a sword distinguished them (in theory) from commoners, and when duelling, despite many prohibitions, was a constant hazard, poor swordplay could cost a nobleman 'his property, his honor, his life, and often his soul, along with the tranquillity of his family'. Dancing was as important – not just for its own sake, but because it conferred graceful deportment, gait and gesture. Drawing could be as useful on campaign as in peacetime, 'especially if he travel ... How many Buildings may a Man see, how many Machines and Habits meet with, the Idea's whereof would be easily retain'd and communicated, by a little Skill in *Drawing* ... ?'[5] These were truly vocational subjects for the nobleman, bringing out his innate superiority, setting his very physical presence emphatically apart from 'the multitude'.[6]

By the eighteenth century, although many grammar schools and colleges continued to retain the classics at the core of their curricula (a 15-year-old at Eton might expect to study Latin for 18 hours a week), they also offered the new subjects as integral or optional extras.[7] The academies proved too expensive for many nobles: deliberately elitist, they might take fewer than 100 students at any one time. This contrasted very starkly, especially in Catholic countries, with the network of colleges run by the teaching orders, most notably the Jesuits. Initially reluctant to go beyond a non-Christian humanist curriculum, the orders soon appreciated the benefits and patronage they could enjoy if they modified their curricula to suit public demand – 'public' because their colleges were usually open to all, regardless of social distinction, but inevitably it was the nobility who set the tone. In France or Italy, where new ideas circulated freely, such establishments were quick to offer even outlandishly modish or modern subjects alongside the classic canon: besides modern languages (mainly French and Italian) and gentlemanly accomplishments, mathematics and the natural sciences came to be sure of a place in the curriculum. It was a well-established practice in the colleges for students to present theatrical performances. In the academies, equestrian displays were put on for a respectable or distinguished audience. By the second half of the eighteenth century, scientific, experimental demonstrations were increasingly part of this repertoire. Not that gentlemen, in principle, were expected to become scientists or scholars: '*Learning* must be had, but in the second place, as subservient only to greater Qualities'.[8] The education they received gave nobles a basic platform from which they could rule their subordinates, perhaps run their estates. John Locke advised any gentleman to study arithmetic and '*Merchants Accompts*' as 'possibly there is not any thing of more use and efficacy, to make him preserve the [landed] Estate he has'.[9]

This was essentially learning aimed at a leisured ruling group, assured of its place at the head of the social hierarchy. Outside the exclusive academies, much of the education on offer was open to anyone who could afford it. The basic educational provision was free – board and lodging and tuition in 'extra' subjects racked up the costs. At the showpiece Jesuit college of Louis-le-Grand in Paris, as many as three-quarters of the students were drawn from the bourgeoisie and the poor. Entry could be from the age of five, though eight to nine was more usual. The school could take around 3000 pupils, who were taught in enormous classes of between 100 and 300. The classes froze in winter. New arrivals took an exam to determine in which class they should be placed before they undertook the standard classical curriculum. Studies were enhanced by generous dosages of 'modern' subjects such as languages, mathematics, the natural sciences. The progressive Fathers of Louis-le-Grand taught a rationalised, enlightened Christianity, where original sin and divine wrath had little place. They were ready to take in protestants and Jansenists. The specially written Latin play performed every August was one of the highlights of the Parisian social year. The school promoted debate on the issues of the day. Louis XIV urged his courtiers to send their sons there. 'Everybody who bears a name in France dates his earliest youth from Louis-le-Grand', wrote the archbishop of Paris in 1762. Voltaire remembered his days there fondly and repaid the Jesuits who had taught him with bitter vitriol. Discipline was comparatively relaxed. A kind of social order was preserved: the richest boys (though these were not exclusively noble – they included aspirants from the worlds of finance and commerce) lodged in their own private apartments, which might include accommodation for their personal staff, even their private tutors. The better-off were encouraged to subsidise their poorer schoolfellows, as an act of charity designed to preserve social subordination. The less well-to-do lived in dormitories for about 20 students; others lodged in cheap outside accommodation.[10]

The Jesuits dominated the education of Catholic Europe. No other religious order could rival them, although a number of smaller ones, such as the Piarists and the Theatines, sought to attract support by giving greater prominence to the 'moderns' (even suitably sanitised versions of authors such as Voltaire were on offer). Much depended on geographic location: the teaching orders of relatively more urbanised and commercialised France and Italy were quicker to provide more up-to-date curricula than their counterparts in the Habsburg lands or in Poland. In 1740 the establishment of an exclusive Piarist boarding school with a modernised curriculum, the Collegium Nobilium in Warsaw, obliged the much better endowed but conservative Polish Jesuits to offer a much wider range of teaching. In the Habsburg lands, Maria Theresa's ministers deliberately sought the overthrow of the near-monopoly of the Jesuits on secondary and higher education.

The classical humanist curriculum remained central, even after the expulsion of the Jesuits from much of Catholic Europe during the 1760s and their abolition by the papacy in 1774. A range of ecclesiastical and secular initiatives helped fill the void left by the order's abolition. France was swept by a wave of *maisons d'éducation* which promised, in newspaper advertisements, posters and semi-philosophical prospectuses, to give a 'new' education to those who could afford it. It is doubtful if what they offered differed substantially from what was already available in the best ecclesiastical colleges. The new establishments were distinguished above all by their claims to offer a 'natural' education, as recommended principally by Rousseau (one prospectus of 1774, for a Parisian establishment, was actually entitled *Théorie d'une éducation républicaine, suivant les principes de J.-J. Rousseau*). Sceptics doubted whether the extravagant promises of healthy, natural and hygienic conditions (usually contrasted with the enclosed 'prisons' of the colleges) and of constant, morally pure individual supervision reminiscent of the fanciful pedagogy of Rousseau's *Émile* were realistic, or indeed whether they amounted to anything other than money-making wheezes to exploit a fashionably gullible clientele.[11] These schools were also complemented by a range of 'pensions' aimed at young noblemen, offering to prepare them for the service of king and state. Such exclusive 'pensions' could be found across the continent. Almost all such establishments remained out of reach of poorer nobles.

The well-to-do were ready to employ private tutors for their children. John Locke preferred this mode of tuition, largely because of his grave reservations about what large numbers of adolescent schoolboys in close proximity to one another would get up to. A private tutor was a status symbol or fashion statement. He need not be too expensive. There were plenty of well-educated persons (or persons who could pass themselves off as such) across Europe of little means who would be grateful for any form of employment. Eastern Europe was a flourishing hunting-ground for these. Individual nobles in Poland or Russia were often desperate to give their sons a 'modern' education, at the very least in manners and French. The quality and experiences of these varied enormously. Tutors of common birth or no means were always at a disadvantage in dealing with a combination of wayward charges and doting parents, who might well be prone to look on these pedagogues as little more than domestic servants. At one end of the scale, Johann Christoph Ostermann, from the family of a poor Westphalian pastor of Bochum, managed to land a post as tutor to the nieces of Peter the Great and provide an entrée to his younger brother Heinrich into Russian government service in 1703: Heinrich eventually rose to be chancellor and one of the most influential figures in Russian foreign policy after Peter's death. Rather more typical were the experiences of Hubert Vautrin, a Frenchman who entered the service of the Polish–Lithuanian Sapieha family between 1777 and 1782 as tutor, only to find himself in the depths of the Polish Ukraine, treated with contempt, his promised remuneration never paid. In short, he felt himself treated little better than a serf. On his return to France, he sought his revenge by writing a damning account of the horrors of Polish–Lithuanian life.[12]

Some families might employ 'governors' of higher social standing, gentlemen in their own right, to direct their sons' education, particularly on the Grand Tour which capped the education of the wealthy. However, the great majority of those who could afford to give their sons a decent education seem to have sent them off, for at least part of their education, to some form of boarding school. If nothing else, they could rely on some form of structured teaching from (hopefully) experienced teachers. Even more importantly, they could expect to make connections and friendships that would be useful in later life and politics (it was, after all, a very small world) and acquire some form of socialisation. Those of higher or wealthier background might expect to continue lording it over their less fortunate contemporaries (poor nobles in Polish colleges might even act as valets to magnate sons in return for being educated alongside their young masters). Thus, amid social intercourse the social hierarchy would be preserved. Presumably, very few preceptors would have dared follow the tone of William Markham, headmaster of Westminster School between 1753 and 1764, who sharply informed an excessively status-conscious aristocratic sprig that

> the only distinctions made here are those that arise from superior talents and superior application. The youth that wishes to obtain eminence must endeavour to deserve it. Therefore your place at present is the lowest place in the lowest form.[13]

Quite what attending the right school might mean is shown by some data from England. Of 460 peers born after 1711, over half attended Eton or Westminster; a good third of MPs who sat in the Commons after 1750 went to Eton, Westminster, Winchester or Harrow. 'If to be first minister of the crown was an object of ambition, education at Eton or Westminster was a sound investment.'[14] Eton and Winchester (unlike Westminster) quite deliberately gave pride of place to sons of peers, placing them at the head of class or of the whole school. Eton also prepared its boys for the rough-and-tumble of politics by other means: at least unofficially, the staff turned a blind eye to the occasional riots between boys and the local butchers and bargees – though when, in 1768, the young George Grenville led an uprising against the school's own staff, that was deemed excessive. He was flogged and expelled. He received no sympathy from his father. The local drinking-dens and brothels furnished introductions to other sides of life.[15] In terms of local social relations, the reputation of Etonians was no worse than that enjoyed by their counterparts anywhere else in Europe. The ideal of a self-enclosed college establishment that would protect its inmates from the vices of the outside world remained just that – an ideal.

Universities were something of an optional extra. Their reputation as centres of learning was decidedly mixed. A nobleman who had attended a college, grammar school or academy did not, unless he was entering the Church or, in some countries, the legal profession, need a degree. Once he had a modernised, humanist curriculum behind him, he hardly needed anything else. A psychological obstacle to nobles entering universities was that they were, in general, open to other orders of society. If nothing else, there might not be enough of their own kind to make them congenial to nobles and gentlemen. A strongly scholastic, medieval curriculum (at least on the arts side) dominated most European universities until the second half of the century, and this was quite enough to deter those who had access to the alternative, more modern curricula of the better colleges and academies. But as ever, the picture varied. The colleges of Oxford and Cambridge were cosy enough to attract the British gentry and peerage in increasing numbers. They acted as a kind of finishing school to the sociability already acquired at Eton or Westminster, rather than as places of intellectual stimulation. Around 1700, barely one in twenty descendants of English peers went to Oxford; by 1800, it was closer to one in five; the story was much the same at Cambridge. They may have formed only a tiny minority of all matriculating students (at their highest, never quite reaching 2 per cent, although this proportion would rise sharply if sons of non-peer gentry were included), but in relationship to the peerage families themselves the numbers were significant.[16] Attendance among French nobles at university must have been significantly higher, if only because of the requirements of the sovereign (and other) law courts, which stipulated at least three years of legal study and the passing of the appropriate examinations. Though these demands were often waived, the French *robe* never questioned their necessity for their future careers.[17]

Germany, with 31 universities by the 1750s, the most extensive such network in Europe, had a dismal record of attracting noble students. Even where more innovative curricula were introduced, as at Halle, Göttingen or Erlangen, the reputation of the majority of universities, with their antiquated, scholastic curricula, remained offputting. At Halle, in 1694, Christian Thomasius began to graft the curricula of the 'knightly academies', or *Ritterakademien*, onto the university's law courses, with a view to educating nobles for responsible positions within the civil service.[18] Halle's reputation suffered a major blow, however, with the expulsion of one of Germany's leading philosophers, Christian Wolff, in 1723. George II of Hanover, ever eager to put one over on his much-hated Hohenzollern relatives, tried to fill the vacuum by founding a similar type of university at Göttingen in 1737 which was aimed not only at Hanover's own nobility (acknowledged by his own ministers as being woefully deficient in education) but at adding lustre to the Hanoverian dynasty by drawing in students of noble birth from across Germany. Among the attractions, in addition to a curriculum that combined traditional learning and the 'moderns' (including natural law, the sciences, pure and applied mathematics, modern languages, politics and modern history), was instruction in a whole range of 'courtly arts'. The university acquired a reputation for unparalleled intellectual freedom; but its biggest single building was the indoor riding hall. Its keynote legal course placed new stress on German common law, with a view to emphasising the rights of the subject, and especially the noble subject (as opposed to the rights of the ruler, emphasised by Thomasius and Wolff at Halle). And, indeed, nobles made up a much larger percentage of the student body at Göttingen than elsewhere in Germany, averaging some 13 per cent (comparable substantial universities were more likely to recruit around 5 per cent of their intake from nobles).[19] The other major university that attracted considerable numbers of nobles was Leyden in the Dutch Republic. Leyden's reputation for excellence was probably unequalled in eighteenth-century Europe.

The fact remains, however, that the overwhelming majority of those who attended universities were drawn from the middling sort. On the other hand, in Germany in particular, a university education could facilitate ennoblement. To rise through state employment and administration to serve in the ranks of the *Dienstadel*, the 'serving' nobility, was a recognised career path for talented commoners. The Russian polymath (and noble) Mikhail Lomonosov, one of the founding fathers of Moscow University, clearly hoped the same would happen in his own country. At the foundation of the university in 1755, he wrote:

The sciences are a path to nobility, and all entering [the Gymnasium attached to Moscow University] should look upon themselves as on those entering a nobility. Therefore all accepted [for study] and not already belonging to the nobility should in their relations with others, and even in the clothes they wear, assume a posture as if they belonged to the nobility.

In fact, Moscow University attracted pitifully few nobles, not only because of the presence of commoners, but because of the absence of the classical, humanist intellectual bedrock that underpinned the Latinate culture of most of Europe.[20]

The state in Germany contributed directly to the education of the nobility only sporadically, mainly through establishing its own specialised *Ritterakademien*. Most of these were aimed, at least in theory, at preparing nobles for the increasingly technical demands of warfare. They were also seen as a means of reviving the noble ethos where it was perceived to be in decay and of binding the nobility much closer to the state. Institutions founded by rulers or governments aimed not merely to duplicate the sort of cultivated education available in the private or clerically run academies, but to add a much more practical twist to them by treating them as seed-beds for future military and civilian officials. The Great Elector's Academy at Colberg, founded in 1653 and relocated to Berlin around 1705, initially concentrated on the turning out of artillerymen. During the eighteenth century, it was much expanded to accommodate some 400 'cadets' (the original establishment had held fewer than 30). Frederick William I used it as a deliberate instrument to inculcate a military service ethos into selected nobles (youths aged about 13 were normally taken in, often forcibly). But even during Frederick the Great's reign, when the involvement of the nobility with the army reached a new height, only around 15 per cent of Prussian adult male nobles received this kind of formal military preparation. Overall, two-thirds of the Prussian nobility had no proper preparation for either the army or the less prestigious bureaucracy.[21]

The eighteenth century saw a plethora of such establishments: in Russia, the Empress Anna, prodded by Field Marshal Burkhardt Christoph von Münnich, set up a cadet corps in St Petersburg in 1731–2; Maria Theresa set up a military academy at Wiener Neustadt in 1752; Stanisław August of Poland created a cadet corps in 1765. In the same year, Frederick the Great set up an *Académie des Nobles* in Berlin to train 20 selected students each year for plum diplomatic and military posts. The largest number of such schools under state control was set up in France, spearheaded by the founding of the *École Militaire* in Paris in 1750 – the immediate source of inspiration for this was the Cadet Corps in St Petersburg. By the late 1770s, another twelve such establishments were acting as feeders for the Paris school. These military academies were meant to provide places in part, or even primarily, for poorer nobles. The *École Militaire* was supposed to cater for 500 poor nobles

with four generations of noble ancestry behind them, offering an extensive course of 'noble' and military studies for boys between the ages of 9
and 20. Ten years after opening its doors, it had barely 40 pupils. The
combination of costs of board and accommodation in Paris and the
demand for written proofs of noble ancestry made it almost impossible
for poorer gentry to send their sons to the capital. Almost inevitably,
such establishments became dominated not just by wealthy nobles but
by wealthy commoners as well.

More successful in this respect were the establishments in Prussia and
Austria, not least because the Hohenzollern and Habsburgs took a
direct, personal interest in the cultivation of a loyal military elite.[22] But
everywhere, the very poor among the nobility had little choice but to
enlist as ordinary soldiers, serve among the rank-and-file and then look
forward to rising no higher than non-commissioned status. Without
luck, money or patronage, the same fate could even await the graduates
of the military academies. It is, in any case, a moot point whether the
technical quality of the products of these schools was necessarily any
better than those who had not frequented such establishments. Britain,
after all, demonstrated that it could gain spectacular military successes
without the benefit of such colleges. Napoleon went to military school at
Brienne; the duke of Wellington learned as he went along and his officers
made do with the playing-fields of Eton. Napoleon was an exceptional
product; by and large, the best French officers learned not in the academies but, like Wellington, on the job.[23]

The state offered its elite other direct educational opportunities:
attachment to the court, with some kind of education there, and the prospects of connection and preferential advancement. A number of grander courts (France, Russia, Austria) had a *corps des pages*, which, besides
excellent connections, offered a fashionable education. Among the great
aristocracy, the tradition of taking in the sons of lesser nobles and providing them with an education with a view to tightening bonds of fidelity and
clientage was on the wane (though in countries like Poland or Hungary,
where court life was less prominent among the great nobility, it survived):
those placed as pages at court could expect to receive an academy-style
education plus, of course, preference and promotion through their court
connections. In France, at least, such placements tended to be restricted
to scions of the greater aristocracy, if only because they were increasingly
expensive investments. Lesser nobles had to be satisfied with service as
ordinary soldiers in household regiments and might never be able to
attain senior rank because of the high costs of commissions.

A more functional education was available under state aegis in Prussia and Russia, two states whose modernisation aspirations were constantly hampered by the shortage of educated commoners and the generally low levels of education prevalent among the nobility themselves. Even in the 1750s, it was not unusual for comparatively high-ranking Russian officials, the provincial *voevody*, to be illiterate.[24] Signatures to instructions to Catherine the Great's Legislative Commission of 1767 suggest around one-sixth of the Russian nobility were illiterate. Peter the Great vainly stipulated that nobles could not marry before receiving a certificate in mathematical proficiency. Given his own interests in mathematics, engineering and artillery, and painfully aware of his servitors' deficiencies, he was determined to make these shortcomings up no matter how reluctant his nobles were. In 1701, he founded a specialist School of Mathematics and Navigation in Moscow, the senior parts of which were hived off to St Petersburg as the Naval Academy in 1715. These establishments were extremely unpopular: most of their inmates were simply press-ganged youngsters above the age of ten who, on graduating some five years later, could expect either to be placed in the unpopular navy or, almost as bad, deployed as teachers in Peter's unsuccessful 'cipher schools', which were geared to providing a rudimentary arithmetical education for the sons of provincial nobles and officials. At its peak, in 1724, the Naval Academy had almost 400 students; by April 1725, barely two months after Peter's death, the number had slumped to under 200. In 1714, betrothal and marriage were barred to nobles who failed to secure a certificate of satisfaction from these establishments. Such injunctions remained on paper. Even during Peter's lifetime, the cipher schools began to be taken over by the Church, largely to provide a preparatory education for the sons of clergy. Other considerations apart, the intellectual classical platform and the appreciation of the value of learning was, except in the case of a few individuals, utterly lacking in Russia. That is not to say that Russian nobles were uninterested in some form of education. Their instructions to the Legislative Commission of 1767 demonstrate a real awareness of its value for personal advance. But in the financially and intellectually under-resourced vastnesses of European Russia, the provision of such educational facilities was utterly beyond the capacities of the state; the basic infrastructure that made a measure of private education available elsewhere in Europe was almost totally absent. The Orthodox Church, itself in dire need of educational improvement at every level, was in no position to rectify the situation, especially as it was chronically suspicious of both

Peter's intentions and almost any outside influences. In practical terms, the situation changed little even under Catherine.[25]

No nobleman's education could be considered truly complete unless he undertook a Grand Tour abroad. On the continent, the enormous costs involved of necessity restricted such a privilege to the rich. Poor nobles could tap into it only as servants or adventurers (private tutors, army volunteers, mountebanks, con-men) – but the latter options implied (even if they did not necessarily formally lead to) a loss of noble status. The situation was rather different for the British, the most numerous travellers of all. Edward Gibbon guessed there were some 40,000 Englishmen travelling in Europe in 1785. Over the century as a whole, the number may have increased tenfold. Throughout the eighteenth century, the pound sterling's exchange rate against continental currencies was extremely favourable, sufficiently so to put travel abroad within the scope of most persons who had any pretensions to gentility. Thus, an annual income of £500, very modest indeed by the standards of British landowners, given an exchange rate of 22 *livres* to the pound, was sufficient to bracket its beneficiaries with the top 13 per cent of French nobles. In provincial France, this was the income of 'high and powerful seigneurs'.[26] Arthur Young reckoned, in 1787, that a noble family in southern France with an annual income of 1500 *louis* (approximately £750–£1500, depending on the rather variable rate of the *louis d'or*) 'lived as handsomely as in England on £5000'. In 1764, Gibbon paid 6 guineas a month for a four-room apartment in Paris's fashionable faubourg Saint Germain. In Rome, two people could get by in modest comfort on £30 a year; and a large, well-appointed, centrally situated apartment could be rented for just over £12 per annum – its equivalent in London would cost around £200.[27]

Richard Lassels, who first coined the expression 'Grand Tour' in 1670, stressed the desirability of visiting France, which indeed was, to many continental travellers, if anything even more important than Italy. Yet few men of culture would have disagreed with Dr Johnson that 'a man who has not been to Italy is always conscious of an inferiority, from his not having seen what it is expected a man should see. The grand object of travelling is to see the shores of the Mediterranean.'[28] Stanisław Poniatowski, who travelled extensively through Germany, France, the Low Countries and England in 1753 and 1754, regretted to the end of his life that he had never gone to Italy: he hoped to remedy the defect after his enforced abdication from the Polish throne in 1796, but his Russian minders had no intention of allowing him to round off his education. The lure of Italy was so strong that Polish nobles of very moderate means made determined efforts to visit it. Such supposedly improving foreign travel did not always improve – in most countries, there was some kind of debate during the eighteenth century as to whether it was desirable or not, or whether the Grand Tour, or *Kavalier-reise*, should be undertaken at some later stage in life. Eighteenth-century moralists worried about unleashing well-to-do teenagers on foreign parts. Fear, in particular, of frenchified fashions and ideas undermining honest native ways and traditional modes of thinking were voiced across Europe. Conservative Frenchmen worried about the influence of anglomania in their own country. All that can sensibly be said about such concerns is that travel was as likely to broaden or narrow the mind in the eighteenth as it is in the twenty-first century. There is no doubt that there was an immense amount of cultural cross-fertilisation. If much of this was abetted by the circulation of just about any text worth reading (and many more not worth reading) in the French language, much, too, derived from personal appreciation. Art, architecture, garden design, theatre and music across Europe were enriched by the patronage of more or less discerning gentleman-connoisseurs.

Not every *Kavalierreise* was a glorified exercise in sight-seeing: a substantial number of places in private and state-sponsored academies were always taken by foreign nobles who might spend several months buffing up their manners and linguistic skills there. Until 1762, Russian nobles were unable to travel abroad without official permission. Despite this, the Russian government itself made provision to send a small number of nobles to approved educational establishments in western Europe (though such trips did not, strictly, amount to a Grand Tour proper). England exercised a particular attraction for continental visitors, curious to sample the country so extolled by Voltaire's *Philosophical letters* (1733) and Montesquieu's *Spirit of the laws* (1748). By the 1780s its industrial centres, such as Matthew Boulton's Soho Manufactory in Birmingham or the Coalbrookdale iron works in Shropshire and the astonishing iron bridge over the River Severn, were as much *de rigueur* for the discerning visitor as any stately home or great cathedral.[29] There were, of course, impressive industrial establishments elsewhere in Europe, such as the mines near Freiburg in Saxony or at Anzin in northern France, but there was not yet anything quite like the leading-edge industrial establishments of England.

5

RESOURCES

'Nobility is kept alive and strong when it is attached to wealth, and without money it is like a dead thing, for those who are in need have often to turn their hands to vile things.' So wrote the Spaniard Martín de Viciana in 1629. The same sentiments were pronounced by a Prussian minister, Eberhard von der Reck, in 1802: 'The name of a nobleman without sufficient estates is only a nominal title, a nobleman who lacks the power and the vital interest to fulfil the purpose of the state.'[1] Amid growing diversity of forms of wealth, it was not surprising that land should retain its pre-eminence. For land was much more than an economic resource: it conferred power, jurisdiction, responsibility, lustre and prestige. The management of broad acres, for that minority who owned them, was not and could not be a mere matter of economic rationality. It was all very well being a marquis or marchese, but unless the appropriate levels of spending were maintained, not only for social, but for political purposes, a social and political abyss beckoned. Estates were not just landed properties: they were the patrimony of the noble house and, as such, had to be transmitted intact, as far as possible, from one generation to the next; younger children had to be provided for, daughters dowered, widows' portions assured and at all times appearances maintained. Social, dynastic and political considerations took priority over economic.

Great landowners were safer, and more sensible, to cling on to what they had, rather than to undertake expensive and dubious improvements and innovative investments. In fact, there was no pressing need for wealthy landowners, or even those reasonably well off, to involve themselves in the toils of making a living. Broadly speaking, despite some vicious fluctuations stemming from the vagaries of climate and harvests, real prices for agricultural produce were stable, or even declining, across most of Europe from the 1650s to about the 1730s. From then on, but especially from the end of the Seven Years War to the end of the Napoleonic wars, grain prices, and with them rents, rose, and fast. By the 1780s, Danzig wheat cost almost half as much again in Amsterdam as it had done in the 1740s; by the 1790s, it was fetching twice as much, if not more. Better still from the point of view of landowners and producers, real wages failed to keep up.[2] In his study of the Thrumpton estate in Nottinghamshire's Trent valley, Gordon Mingay wondered at the benevolently lackadaisical attitude of the Emerton family. They did little or nothing in terms of direct management, yet the rents from their larger tenant farms grew between 30 and 70 per cent between 1750 and 1790 and between 90 and 100 per cent between 1790 and 1825.[3] In France, the great family of Bourbon-Conty pursued a deliberate policy of borrowing in order to purchase more lands, from which, given rising prices and rising demands among tenants, it could extract ever higher rents, without any productive investment at all.[4] On their remote estates in the kingdom of Naples, the Carraciolo di Brienza barons invested virtually nothing and changed almost nothing between the late sixteenth and the early nineteenth centuries. They lived mainly off the profits of their jurisdictional rights and off rents and dues supplied in kind, stored in granaries which their own vassals administered and which enabled them to keep abreast of rising agricultural prices and demand from their own peasantry and the city of Naples.[5] It was much the same over the rest of Europe. German rents rose rapidly in the last two decades of the eighteenth century, to stand at between two and three times the level of the 1730s by 1800. French grain prices rose by well over 150 per cent between 1730 and the Revolution. Taking a longer-term view, the Polish historian Witold Kula calculated that between 1600 and 1750, so even before the price boom of the second half of the eighteenth century, the real value of their estate produce had doubled for the great Polish–Lithuanian nobility, and risen by almost half for lesser landlords.[6] Some of the steepest gains took place in Russia as its prices began to come into line with European norms. Over the century as a whole, agricultural prices rose by over 500 per cent; during the reigns of Catherine II and Paul, by 250 per cent relative to the prices of the 1720s.[7] Landowners could get rich by doing virtually nothing.

On the other hand, the demands of maintaining a noble lifestyle grew more onerous as the century progressed. Houses, clothes, carriages, receptions, amusements, as well as marrying off and providing for sons and daughters, consumed ever greater sums. If landlords wished to raise more revenues from their estates, they were in an excellent position to do so: *nulle terre sans seigneur* ('no land without a lord') ran the French adage. The gamut of lordly rights, privileges and jurisdiction that went with their estates gave landowners a formidable array of powers to deploy to secure extra revenues from tenants and 'subjects'. Some 35 per cent of the cultivated land in France belonged to a notionally free, unenserfed peasantry. Yet most of that peasantry owed a range of dues to their seigneurs, supposedly in return for their protection and the provision of justice and order. Thus, in the Lauragais, the rich agricultural area stretching south-east from Toulouse, in addition to the basic ground rent (*cens*) for farming the holdings within the jurisdiction of the *seigneurie*, peasants were usually obliged to make use of the seigneur's mill, smithy or even bakery – for which of course they were charged fees, often by entrepreneurs (who might well be well-off peasants) who had, in their turn, leased these monopolies (*banalités*) from the seigneur. The seigneur could claim a cut, the *agrier* or *champart*, of the harvest. Peasants were at liberty to sell their tenures – but the right of *retrait féodal* allowed the landlord to buy back for his own purposes holdings that might have been recently sold; he could in any case impose a transfer tax (*lods et ventes*) on such land. If the holding passed to the peasant's son, the landlord was entitled to an inheritance fee, or *acapte*, equal to twice the annual *cens*. Peasants might still be subject to a few days' unremunerated labour services (*corvées*) for the seigneur.

Broadly speaking, landowners of any substance in western Europe did indeed live off rents, in the sense that these were revenues supplied by tenants; in Germany and eastern Europe the picture was much more complicated, with cash rents, direct labour services and dues in kind all contributing to the landlord's revenues. The crucial factor here was the relationship between the landowner and the peasantry: by and large, unless the peasants belonged to categories specifically recognised in law as free, they were serfs: *glebae adscripti, an die Scholle gebunden* – that is, legally tied to the land and the estate on which they lived, possessed of minimal rights, *de facto* and sometimes if not always *de jure* the property of their landowners. These central and east European lands – much of Germany, Prussia, Bohemia, Hungary, Poland, Russia – were the territories of *Gutswirtschaft*, the direct administration of the estate by the landowner or his managers. Even where peasants in these lands were technically free to leave, they could still find themselves legally subjected to a variety of sometimes arbitrary labour impositions and dues in kind. Even free peasants could not legally leave unless they had discharged all outstanding obligations to their landlord.[8] Since the mid-sixteenth century there had been a growing, if irregular, increase in demand from the west for eastern European grains; and in the eighteenth century, particularly its closing 20 or 30 years, this demand surged. If direct, large-scale involvement in the export trade remained the preserve of a tiny minority of nobles whose territories were well placed to take advantage of waterway communications (even in the late sixteenth century, the heyday of the Polish grain trade, only around 2.5 per cent of landowners were actively involved in the grain export market), lesser landowners and even peasants were able to take advantage of the great fleets of barges that carried cereals down to the ports. As far as possible, landowners in this area sought to appropriate for themselves the profits of sales, be they exports or for the domestic market. Although there were exceptional areas, such as Saxony, the course of economic development throughout most of eastern Europe since the sixteenth century had given landlords little reason to hope for profits other than by creaming them off from the peasantry. The towns were too weak to provide an adequate source of revenues via the mechanism of rents, as in much of western Europe and the Mediterranean region.

The inevitable tendency was for landowners to rely on such tied labour. The more extensive the peasant holding, the more labour that peasant was supposed to provide for the seigneurial domain. In one extreme case in the Podlasie region of Poland, large peasant holdings were supposed to supply the equivalent of 17 days' labour per week: that is, the peasant would have to supply two or three ploughing teams (drawn from smallholders or cottagers with few or no labour obligations) per week. During the 1770s, Maria Theresa's government laid down maxima of three days per week across the Habsburg monarchy – paradoxically, a measure that allowed some landlords to increase the demands they made on their peasants for labour. More or less sophisticated calculations aimed at demonstrating the superior efficiency of hired labour probably had the opposite effect on nobles in an area of Europe notorious for cash shortages and dubious currencies, who feared that they simply would not be able to raise the monies to pay a peasantry that daily experience taught them was idle, shiftless and untrustworthy. Even on the relatively progressively administered estate of Stavenow in Brandenburg, where Friedrich Joachim von Kleist accepted that labour services (*Fron*) were so badly performed that it would probably be more efficient to employ day labourers, the lure of obligatory and unpaid service remained an irresistible attraction.[9]

To the so-called physiocratic reformers, so in vogue during the reconstruction that followed the Seven Years War, agricultural reform was essential as a means to both a wealthier state and one in which the injustices of seigneurialism could be eradicated while seigneurial incomes were boosted. The transition to cash rentals was something of a holy grail. The prevalence of money rents in England, so often held up as a model of progressive, remunerative agriculture, underlined the arguments in their favour. There were, however, very serious problems with the flattering English paradigm. In 1813, the agricultural writer William Pitt noted that real improvements came from landlords with estates of less than 300 acres – that is, from those who had to take careful, measured and innovative steps if they were to increase their incomes.[10] But such steps made sense only in the right conditions: primarily, access to ready, reliable markets. England's 'agricultural revolution' was a long-drawn-out process which adapted and borrowed elements of agricultural development reaching back to the Middle Ages. The kind of measures that helped to make large swathes (though by no means all) of farmland in England prosperous were certainly not confined to that country. Generally speaking, farming in the vicinity of towns was a profitable occupation because increasingly even lesser provincial towns offered a more demanding and diverse market. Travellers regularly commented on the more flourishing fields around town peripheries. Productivity was more likely to come from the careful, conscientious application of existing practices than from radical, uncertain experimentation.

If urban-centred islands of prosperity were less evident in the east than in the west, it was largely because of the small size of eastern European towns. Across the River Elbe there was no shortage of settlements with legal, municipal status. Most, however, boasted populations of a few hundred people. By western standards they were little more than villages, and much of their economic activity was, in fact, centred on agriculture. They constituted scarcely more of a market than the villages in which 'proper' peasants lived. It is not surprising that agriculture should have been seen as especially flourishing in much of England and Holland. Their towns and the generally well-developed state of communications (not necessarily roads – waterways and the sea were more important) facilitated the marketing of agricultural produce in a way that was out of the question in the interior of Poland or Russia (or, for that matter, Spain). Landlords in eastern Europe who owned estates far removed from navigable rivers could indeed overcome the distances by simply obliging their serfs to transport grain to the nearest points of shipment, even if this meant travelling dozens, occasionally hundreds, of kilometres. The serf was thus made to bear the costs – but it was a horribly inefficient mode of marketing and a huge drain on peasants' (and, ultimately, landlords') resources. This is not to say that cash rents did not exist in eastern Europe: they did and were widespread; and some areas, such as Saxony or the Vistula delta, were dominated by them; but the presence of particular factors (in Saxony, a healthy market in Leipzig and Dresden, in the delta, the Royal Prussian towns and exceptionally fertile soils) kept areas where rentals predominated fairly small.

Even where markets were more readily accessible, investment in agriculture still suffered from the almost unbearable expense that was so often involved. Historians are increasingly cautious about the English model and its favoured circumstances: 'The combination of an enlightened landlord ready to venture capital in his estate, a forward-looking and enthusiastic agent, and farmers both able and willing to promote better agriculture, was more likely to bring progress when economic conditions and terrain permitted.' This was the exception rather than the rule: for most of the eighteenth century, most managers on large estates remained anxious 'to secure the maximum financial return from the estate at a minimum cost in landlord re-investment'.[11] French agriculture could be both diverse and productive provided it had ready access to markets – but the geography of France was far less favourable to the easy transport of goods than that of Great Britain. A network of internal tolls and duties hampered not only French agriculture but French economic development in general. The price of wine shipped from Clermont to Paris was increased four times by such imposts.[12] On his model estate at Fréchines in the Loire valley, Antoine Lavoisier concluded after nine years of experiment and observation that returns in agriculture simply could not begin to compare with his investments in France's General Tax Farm.[13] It was much the same in Spain: reformers accepted that without massive state initiatives, the internal markets of Castile were so underpopulated that little improvement could come about in agriculture. If the average returns on land in Castile were at about 1.5 per cent per annum, how many landlords would seriously invest in agricultural improvements when they could get returns of 6–8 per cent by government bonds and mortgages?[14]

In Britain, landowners more or less had to concentrate on landed improvements, or at least facilitate them for their tenantry, because the panoply of feudal rights enjoyed by their continental counterparts had withered away and reliable tenants were in short supply. The great age of agricultural investment was to be the nineteenth, rather than the eighteenth, century. The visible evidence in England was that improvements, even if limited to enclosures, generally paid handsome returns – rents for an enclosed property could double, triple or even quadruple compared with its unenclosed condition. Landlords were increasingly reluctant to let their hands be tied by agreeing to hereditary leases 'for lives', especially against a background of rising agricultural prices in the second half of the eighteenth century, preferring to let tenancies on more open-ended, easily renegotiable terms.[15]

The implementation of new techniques was hugely expensive and disruptive of old ways. Success in one area was certainly no guarantee of equal success in another. Peasants all too often feared that the 'improvements' were primarily there for the landlord's benefit and would involve greater demands on them – and rightly so. Agriculture across most of Europe was, by modern standards, desperately unremunerative, and geared to one overriding aim: subsistence. In the exceptionally rewarding agricultural frameworks of Britain and the Low Countries, average return on seed (after harvesting, threshing, cleaning and storing) sown about 1700 stood at a ratio of 7:1 for the three principal cereal crops of wheat, rye and oats; in France, Spain or Italy it stood at around 6:1 to 4:1. In much of Germany, Switzerland, Denmark or Sweden it was barely above 4:1; in Bohemia, Poland, the Baltic states and Russia it was between 3:1 and 4:1. By the 1750s and 1800s, the British and Dutch regions were producing average yields closer to 10:1 and 11:1 (probably less than a quarter of modern yield ratios). These figures conceal immense variations: if wheat alone were to be considered, the productivity of the British Isles and the Dutch would be much greater; rye was the principal crop of eastern Europe, less demanding to cultivate, but less generous in yield.[16] Most peasants, apart from a fortunate wealthy few who often worked in collusion with the landlords to facilitate the running of the agricultural economy, endured appallingly difficult conditions on the margin between material adequacy and destitution. They kept going because they had to. Even supposedly well-to-do peasants in Brandenburg, at a time when the markets for their produce were expanding as never before, might easily find that their annual 'profits', after dues, taxes and necessary reinvestment in their holdings, would run to around 15–20 *Thaler*, or no more than a hired farmhand might earn in a year.[17] Production for the market came second to the need for survival.

Europe's arable lands were divided into open strip fields, which in some cases could be up to a kilometre long but only a couple of metres wide. The strips would belong to different proprietors or tenants; those of the seigneur would usually be found side by side with any number of those of his tenants or serfs. One-third or even one-half would lie fallow every year, to allow soils starved of fertilisers to recover. These layouts corresponded to communal needs (notionally, in some golden past, every family would tend sufficient land for its survival and generate a sufficient surplus for the seigneur, the Church and the state to take their cut); they also corresponded to the primitive agricultural technology on offer – at best, horse-drawn ploughs, though these were not freely available to all villagers; at worst, a hand-pulled plough that scratched the land. Long, narrow strips made ample sense in these circumstances. If more land was needed, then more uncultivated land could usually be taken in – although one of the problems facing France in the eighteenth century was that suitable marginal land was becoming increasingly scarce. Advice books, especially in central and eastern Europe, stressed the need for careful management – but predominantly within a patriarchal, non-market-orientated sphere. The well-run estate was one that was self-supporting as far as possible and required minimum expenditure on infrastructure or seed grain or livestock: on the contrary, such purchases were often viewed as a financial disaster. On the other hand, such advice books reflected the low productivity of much of the agriculture of the region. The best advice that Ivan Bolotov – by Russian standards an exceptionally well-educated and well-travelled individual – could offer his fellow-landlords for maximising their income in 1765 was for them to 'exchange' any superior harvests on peasant strips for inferior ones on seigneurial soils.[18] In their bones, most landowners in most of Europe would have agreed with the comments offered by Feodor Udolov to the newly established Free Economic Society of St Petersburg:

> Above all, the farm people must realise that it is not for their own benefit that they are given to agriculture and the other tasks appropriate to their condition; but that it is their duty to serve first their sovereign, then their landlord and all society, to which they unconditionally owe tribute ...[19]

Not surprisingly, then, peasants were suspicious of landlords' initiatives. A 'good' landlord who took a close interest in the running of his estates was one who did not exploit his peasants excessively and did not interfere with existing practices. To the landlords themselves, 'improvements' meant, at the least, not spending money on dubious improvements. As the duc de Choiseul noted on his bailiff's report for 1752 against an expenditure of 15 *livres* (less than one pound sterling) on nails for roof repairs: 'Allowed. Another year I do not want one nail driven in without my particular order.'[20] Like most nobles, even the great Choiseul was chronically short of ready cash. Dubious long-term investment was not going to help him with 'living nobly'.

An alternative and acceptable 'investment' route was taken by Charles-François-Casimir de Saulx, comte de Tavanes. He was one of the great seigneurs of France, even if his landed income in 1780, of some 90,000 *livres*, or not quite £4100, though not to be sneezed at, was small by the standards of the English peerage. Unlike the *gentilshommes-campagnards* of Toulouse, he was an absentee who spent most of his time in Paris and Versailles. He let his estates on nine-year leases, leaving his tenants the trouble and expense of management and collection of seigneurial dues. His estates were a milch cow, requiring minimum maintenance (by some measures, therefore, he was a 'good' landlord). His sole major capital investment was the drainage of a few hundred acres of marshland abutting his estate at Arc-sur-Tille in Burgundy – he shared the costs with 66 other local proprietors. Between 1758 and 1761, an unusually entrepreneurially minded tenant farmer, Jacques Huvelin, proposed a series of capital investments, including further drainage improvements (dykes and canals). These required not only his own but the count's financial input. The count was asked to put up 10,000 *livres* – the price of one of his wife's court dresses. Another 10,000 *livres* would buy potash to improve the yields of the hay meadows, and would bring in an extra 2000 *livres* income. New stables would permit diversification into cheese production (the count was asked for another 2000 *livres*). Charles-François-Casimir's response was discouragingly rational: all the proposals would cost him money; the results could not be guaranteed and, in the case of the hay meadows, he would get the extra 2000 *livres* Huvelin was promising by the simple expedient of adding that sum to his lease when it came up for renewal.

This is not to say that the count did not invest in his property. He did – by the revival and stricter enforcement of the feudal rights associated with his *seigneurie*. During the 1780s, he was prepared to spend 5000 *livres* or more per annum on the services of *feudistes* – surveyors-cum-lawyers – who would recalibrate in detail all that peasants living within his jurisdiction owed him. The results were far more spectacular than anything that 'improvement' could achieve: the Saulx-Tavanes Burgundian estates yielded around 50,000 *livres* in the 1750s; in 1788 they were yielding over 82,000 *livres* net, an increase of the order of 75 per cent – during a period in which wheat prices rose by only 22 per cent. This amounted to an increase on the same scale as could be expected from enclosure in England, but at a fraction of the cost. Given the problems of rationalising agriculture and the uncertainties of the return on investment, it made far more sense, or it seemed to make far more sense, to invest in something sure to bring a guaranteed return: feudal rights. If tenants and sub-tenants went bankrupt – and the Tavanes saw no reason why even a large tenant should make more than 1000 *livres* profit each year – then others were desperate enough to offer the ever more outrageous asking prices. When, in 1784, no-one could be found who was prepared to lease the Tavanes' Beaumont estate as a whole, Charles-François-Casimir found a simple solution by splitting it into eight smaller leases, for which takers could be found. Few of the new tenants made it to the end of their nine-year leases (defaulters were pursued through the Tavanes' own seigneurial courts).[21]

The same processes were at work in the Europe of the serfs. The stock advice from the Free Economic Society of St Petersburg to those nobles who felt the need to read its publications was that the first task of any estate manager was to inspire fear into the peasantry: only then could the estate be run efficiently.[22] A wide variety of methods was tried to improve productivity within such constraints: setting work quotas and quality standards, insisting that peasant proprietors should perform labour in person, and so on. Even medium-sized estates required a complex administrative machine employing dozens of officials to supervise peasant labour and manage the sales of agricultural produce. In Poland and Hungary, these positions were almost invariably filled by lesser nobles, who constituted an important political interest. Large tracts of great estates were regularly leased to such gentlemen. A generalised transfer to rents would only serve to blur even further the differences between serfs and petty noblemen. Politically and socially, reform of agriculture was, if not impossible, monstrously difficult. Where progress was made, it was either small scale, with enlightened landowners experimenting on selected properties, or because market conditions (proximity to larger towns) permitted. Otherwise, an inefficient subsistence agriculture lurched along: every imposition was a disincentive for the peasantry to work and engendered an utter lack of faith on the part of landowners in their serfs and tenants. Rulers in particular, confronted with the responsibility for steering their societies as a whole, might take the view expressed by Frederick the Great, that the peasantry formed 'the most useful part' of the state, but such worthy sentiments did not lead to more productive farming. Agriculture suffered and stagnated, but at least the social order remained unscathed.

Reliance on jurisdictional *force majeure* was an uncertain game: peasants might and did react by malingering, decamping or, at worst, by resorting to violence and revolt. Few could have foreseen the advent of the French Revolution, but there is ample evidence of the growing strength of peasant resistance to what was perceived as the utterly unjustified burden of seigneurial demand and exploitation.[23] More market-orientated economies had their own checks: for much of the eighteenth century, in England, good, reliable tenants were not easy to find. Moreover tenants, who might well be freeholders in their own right, with enough land to qualify for the franchise, might have to be kept politically sweet and not unduly burdened.

Land was not the only source of wealth. In 1756, abbé Gabriel Coyer's *La noblesse commerçante* (*The nobility in commerce*) touched off one of the widest-ranging disputes of the century. Within ten years, translations had appeared in Spain, Germany and Russia. Should the nobility abandon its traditional 'prejudices' against more active involvement in commercial life? Where, in any case, were the lines to be drawn? Charles Loyseau's much-repeated sixteenth-century formulation, found in various guises across Europe, that 'It is, properly speaking, base, sordid profit which derogates from nobility, whose true mode of life is founded on living off its rents', raised more questions than it answered.[24] Looked at closely, the dividing line between running an estate and managing a commercial business was disconcertingly blurred. It might work up to a point on autarchic estates, those that struggled towards an entirely unreal goal of total self-sufficiency, much praised by conservative landowners especially in the less commercialised parts of eastern Europe – parts of east Elbia, Poland, Hungary or Russia; or on the properties of lesser nobles who could just about keep body and soul together from their tiny plots of land. But autarchy was unrealisable: agricultural produce had to be sold if the trappings of noble life were to be bought.

Landowners perforce had to engage in business, directly or indirectly. Nor was it possible to maintain the fiction that agricultural products were all that landed nobles should concern themselves with. For grain was converted not only into breads, but into beer and spirits; grapes into wines. Noble fortunes, great and small, across Europe floated on an ocean of alcohol. That meant breweries, distilleries, ale-houses, inns and taprooms. In Russia after 1754, the nobility were given the monopoly of the supply of alcohol to the state; its retail was, in turn, a state monopoly, in practice shared with the nobility, in part as a device to prop up noble revenues. Though lesser nobles could benefit, largely by banding together into suppliers' syndicates, once again it was the owners of larger estates who benefited most. Landless nobles were barred from the business altogether. The same, almost by definition, was true in Poland–Lithuania, where nobles enjoyed the monopoly of alcohol production and sales (usually leased to Jewish middlemen) on their estates.[25]

And what of mineral wealth, forestry products? The effective exploitation of these required close involvement in the market, in the industrial processes that converted these commodities into saleable products, perhaps even in the logistics of distribution and retailing. The passive 'Living off rents' was a fiction, at least if one wished to live well. If it was at all realisable in any pure form, then it was by investing in government stock – but truly secure investments in government bonds were limited largely to Britain and the Dutch Republic. It was possible to live off rents drawn on private individuals (in France, indeed, such *rentes* were viewed as a form of real property), but such income too ultimately derived from sales in the market. Many nobles may have affected a disdain for business, but if they wished to be nobles in the sense of maintaining a suitably impressive lifestyle, they could not, in mundane reality, divorce themselves from it. The only alternative was to borrow – but if borrowings were outrun by the capacity to service the debts, landowners would become overwhelmed.[26]

The problem of securing an income was rendered more complicated by the existence of what the French called *dérogeance*. In general, a more or less disparate battery of laws existed which reinforced prejudices against nobles being involved in 'the mechanical arts', 'service deemed abject', and so forth, for to practise them would detract from the noble's capacity to form part of the ruling order. Such legal generalisations reflected noble prejudices and fears rather than addressed specific issues. Oddly enough, French nobles were permitted to involve themselves directly in one specific industry – glass-making (leading some commoner glass-makers to claim that by virtue of exercising this activity, they, too, belonged to the *noblesse verrière*).[27] Polish laws, reiterated over the sixteenth and eighteenth centuries, barred nobles not only from participation in artisanal trades, but even from holding municipal office. If specific prohibitions did not always exist, it was because the expectation was that nobles would simply not involve themselves in mean occupations in the first place.[28]

In the sixteenth century, France's sword nobility looked on the upstart *noblesse de robe* as belonging to the Third Estate, royal edicts to the contrary notwithstanding. Some of these attitudes persisted into the eighteenth century.[29] The mud stuck sufficiently for France's sovereign courts explicitly to forbid their officers from engaging in commercial activities. The Ordinance of Orléans of 1560 barred 'all gentlemen', '*tous gentilshommes*', not only from any 'dealings in merchandise' but from involving themselves, even through intermediaries, in the management of tax farms. Louis XI of France had tried to tackle such prejudice by issuing edicts which specifically stated that commercial activity and nobility were not incompatible. Richelieu, in 1629, secured an ordinance whereby maritime trade, because of the dangers from war, piracy and shipwreck that so often accompanied it, was not to be regarded as dishonouring for nobles. But this only caused fresh problems. Social prejudice against a *noblesse commerçante* remained extremely strong. Other ordinances of the States-General and the crown (1560, 1579, 1606) affirmed blanket bans on noble participation in *trafic de marchandise*. Commercial activity could well lead to a decision by royal officials to levy *taille* on the lands of the 'offending' noble; and once *taille* was levied, noble status might be lost, especially if no formal documentation of that status was available. Brittany boasted the peculiar safeguarding device of *noblesse dormante*, 'sleeping nobility', which allowed nobles to place their status into a kind of suspended animation while they pursued commercial activity and paid the regular taxes. Then, on affirming before a magistrate that they were no longer commercially active, they resumed their 'normal' noble status. The *arrêt du conseil* of 30 October 1767 formally declared that bankers and manufacturers were on a par with wholesale or maritime merchants, so no longer taking part in derogatory activities; but old prejudices could not be overturned by mere acts of legislation. The fact that the decree made specific provision for the ennoblement of only two wholesale merchants every year by royal letters patent did nothing to enhance the prestige of a 'business nobility'.

Even those who made money from commerce and used it to acquire nobility preferred to invest in land and sever their commercial links, if only because commercial enterprise was far more risk-laden than land-ownership.[30] Non-noble merchants opposed nobles' involvement in trade, fearing they would have a significant advantage through their tax exemptions (which many nobles, in turn, feared they might lose if they involved themselves in commerce), privileges and connections. Even successive royal edicts (when not contradicted by other decrees) permitting nobles to undertake commercial activities were highly ambivalent, invariably drawing a distinction between wholesale or maritime commerce (*négoce*) – portrayed as risky, adventurous – and the less glamorous retail trade (*détail*), which remained off limits.[31]

In any case, commercial and industrial ventures required capital which lay beyond the grasp of the overwhelming majority of nobles. Even in England, mining and industrial ventures were not for lesser gentry, if only because of the expense and uncertainty involved. Most English landowners preferred to lease mining rights or cream off royalties on coal sales rather than become too closely involved. By 1800, the single largest source of revenues for the earls of Dudley came from coal sales – but in this, and in the extent of their direct involvement in the industry, the family was quite exceptional. As it happened, their estates in Staffordshire and Worcestershire straddled a 10-metre-thick shallow seam – not every aristocratic landowner was so fortunate, nor able to count on an expanding, regular market of at least 400,000 tons of coal sales. New pits cost tens of thousands, even hundreds of thousands, of pounds to open, even in well-endowed coal areas.[32] A fair mirror image of the British scene was to be found in Sweden, where good agricultural land was in short supply, particularly after the loss of the Baltic provinces to Russia in 1721. The country's extensive deposits of high-grade iron and copper ore meant that the extraction and processing of iron, for which there was a seemingly inexhaustible European appetite, was a major component in many noble incomes, especially as a source of liquid capital; entrepreneurship in the iron trade was a recognised avenue to respectable ennoblement. It was also an area of active partnership between nobles and commoners: neither in Sweden nor in Britain could aristocrats have gone in for the development of mineral resources without the co-operation of merchant and professional capital.[33]

One does not have to look too hard to find nobles involved in trade elsewhere in Europe. Indeed, it could be said that nobles in the poorer, less accessible regions of the continent showed significantly greater industrial drive than their more fortunately placed British or Swedish counterparts. The advantage that these possessed was precisely access to reasonably stable, dependable native or foreign markets. There were great iron-masters in France – Babaud de la Chaussade in the Nivernais, the Dietrich and the Wendel families in Alsace, the Barral in Dauphiné – but they were newcomers, families of commoner origin, who had acquired noble status through purchase of the post of *secrétaire du roi*. Marc-René, marquis de Montalembert, with a pedigree reaching back to 1050, was very much an exception. He was also one of the weaker producers, relying on connections with the state to bail him out of trouble – which the state had to do as early as 1755, when his foundry at Montalembert ran into quality control problems. The state could not afford to let an establishment supposed to be producing 800 naval cannon per annum go to the wall.[34]

Most of the metallurgical works scattered across the ore-bearing areas of France were small scale, and almost invariably leased out to non-noble forge-masters. But even the largest and most successful manufacturers, the Wendel family, one of the first to introduce English iron-making techniques and steam engines to their coal mines, just before the Revolution, were perilously dependent on orders from the government to keep their enterprises solvent.[35] One of the most enterprising of Spanish nobles, Don Juan de Goyeneche, discovered just how difficult it was to marry traditional noble management with the demands of primitive capitalism. For the last 25 years of his life he involved himself in timber and paper mills, textile development (woollens, silks, millinery), leather-working and glass-making. One of his entirely worthy motivations (apart from self-enrichment) was to locate his enterprises on his properties with a view to alleviating rural poverty. But situated in remote parts of Spain, far removed from consumer markets, his projects either failed or staggered along, kept afloat by orders from the court or the army. When Juan Fernandez de Isla's patron, the marquis de la Ensenada, fell from grace in 1754, he found himself ruined, for the orders for his dockyard at Guarnizo dried up.[36]

Contacts with the court should not be underestimated: without them there could well have been less industrial growth than there was in Europe. Such contacts were vital for the development of what industry there was in Russia and Poland. But that families like the Stroganovs or Demidovs were so dependent on such links served to highlight the weaknesses of a genuine consumer market. That is not to say that the nobility who were in a position to do so did not try to create such a market, but it was usually by reliance on top-down, monopolistic pressure. Thus, Polish nobles sought to exploit their seigneurial powers by forbidding peasants to buy goods from outlets or, in some cases, manufactories outside the seigneurial estate. In some cases, landlords even attempted to impose quota purchases from their own enterprises on their peasants. Most such operations failed after a few years – the only successful market for a genuine, mass-produced consumer commodity in most of eastern Europe remained alcohol, which could usually be produced with little investment. Otherwise, peasants either refused to buy or did so on credit, which they had no intention of repaying, leaving the landlord to pick up the bill. The ensuing mutual dissatisfaction made the creation of a genuine market and the fostering of any significant economic improvements even more problematic.

The prohibitions on *détail*, found throughout much of Europe, meant absolutely nothing to great seigneurs who owned extensive properties, which in Bohemia, Poland or Hungary might run to hundreds of villages and dozens of towns. Territorial magnates still benefited from all manner of base transactions through fees and rents, even if they never did anything as unseemly as setting foot in a shop. One of the reasons why Jews were found in such extensive numbers in Poland–Lithuania was the deliberate policy of magnates attracting them to their numerous private towns. The Sanguszko family's town of Brody in south-east Poland, with a population of over 10,000 Jews (the largest Jewish urban centre in Europe), was an outstandingly useful source of ready cash and credit by the late 1760s. Overall, however, it was fortunately placed nobles in more vibrant economies who benefited from encouraging (or exploiting) urban growth. Few could compare in wealth with the Grosvenors by the late eighteenth century. Agricultural land to the west of London brought in rents of around £400 before 1720; but with the expansion of the capital, the Grosvenors' Mayfair and Pimlico properties, designated for high-class housing, were bringing in some £3000 a year by the 1780s; as leases were renegotiated, income shot up, reaching £60,000 by the 1830s and continuing to rise spectacularly. The same happened on a lesser scale in expanding provincial towns: the Gough family (elevated to the peerage from 1796 as the barons Calthorpe) had their fortune made by the high-class residential and canal development of 2000 acres of land at Edgbaston, upwind of the noisome, metal-bashing, but remorselessly growing Birmingham.[37]

Nobles who did own extensive mineral deposits in any case almost invariably did not involve themselves directly in their day-to-day running, but employed stewards or lessees to do so. A duke of Bridge-water, who poured some £350,000 into his canal projects and took a pas-sionate interest in them, was acceptable in England as an almost one-off eccentric. His case also served to underline the perils of active entrepre-neurship: it was years before he made any profits; his construction of the canals linking Worsley, Manchester and Runcorn brought him to within a whisker of bankruptcy. On the other hand, once his canal invest-ments began to bear fruit, they cut Manchester coal prices by 50 per cent and yielded the duke a 30 per cent return.[38] Otherwise, those nobles who did involve themselves directly in such vulgar activities were almost invariably the poor, who did so because they had to, not because they were going to make any money out of them.

Guy Richard has identified between 300 and 400 'trading nobles', individuals actively involved in commerce, in late eighteenth-century France. Most of them lived in the hinterland of ports. Around two-thirds were concentrated in Brittany, much impoverished inland but with a burgeoning maritime trade centred on St Malo and Nantes. Trading nobles indeed accounted for between one-third and one-half of Brittany's commerce, much of it focused on the slave trade. The ports of Rouen and Bordeaux also saw a sizeable *noblesse commerçante*. Fifty-five out of 175 wholesale traders in Rouen were noble in 1785, 31 out of 455 in Bordeaux in 1777. But all these figures include substantial numbers who had purchased their noble status, principally through the post of *secrétaire du roi*: although the crown declared nobility and trade to be compatible, it was in practice extremely sparing in conferring ennoble-ment through commercial activity.[39] All this demonstrated one thing: beneath the rhetoric about *dérogeance* and the attendant snobbery, nobles were opportunists. Philip Jenkins's comments on the gentry of Glamorgan have a much wider applicability:

> the main lesson that emerges from studying gentry economic activities is their total opportunism. If a squire lived in coal country, he owned mines; if near the sea, he traded; if neither of these, he prospected for what minerals there might be. Finally, if all these resources failed, he loaned money at interest.[40]

There was an alternative route to making money which enabled its practitioners to play the role of *rentiers* and so remain at one remove, as it were, from the grubby business of dirtying their hands. This was involvement in the world of financial capitalism: not only buying and enjoying the fruits of government stock, but also involvement in the new joint-stock companies, or even outright involvement in financial transactions. The governments of Britain, France and Spain were, by the mid-century, reckoned sufficiently trustworthy for their subjects to lend monies to them on a considerable scale: there is a plausible argument for the case that the French Revolution might have been avoided if the government of Louis XVI had been prepared to do what those of Louis XIV and XV had done and not have honoured its all-too-expensive obligations.[41] But the court at Versailles also provided an example of the cohabitation of the great court aristocracy and the world of finance, not just in the sense of supplying royal mistresses, but as a financial hothouse where favoured members of the aristocracy could buy and trade in shares in such state-chartered businesses as the Indies Company or the Paris Water Company. Among the most lucrative of such enterprises was the General Farm, the private corporation responsible for the collection of the bulk of indirect taxation in France. On the eve of the Revolution, it may even have had a majority of noble shareholders, often acting through frontmen. According to long-standing prejudice, involvement in money-making was supposed to be incompatible with noble status, and the stigma clung on, despite royal edicts to the contrary. Even Louis XVI had a share in the General Farm (that is, in his own taxation), and his sister had a half-share. Thus, beneath the pretence of 'living nobly' was (once more) the sordid reality: the great aristocracy were no different to anyone else in their money-making activities, save, perhaps, that they had a much greater range of opportunities. The duke of Bedford, who helped negotiate the peace of Paris in 1762–3, bringing Britain's war with France to an end, provided a nice example of what inside knowledge and connections could do: on his instructions, just before he signed the peace preliminaries, news of which was bound to lead to a rise in the value of government stock, his broker bought £200,000 worth of government securities.[42]

Even in backward Poland, such connections between finance and court nobles existed, but they were no more motivated by the desire to build up industry for its own sake than among their French counterparts. Polish magnates would invest in royally sponsored factories, promoted by the king because they seemed to offer a key to boosting Poland's economy. Their aim was, however, to win royal favour, with a view to securing contracts for their own enterprises or just the considerable fruits of royal patronage. In exactly the same way, Russian nobles joined the Free Economic Society of St Petersburg not because they were seriously interested in innovatory agricultural methods, but because they hoped to attract Catherine II's attention and favours or secure useful court contacts.[43]

The most acceptable mechanisms, however, involved the painless use of the family inheritance itself. Any nobleman with a landed estate of any size was likely to have some familiarity with credit mechanisms, investment, speculation and loans. Almost all propertied nobles borrowed, and many lent, money. Their lands, houses and moveable belongings may have made them asset-rich, but cash poverty was a chronic problem. It was one that had to be solved if daughters were to be dowered and sons provided for, mansions remodelled and consumer inclinations and competition indulged. Across Europe, traders, merchants, townsmen, petty nobles were ready to lend money in huge quantities not simply to indulge their social betters but because their social betters' ownership of land offered a far better form of security than almost anything else. True, there was supposed to be no lending at interest in Catholic countries, but it was an injunction that was readily ignored or evaded, not least by the very institution that proclaimed it, the Church. Instead, a lender might buy an annuity, a set annual income, in return for paying over a lump sum to the 'debtor'. In France, where lending at interest was only legalised in October 1789, it was helpful to avoid the word 'interest' in any contract. Alternatively, various theological gymnastics made interest acceptable, such as insisting that the principal was never repaid. A 5 per cent *rente* that ran for 40 years would, in fact, repay the equivalent of the principal as well as an equal sum in interest.[44]

Lending to French landowners was all the more desirable in that the *rentes* purchased by such loans derived ultimately from the landed revenues of the debtor/annuity-provider; they even had the same legal status as land itself. It has been calculated that an investment of 12,000 *livres*, with the annuities reinvested annually over a period of three generations, or 100 years, could be expected to yield a sum of 1 million *livres* – easily enough to afford the purchase not only of nobility, but of the necessary trappings that went with it. In a slow-moving agricultural society obsessed by ancestry, it was not abnormal for well-to-do families to think in terms of strategies of social advancement spanning the generations.[45] From the landowners' point of view, such loans were desirable in that in most cases, the rate of interest (at least in western Europe) was comparatively low – around 5 per cent in France, closer to 4 per cent in Britain – and so, in return for a comparatively modest annual outlay, a landowner could secure a useful, sizeable cash sum. At 4 per cent (excluding repayments of principal, which could be factored in at an insignificant rate) a lump sum of £1000 required only an annual outlay by the lender of £40. Again, the rising prices of the eighteenth century helped make such repayments negligible in real terms; moreover, some lenders were so impressed by the certainty of income from such sources that, rather than risk the loss of income by repayment of the principal, they might be willing to renegotiate their terms at a lower rate of repayment. In France, indeed, the rate of return on such so-called *rentes constituées* was consistently below the prevailing rate of interest from the middle of the sixteenth century.[46] There was, of course, the danger that a landowner might take up so many of these obligations as to make it difficult for him to keep up repayments. In 1787, Paul-Charles Depont, seigneur of (among others) Aigrefeuille near La Rochelle, found that more than a quarter of his income of 30,000 *livres* was going in interest payments. The following year, he inherited 340,000 *livres* from a related branch of the family and his financial problems were temporarily over.[47]

The other obvious risk was to the lender. By and large, where there was competition for loans, then the chances of default on such loans were less likely than on most others – after all, where else could defaulters raise money? If there were exceptions (no-one in the Polish–Lithuanian Commonwealth could make Karol Radziwiłł, blessed with properties the size of Belgium, repay his debts – but then it took a good 100 years after his death to sort out the various claims on the estate), they were sufficiently infrequent not to discourage lending. Everyone with spare cash lent to landowners: their tenants, their officials, their friends, their lawyers, even their servants. That was as true of England as it was of Poland. Even small 'depositors' gave territorial magnates a measure of useful liquidity. The first Austrian governor of Galicia, Count Anton Pergen, reported that one of the greatest landowners in the region, Prince August Czartoryski, both had abundant access to such cash and also assured himself of a steady political following by paying out a return of 10 per cent on sums lodged with him by local nobles.[48] This extraordinarily high rate of return reflected the very primitive credit conditions in Poland, but it was, none the less, indicative of the 'banking' role of great nobles (in Polish conditions, even a magnate who defaulted on such obligations would not necessarily lose his political support – those who had invested in him stood little chance of ever seeing any returns if they turned against him politically). Such loans were more than a highly convenient source of ready cash: they were also an investment by much of the rest of society in the ruling, landed, sector, and they contributed not only to its dominance, but to the social acceptability of that dominance.

In more prosperous and financially far more sophisticated Britain, new-style corporate lenders emerged by the end of the century. By 1800, the two leading insurance companies, the Equitable and the Sun Fire, had lent a staggering £776,000 in mortgages to aristocratic landowners, tens of thousands at a time (near the top of the scale, the duke of Leeds secured £50,000 in 1780). With rising rents and rising prices until 1815, repayments could be easily absorbed, and even the most indebted individuals could usually dig their way out of their financial holes. Out-and-out bankruptcies of landowners in Britain were rare.[49] The legal doctrine of 'equity of redemption', developed in the late seventeenth and early eighteenth centuries, made foreclosure for non-payment of debt, even where land had been specifically pledged as security, almost impossible to exact – the borrower could simply get away with interest repayments. The land itself would remain 'safe' in the hands of its 'natural' owners, out of the hands of mere money-grabbers.[50]

Such transactions accustomed the nobility, and others, to lend to governments. Indeed, the returns on loans to governments, at least on the continent, were usually higher than on any other form of investment. In 1761, at the height of the Seven Years War, the French government was offering perpetual annuities of 10 per cent per annum on loans.[51] That of course was a measure of desperation – such tempting rates of return carried with them a correspondingly high risk of default. By the end of the eighteenth century, even those hitherto recognised as poor credit risks (mainly in eastern Europe – Prussia, the Habsburgs, Russia, and even (before the Second Partition of 1793) Poland) were deemed sufficiently creditworthy by international bankers (whose unerring inability to foresee massively destabilising credit crises has a long ancestry) for them to loan money to them. The governments of western Europe increasingly developed sophisticated credit systems from the sixteenth and seventeenth centuries onwards which encouraged their subjects to invest in government stock – in effect, to lend monies to those governments in return for long-term interest payments, giving assured returns. Much of this lending came from commoners; much of it was also intimately tied up with the nobility. Lending to the government did not feature as highly among the British aristocracy and gentry as it was to do in the nineteenth century, but it helped diversify portfolios, and, especially in wartime, when interest rates were higher, it was seen as more lucrative than investment in or purchase of land. It was more than likely, however, that the scale of such lending by the landed classes was easily eclipsed by their lending and borrowing among themselves. The return on such mortgage lending in Britain in the latter half of the eighteenth century (around 4–5 per cent) at least matched that on government stocks, save in wartime.[52] The purchase of venal office in France and the periodic, if haphazard, revaluations of those offices, obliging purchasers to advance supplementary sums to the French government, was a form of quasi-forced loans that did nothing to endear the French monarchy to a sizeable and important section of its subjects. The Spanish government, too, was seen as an increasingly reliable credit risk, although as a result of the war against revolutionary France, in 1798 the only way the Bourbon monarchy of Charles IV could avoid bankruptcy was to order the sequestration and sale of ecclesiastical lands.[53]

If credit was otherwise unavailable, an alternative source could be found in the state. From their point of view, governments and monarchs might feel they had little alternative but to bail out impoverished nobles. It was not only in England that noble and gentry land held a privileged place vis-à-vis creditors. After the Seven Years War, Frederick the Great could not allow nobles, who he was convinced were vital to supply his officers, to go to the wall. He refused them leave to sell estates to commoners to alleviate their plight. As early as 1759, he had banned foreclosures on property for debt. Between 1763 and 1765, he gave landowners in all provinces a five-year moratorium to clear their debts. From 1769, he began to create a network of *Landschaften*, institutions intended to give nobles easy loans secured against their estates. All the major Prussian provinces had these by 1788. The landowning nobles in each province assumed a common liability for the credit of each individual: each landowner could obtain a bond to the value of one-third, one-half, or even two-thirds of his property, provided his nearest male relatives (agnates) agreed. Rates of interest were kept low, at around 6 per cent, eventually dropping to 4, the money itself originating from merchants and townsmen who viewed the arrangements as secure.

The whole purpose of the *Landschaften* was to enable the nobility to reconstruct their war-ravaged estates. Instead, most of the money went either on consumption or on speculation. Rapidly rising grain prices in the last 30 years of the century meant that landowners' incomes would probably have doubled anyway. In reality, many were tempted to use their mortgages to buy additional land, then remortgage it, then buy further land. The restrictions on borrowing were largely ignored – 100 per cent mortgages were easily obtained. Colonel von Hülsen paid only 100 *Thaler* for an estate in East Prussia, valued at 16,000 *Thaler*, in 1788; the balance was financed by interest payments on the mortgage secured on the property.[54] The effect of all this was to build up a fevered speculation in land, as (as ever in such cases) those involved were convinced that they could not lose. In two *Kreise* (districts) of Silesia, there was not an estate that had not changed hands between 1766 and 1800; the price of land in the province rose by over 200 per cent in the same period, and by almost 500 per cent in Brandenburg. The speculation affected neighbouring areas, such as Mecklenburg; and the idea of land banks, as an easy credit source to nobles, was widely adopted across eastern Europe. Booms end, usually in tears. In Silesia, the crash came in 1800. One insolvent landowner who had bought an estate for 30,000 *Thaler* found that he could sell it only for 10,000. In the rest of Prussia, the speculation flourished until 1806.

Despite the prohibitions on the purchase of noble land by commoners, those who lost out often had little choice. Already in 1800, 9 per cent of the owners of properties designated as 'noble' in the Kurmark were townsmen; elsewhere in the Brandenburg heartlands, it was closer to 5 per cent. The real figures were probably higher, since many estates were almost certainly purchased clandestinely or under fictitious noble names. In 1807, noble insolvency and the shock of catastrophic defeat at the hands of a non-*Ancien Régime* army meant that all restrictions on the commoner purchase of land in Prussia were dropped, although the legislation specified that the purchase of noble land was not to lead to ennoblement.[55] Even so, the real problem was not so much that there was an influx of commoners into what had hitherto officially been a noble preserve, but that internal differentiation within the Prussian nobility increased markedly: inequalities of wealth, hitherto relatively muted by European standards, became much more striking, and poorer nobles became more dependent than ever on the limited opportunities offered by state service to maintain their status.[56]

In Britain, a couple of dozen or so 'of ancient noble families, whose peerages happen to continue after their estates are worn out' were maintained in some form of decency by the 'aristocratic dole' – handouts and pensions from the royal civil list.[57] Likewise, the Russian nobility looked to the state to bail them out. Caught between a particularly unremunerative economy and the demands of state service, it was probably inevitable that they should get into debt, even without demonstrating any extravagance or financial irresponsibility. 'Luxuries apart, most members of the [Russian] gentry lacked the money income necessary to carry on their lives, and the most common means used to bridge the gap between income and expenses was credit.'[58] Only a minority owned estates sufficiently extensive to permit them to benefit from Russia's rapidly rising real prices for agricultural products – and those who did could only have been encouraged to consume more. Between 1729 and 1785, successive rulers set up a variety of institutions, banking or pawn-houses, to offer nobles credit at comparatively low rates. Compara-tively, that is, by Russian standards: 6–8 per cent loans were normally on offer in an economy where purely private credit was obtainable at rates usually at least three times as great. Most of these state credit insti-tutions were based in Moscow and St Petersburg, and were hardly easily accessible to most nobles. Most of the loans went on consumption – unless they were within easy reach of the capitals, it is unlikely that direct investment in land would in any case have yielded any positive results, and many were simply loans incurred to pay off old ones.

The Russian land market was not sufficiently active to allow specula-tion in it to lift nobles out of trouble in the same way as in Prussia, but the serf market was. The banks set up to assist nobles used their serfs as collateral; the pressure of demand from nobles was such as to help prod Catherine II's government into printing paper roubles from the 1770s. The resultant inflationary pressures worked to well-born debtors' advantage by allowing them to pay off existing loans with cheap money while continuing with the debt cycle. In 1786, the government simply forgave a large slice of noble debt, but, even so, by 1792 the govern-ment-sponsored banks alone were owed at least 45 million roubles, which if they were to be repaid at all could only be in ever less valuable paper assignats. The extent of private debt, run up at punishingly high interest rates, was incalculable. Paul I tried to stop the rot in his own way, by instituting a scheme which would impose forcible repayments on debtors. Had it been implemented as originally intended, it would have swallowed up some three-quarters of the incomes of even well-off landowners. As it was, by 1800, as many as one in nine of all privately owned serfs may have been mortgaged to various banking institutions. Though much diluted, Paul's scheme did nothing to enhance his stand-ing among the *dvorianstvo*, who continued to borrow against their serfs well into the nineteenth century.[59] But wherever serfdom existed, in the sense of peasants being tied to the land, not free to move, then it was the serfs who bore the consequences of their masters' indebtedness, in the form of more demanding or more refined impositions.

Did the nobility do more for the economy, by investment and management, than the economy did for them, through rising prices and expanding markets? The answer to this question must be a qualified negative. Those genuinely engaged in agricultural, industrial or commercial development were few and far between. The best that could be hoped for was that they might help provide the conditions in which already favourable economic developments could continue to unfold. Their role in the Industrial Revolution in Britain, for example, was essentially secondary, providing a useful legislative framework (helping to pass enclosure acts, canal and turnpike acts) – but even this should not be overstated. Landowners who appreciated that they might benefit personally from such improvements were happy enough to sponsor them. Where they saw a chance to make money by selling land for such development at outrageous prices, they were equally glad to do so. Otherwise, in general, landowners adapted to the opportunities open to them; and, because a few were rich, powerful and owned extensive landholdings, they had, in reality, far greater scope for profiting from economic developments than others. On the other hand, noble and even ennobled landowners were not, nor were they intended to be, entrepreneurs. Even in England, it is doubtful how far entrepreneurship was valued for its own sake. On the contrary, there as everywhere else it served as a rather risky avenue to buy into the landed sector, to become absorbed into the gentry, rather than to stay in the ranks of the 'middling sort'.

The well-off great and good had the resources and connections to keep afloat and prosper. Those with only a few peasants, or none, or with little or no land, found the going much harder. In extreme, but none the less universally telling form, the problem can be seen in Russia, which was supposedly opened by Peter the Great at the beginning of the century to Western influences. Genuine access to even the trappings of a Western lifestyle, which involved such desirable things as fashionable clothing, a modest carriage, the purchase of imported luxuries, was utterly beyond the reach of most Russian nobles. Arcadius Kahan has estimated that if such a lifestyle was to be comfortably sustained, then the minimum requirement was an estate disposing of some 100 (male) serfs and returning an annual income of at least 500 roubles – but over 80 per cent of Russia's 60,000–70,000 noble households in 1795 had fewer serfs than this. The average income, of 225 roubles per household, would come from around 45 serfs: this was less than half of what was required to afford that desirable Western lifestyle. Over half of Russian noble landowners owned fewer than 21 serfs. At least comparable problems existed in Poland, Hungary and Spain; almost everywhere in continental Europe, the straitened circumstances of many of the lesser nobility gave cause for concern.[60]

Governments and nobles responded to the problem of the poor nobility by breaking, bending or ignoring their own laws on derogation or by pretending that a problem did not exist. In 1764, the Polish *Sejm* ruled that nobles were allowed to retail, even hawk, certain types of beer. A career as cook or butler was not deemed dishonourable. In Spain, it was accepted that *hidalgos* in the Basque provinces would practise manual trades en masse – smithying, shoe-making, carpentry, and so on. Another solution was for the state to provide support, something that it did on a very wide scale in Russia and Prussia, to the extent that, from the nobles' point of view, these were almost welfare states for the nobility. But such support came at a high price: service to the state, and that meant predominantly military service. Almost all Russian males of noble origin were expected to serve for life in the armed forces. The provincial and central bureaucracy offered a considerably less prestigious alternative. In 1736, the lifetime service was reduced to 25 years and service in the considerably less prestigious local bureaucracy was formally opened up as an alternative for noble families with a son already in the forces.[61] The 'emancipation' from service proclaimed for the nobility by Peter III in 1762, reaffirmed by Catherine II in 1785 (and *de facto* abolished by Paul in 1797), meant little, other than psychologically: the great majority of Russian nobles continued to need state service to support themselves. To those who owned thirty, ten, seven or just one serf, a state salary or some form of state subvention was crucial if they were to avoid utter penury.[62] It was little different in Prussia. As early as 1724, the nobility of Pomerania, almost entirely petty or even landless nobles, consisted exclusively of serving or retired soldiers; in 1767, 960 of the 1700 nobles of Prussia's Kurmark were in the army; by 1800, 68 per cent of the Kurmark's landed proprietors had served or were serving in the army and another 7 per cent in the civil service. Some 60 per cent of nobles in East Prussia served in the military. No officer anywhere in Europe could expect to earn anything like a decent salary before reaching the rank of captain, when substantial opportunities for the fiddling of company funds began to appear. And in Prussia, where opportunities for promotion for poor nobles compared well with other states, that might easily take up to 15 years in lesser commissions. Indeed, if anything, except for those who obtained senior commissions, the economic security of a commission might prove illusory – even in the comparatively well-financed British forces, officers had to rely on subventions from their family estates not just to help eke out their own salaries but, especially in wartime, to help keep their own men together. Very few nobles could realistically hope to emulate the fortunes of General Bogislaw von Tauntzien, who from a modest background was able to amass 150,000 *Thaler* (at a time when most estates yielded between 1000 and 5000 *Thaler* per annum) through his career in the Prussian army.[63] The clamour to reserve places in the army for the poor nobility in France or in Poland was a reflection of the same problem. It is true, of course, that nobles had rather different expectations of what constituted 'poverty' than commoners: but their complaints of poverty were real enough.[64]

Across Europe, the choices of impoverished gentlemen were few. They could ideally (though not, of course, in practice) maintain a kind of Cincinnatian dignity by working their own land: French law indeed allowed nobles in most of France to work their own land without subjecting them to the *taille*, up to a limit of four *charrues*, leaving their swords (even wooden ones – steel was expensive), their sole status symbol, hanging from a nearby branch. But this was pretty desperate – there was no doubt that these people were really peasants, and poor even by peasant standards. There were some 20,000 noble families in Prussia even before the First Partition added another 30,000 in 1772, but only 11,500 noble properties (and an increasing number of families owned more than one estate) – which meant that a good half of the Prussian nobility were near destitute. By the 1790s, the number of noble-owned estates had about halved.[65] Frederick the Great of Prussia had to issue an ordinance forbidding officers – nobles – from begging in the streets of Berlin.

'By birth a landowner, from need a miller, a shoemaker, a tailor, a cooper ... and from necessity a peasant', wrote a Polish nobleman, Jacek Jezierski, of those who failed to share his good fortune. Jezierski himself succeeded in escaping the poverty to which the subdivision of the small family estate would have condemned him through a mixture of luck and guile: it took embezzlement, pimping and entrepreneurship. In Britain, the Catholic Scot Lord Aston was reduced to seeking employment as a cook and a watchmaker (George III gave him an annual pension of £200 in 1761).[66] Many who enjoyed noble status but could not afford the trappings simply gave up the struggle and sank into a mass of petty landowners, peasants and indigents. It happened in Spain, where the number of nobles fell from 722,794 to 402,059 between the censuses of 1768 and 1797 and thousands of *hidalgos* 'disappeared'; thousands more remained noble – but only at the price of the contempt of rulers, ministers and the well-to-do. In Denmark, between 1660 and 1720 the number of nobles declined from 1500 to 864 – not just through biological extinction but also by the sheer inability to afford to maintain their status. It happened in Russia, where thousands of those who could have laid claim to noble status if only they had had the resources dropped into the peasantry or into the ranks of *odnodvortsy* who struggled desperately to preserve some form of vestigial noble privileges. In England, once comfortably off gentry sank to the level of tenant farmers.[67] Those not so fortunate were reduced to arguing over which peasant owed them what services on what day from what fraction of a village, subdivided by generations of inheritance. In Poland and Hungary, petty nobles found employment as stewards, bailiffs, or worse. Around 1720, an illiterate swineherd living in the Hungarian village of Ruda-banya regaled his amused fellow-villagers with his most precious possession, an old parchment confirming bestowal of noble status on his family. It had probably been gained during the late seventeenth-century Turkish wars.[68] Without wealth and its trappings, nobility was indeed 'like a dead thing'.

6

INHERITANCE

The noble house was a nexus of dynastic connections that reached far back into a past that was often mythical, if not consciously fabricated; it also reached forward into a future where the patrimony and the name were to be preserved. Ancestral deeds, lauded in family histories and proclaimed for all to see on family tombstones and funerary monuments, served as a continuous, almost living, example and inspiration. It was the duty of the present generation to ensure that what had been received from the past should be passed on intact, preferably increased, to posterity. Family histories, commonplace books, *livres de raison*, almanacs and public panegyrics and eulogies extolled the virtues of glorious forbears and relatives. Jean Étienne Gautier, canon of Cavaillon, kept such a record between 1634 and 1704 for the edification and instruction of his nephews and grand-nephews. He leavened a seemly pride with a discreet prudence in not carrying his explorations beyond the eight previous generations, 'since this is pointless in the case of a family which has no need to prove nobility, and which is known in this town as one of the worthiest and most ancient'.[1] More than any economic ratiocinations, the need to preserve, consolidate and extend the inheritance of the past for the present and the future dominated the thinking of the nobility, providing them with their most immediate worries and, for a lucky few, with their greatest opportunities.

Nobles had to contend with the laws and customs of their country or region, which almost invariably created a degree of constraint on the disposal of their patrimony. Many of these reached back to the early Middle Ages and were not necessarily appropriate to noble concerns in the eighteenth century. Such local laws and customs laid down how testamentary property was to be divided, insisting on the rights of all children, male and female, to benefit. On the other hand, since nobles had access to the centres of power, and since the ruling dynasties saw nobles as indispensable to the maintenance of their own power, even the most hallowed laws could be manipulated or evaded, or opposed by different legal frameworks. Thus, across much of France the so-called *droit d'aînesse* ('right of the elder') was used to allow noble fathers to make arrangements which favoured the elder son, irrespective of what local custom enjoined. Even where *droit d'aînesse* did not apply, as in Alsace, in practice arrangements favouring the eldest son could always be made. Not that such evasion or manipulation was confined to the nobility – it was found at all levels of society.

The most obvious way in which the name and patrimony of a noble house could be preserved was by ensuring that the property descended to one son, usually the eldest, by the path of male primogeniture. Women were unsuitable, since they normally took the name of the husband. In the normal way of things, heiresses could expect their estate to pass to the line that was emphatically the husband's. The principal, if partial and spectacular, exception was Castile, where in default of direct or close male heirs the family name and titles, as well as the properties, would descend through the eldest daughter. Where this happened, she and her spouse could then expect a barrage of lawsuits from other relatives, unless, perhaps, she married a relative in the first place. Europe's monarchs all married each other's relatives, and found themselves engaged in wars of succession on that account. Litigation through the courts, if often more protracted than a war, was at least more civilised, but it could be extremely lengthy: individual disputes might drag on, as in Naples, for centuries. Or, for that matter, in England.[2] Almost any land in outright ownership in Poland was liable to legal challenge from supposedly cheated, if distant, heirs. After 1588, as a measure to prevent noble land from reverting to the crown, claims were allowed to the eighth degree of kinship, but this furnished almost limitless scope for litigation from would-be claimants. Lawyers across Europe, who themselves numbered many nobles, did nothing to discourage such lucrative sources of business. Few nobles were prepared, however, to go as far as the fourteenth Lord Willoughby de Broke, who, in 1802, ordered the demolition of Chesterton House in Warwickshire, inherited by his father from a cousin in 1746, in order to prevent rival claimants to the estate from getting their hands on it. Lord Willoughby himself could continue to lead a perfectly agreeable existence at his nearby family seat of Compton Verney.[3]

Excessive subdivision among heirs could impoverish and eventually destroy a noble family. The English government and the Protestant Ascendancy well knew what was at stake when the Dublin parliament ruled in 1703 that the lands of Catholic landowners should be subject to equal division among male heirs – unless one of the heirs converted to Protestantism, in which case he would scoop the lot (even his father, if alive, would be reduced to the status of life tenant).[4] The obvious antidote to uncontrolled subdivision was the entail – subjecting the property to a legal device that would prevent its alienation, sale or diminution in favour of anyone outside a specified family line. It was in Spain that the most determined steps were taken to preserve intact the family patrimony, and it is there that the problems involved can be seen most clearly. In Castile, the norm of partible inheritance with equal division among sons and daughters did not suit the nascent aristocratic families of the Middle Ages. From the late thirteenth century, these great houses began to prise from the then weakened monarchy *mayorazgos*, entails comprising not only land, but even jurisdictional rights usurped from the crown. The intention was to ensure that the family would never lack either fame or means. The act setting up the *mayorazgo* of Vilverde in 1581 boasted that it was done

> in order that in the absence [of the *mayorazgo*'s founders] their memory will endure among their descendants and successors, which memory would be erased if such property would continue free and unbound, because it is notorious . . . that free possessions . . . are consumed and damaged in many ways by prodigal successors who disperse them, or imprudent ones who do not preserve them, or by a multitude of heirs who partition them, so that . . . *mayorazgos* were instituted for the preservation of their memory and so that all the children, descendants and kin of that line may be favoured and can serve our Lord God and his natural kings and defend the honour of the House whence they descend.[5]

The establishment of this type of entail was everywhere a truly monstrous act of family pride. It subordinated the individual to the preservation of the name and house, and demonstrated an utter lack of confidence in the future generations the founders presumed to bind. Successive possessors of the *mayorazgo* (tenants-in-tail, as English law would put it) found that they were unable to sell, or even put up, land as security for loans and mortgages. Even the most careful seigneurs found that, as they had to provide for siblings, sons and daughters and older relatives, their often massive landed assets generated too little cash to meet their obligations. On the other hand, since the terms of a *mayorazgo* could be altered only by a monarch (for example, to raise a mortgage against security of land within the entail), Spanish kings found that manipulation of *mayorazgos* could serve to control and curb and make even the most powerful grandees dependent on them. When the financial charges against *mayorazgos* threatened to engulf all their revenues, kings could even send in administrators and judges to adjudicate between tenants-in-tail and their creditors.

The effect of *mayorazgos* was often the opposite to what their founders had hoped. Far from preserving family fortunes, they were a millstone around posterity's neck. Yet these inflexible entails continued to be created partly to satisfy family pride, partly because they were so widespread, and partly because of the illusory security they seemed to offer to the family name and possessions. In Spain, the practice rapidly spread to lesser nobles and even to commoners. Creditors were able only to distrain rents (if the courts agreed) – they could not make off with the land itself. A parallel process took place in Portugal. Perhaps as much as one-third of the land of Castile was entailed by the late eighteenth century. By then, criticism of *mayorazgos* was more widespread and trenchant than ever. Their possessors (so it was widely argued) had no incentive to invest in agricultural improvements. After all, they were, in the final resort, immune from the consequences of bankruptcy. But there was, in any case, little point in investing in improvements (even assuming there was spare cash to be had for them in the first place) since, even if such investments produced higher rents, those returns would be siphoned off by creditors and be swallowed up by the obligation to provide portions, *alimentos*, for other relatives. Where more than one entail passed to one individual, gargantuan landed complexes developed that were beyond effective management and control.

The other extreme, partible inheritance, or equal division of the estate between male children, carried obvious dangers. Peter the Great feared that the ability of the Russian service class (the foundation of the eighteenth-century nobility) to discharge military service was being severely undermined by the practice. In March 1714, the tsar ruled that in future, all the land should go to a single heir (not necessarily the eldest, save in the case of intestacy); other sons could enter commerce without loss of what was still a very poorly defined and uncertain noble status. The following year, however, Peter decreed that all sons should enter state service. The effect was not only to destroy centuries-old inheritance patterns but to place the family entirely at the mercy of a state which under Peter demonstrated itself to be particularly arbitrary and capricious. These *diktats* were widely ignored: fathers continued to find means to bequeath land by partible inheritance. In March 1731, following the accession of the Empress Anna and the agitation for repeal of the Petrine decree in the brief interregnum preceding her accession, customary, partible inheritance was reinstated.[6] Ironically, barely a generation later, in instructions for the Legislative Commission called by Catherine the Great in 1767 there were widespread complaints from the Russian nobility that the process was indeed undermining their position, in some cases yielding insufficient land to support a single peasant, let alone a nobleman. The custom of subdividing scattered villages or estates equally among all male heirs, instead of conferring individual estates on them, did nothing to alleviate matters.[7]

While the Russian nobility themselves offered no coherent solution to the problem, it was one that the state could turn to its advantage, in a way that mirrored the situation in Spain: a fragmented nobility would be forced into dependence on the state and state service (particularly after the formal 'emancipation' of the nobility from this obligation in 1762). The state could rely on its own immense reserves of patronage to reward those it wished. Only one entail, or *maiorat*, was set up in Russia: in 1774, Catherine the Great granted one to the eccentric (he became a Catholic, not something Orthodox Russian nobles normally did) Count Zachar Chernyshev, largely pieced together from confiscated estates on lands annexed from Poland under the First Partition – which Chernyshev had played a key role in bringing about.[8]

Between the two extremes of unbreakable entails and partible inheritances, the nobility developed a wide variety of strategies for family succession and material and status preservation. Entails did not have to be perpetual. They could be made to run for limited periods: in Piedmont after 1598, Naples after 1666, Tuscany after 1747 for no more than the tenancy of four successive holders. Italian law in any case made some provision for the sale of parts even of entailed estates in order to pay off debts.[9] It was the same in France where, after 1747, entails could not be prolonged beyond two generations.[10] In general, entails were favoured by the powerful and the wealthy. The Spanish Habsburg example influenced not only Italy but the lands of the Austrian Habsburg cousins, where, after 1606, the emperor showed himself ready to accord entail status (the so-called *fideicommissum*, or *Fideikommiss*), although it was rarely as restrictive as the Iberian model. The first Hungarian entail was set up by the Pálffy family in 1653. Though lesser nobles could take advantage of entails, it was extremely rare for them to do so – to 1765, only one Hungarian non-magnate family had secured one. But even where the emperor was not prepared to grant *Fideikommiss* status, families sought to leave the bulk of the inheritance to the eldest son and pension off or buy out his younger brothers.[11]

Similar formal arrangements were slower to catch on in Prussia before the mid-nineteenth century, despite active encouragement from Frederick the Great in particular. In practice, many families acted as if their estates were entailed: one son, usually the eldest, would inherit but would provide cash portions for his siblings, in effect buying them out. The establishment of *Landschaften* after 1770 to provide cheap credit against the security of estates, combined with rising prices for land and its products, eased the process. The principal spur to the introduction of new agricultural methods on the Stavenow estate of the von Kleist family north-west of Berlin was the agreement between ten brothers in 1758 that the estate should pass to just one of them, Friedrich Joachim – but he had to buy out the others' shares in the estate. The alternative would have been a drastic fragmentation of the 6400-acre property and its seven villages.[12] The general reluctance with which the middling and lesser nobility of eastern Europe – not only in Prussia and the Habsburg territories but also in Poland and Russia – viewed the entail suggests that an awareness of the disadvantages weighed as much as any appreciation of the benefits.

The most remarkable and flexible development of the entail took place in England after the 1640s, assuming the form of so-called 'strict settlement'. Although the detailed terms and degree of restrictiveness varied from one settlement to the next, the principle was the same: to create a fictitious owner (an as yet unborn heir, or, in legal parlance, a 'contingent remainder') while the current head of the family and his immediate successor (his eldest son) assumed the status of life tenants: their powers over the estate were sufficiently limited to prevent them from disposing of it. The arrangement would normally be made at the time of the coming of age or marriage of the eldest son. He and his father could only draw on the income of the estate and otherwise use it to raise monies (by raising mortgages) for certain specified purposes, usually connected with the business of marriage and inheritance: to ensure financial provision for the bride and future children. Ownership of the estate was vested in trustees who normally consisted of friends, family, legal advisers, answerable to the court of chancery for their stewardship. These acted on behalf of the yet-to-be-born eldest grandson (or other specified collateral male relatives, in the event of the son's marriage failing to produce heirs). The designated future heir would come into his own only at the age of majority − 21. He would then, as tenant-in-tail (outright owner), have full powers to dispose of the property as he saw fit, subject to whatever legally binding charges (mortgages, provisions for other family members) existed on it. While he was not, in theory, bound by debts incurred by his predecessors, unless he honoured them he would find it almost impossible to find credit essential to his status. An unmarried heir in such a situation would find that no self-respecting family would wish for connections with him (though a wealthy parvenu family might take a different view). At the tenant-in-tail's coming of age or marriage, the entire arrangement would be repeated. Indeed, the occasion would provide an opportunity to break, or bar, the entail, permitting whatever adjustments were necessary to suit the particular circumstances of the family at the time.[13]

It may, after all this, come as an anti-climax to learn that 'the central significance of the strict settlement was that it was not in practice very strict'.[14] It rarely comprised the whole complex of a given family's inherited estates. Peripheral lands, or lands coming in via marriages or inheritances, were usually deliberately excluded from the entail, precisely to endow the settlement with a flexibility, in terms of providing for younger children or sales to meet financial obligations, not found in the Spanish *mayorazgo*. Entails were unnecessary because families on the commanding heights disposed of enough property and enjoyed sufficient access to wealth to make them unnecessary, be it in terms of royal favour, the spoils of office or, most importantly of all, access to heiresses, who fuelled the great carousel of landed turnover. Even if generous provision was made for younger sons and daughters, the influx of great heiresses easily guarded against excessive fragmentation of families' properties. It was also possible, though not necessarily easy, to have strict settlement set aside by the court of chancery or by private act of parliament. Strict settlement was primarily a form of psychological reassurance. Its labyrinthine procedures were useful to ensure both the preservation of the estate and the name and the interests of family members; that they had to be labyrinthine reflects the complex permutations to which family succession, and hence the maintenance of the honour of the family name, were subject. And the more complex and arcane the provisions, the more the lawyers who drew them up stood to benefit. If the merry-go-round of property transfers was in danger of coming to a halt, it could be boosted by the injection of cash. Since only one in three fathers lived to see the marriage of the eldest son, there was always a good chance that eighteenth-century mortality would in any case bar (break) the entail.[15]

Likewise, the Act against Clandestine Marriages of 1753 was designed to meet a danger more imaginary than commonplace, to avoid the risk of sons and heirs making unsuitable (non-dowered) love matches, or heiresses throwing away their affections (and fortunes) on unsuitable youths. Such unions would preclude any possibility of an injection of financial relief or threaten the dissipation of a family fortune: so under the Act no person under the age of 21 could marry without the consent of the father or guardian; banns had to be called; and a month's prior residence in the parish concerned was required. The House of Commons endorsed the measure with some misgivings (it had thrown out several previous bills to this effect), fearing it was designed to mop up wealthy heiresses for the Lords.[16]

That the threat of fragmentation of family inheritances was not necessarily as great as it could have been can be seen in Poland–Lithuania. There, all sons were entitled to an equal share in three-quarters of the estate and movable property, sisters one-quarter. Between 1586 and 1783, only seven families took the 'obvious' precaution of guarding against the splintering of the patrimony by securing entails (which had to be sanctioned by and could only be altered or terminated by the *Sejm*, not the king). In part this was because these *ordynacje* were politically unpopular: the nobility sensed an attempt by individual magnates to carve out favoured treatment for themselves, to the detriment of the *szlachta*'s much-vaunted equality. In part it was because of their inflexibility. By the eighteenth century, at least three of the entails were hopelessly weighed down by debts; during the 1750s, a fourth was illegally dissolved (to pay off the debts of its holder) amid intense political acrimony. But some of the most powerful families, such as the Czartoryskis, the Potockis or the Lubomirskis, were able to maintain vast wealth, estates and political influence without recourse to entails. Wealth married wealth; one great landed inheritance would attract another. There also existed another great buffer against fragmentation. At least 15 per cent of the sprawling territory of the Polish–Lithuanian Commonwealth consisted of 'crown lands' (*królewszczyzny*), divided into hundreds of individual estates, which monarchs were bound by law to distribute to 'deserving' nobles in lifetime tenure. One of the driving forces of Polish politics lay in competition among magnates to secure these – not just for themselves or their clients but to ensure adequate provision for younger sons without biting too deeply into the family patrimony. And for the entail-holder, or *ordynat*, there was always the greater chance of securing a non-entailed acquisition through inheritance or marriage, to provide some additional flexibility in the landed portfolio.

It was among the poor and lesser nobility that the dangers of partible division were all too real. There could be no great heiresses to bail them out. Impoverished nobles of ancient lineage were often too proud to marry the daughters of bankers or financiers, who would, in any case, prefer a rather grander social match for their offspring and were ready to stump up massive dowries in order to buy their way into the highest aristocratic circles. If lesser nobles could not marry their social equals, they might well have to make do with the daughters of peasants or poor townsmen, whom they would socially elevate by the match but who, in their turn, could do little to repair their fortunes.

The preservation of the family name and estate, of course, required heirs, the begetting of whom was also a complex lottery. No individual, however grand, could be sure of his posterity. In March 1711, the succession to the throne of France must have seemed more solid than any in Europe. Louis XIV had a 50-year-old son, three grandsons and two great-grandsons. Within two years, all but two of this impressive progeny were dead, carried off by smallpox and measles. The last surviving great-grandson, the future Louis XV, was at first in too frail health to be expected to survive long, and probably owed his life to the ladies of the court keeping the doctors away from him during one of his illnesses. If he had died, there would certainly have been a major dispute, perhaps even war, over the French succession between Louis XIV's nephew, Philip, duc d'Orléans, and his last surviving grandson, Philip V of Spain. It was a spectre which stalked every family of early modern Europe; its complications were something that all landed families had to take into account in their calculations about the future of the name and estate.

Leaving aside the fact that not all nobles married (almost 9 per cent of English peers in the seventeenth and eighteenth centuries did not do so) and that around 5 per cent of marriages were likely to prove childless, nobles serious about the preservation of the name and patrimony had to play a guessing game with mortality over the number of children they could risk siring. One son was not enough: he had only a one in three chance of outliving his father; too many sons, even if partible inheritance did not apply, would still produce the risk that the estate might be excessively encumbered with provisions for their support; on the other hand, if the name was to be continued, there needed to be a reserve of younger sons to carry on the family if the eldest failed to produce surviving sons. Overall, about one-quarter of the sons and daughters of peers did not marry. Among sons, around one in seven heirs did not marry, around one in three younger sons did not do so. The continental experience suggests the numbers among younger children not marrying were significantly higher.[17]

Too great a reserve of sons would not only be a drain on resources, but could store up future complications as relatives disputed the inheritance. Daughters made things even more complicated. If a union produced only females, then, unless they could inherit in their own right, the ancestral name and estate could well disappear altogether. And even if, as in Spain, girls could inherit, their family's estates might simply be lost amid the plethora of grandiose names and estates accumulated through the female line. On the other hand, where only an heiress survived, the family name could be preserved by her husband dropping his own and taking that of his spouse: it happened not only in Spain and the French Basque country, but there were similar instances in England. Younger sons in particular were less likely to object to dropping their own surname, since it was usually their sole route to a major inheritance. And, of course, the grander the family to which a younger son belonged, the greater the chances of his securing a wealthy match which would enable him to set up a collateral line in his own right. The case of the 14-year-old James Archibald Stuart furnished an extreme example of how a younger brother could leapfrog to pre-eminence through the vagaries of inheritance. His maternal grandfather, Edward Wortley Montagu, had disinherited his own dissipated son, Edward. He then earmarked the most lucrative part of his estates, valued at at least £800,000 and built on the backbone of Tyneside coal, for young James Archibald; to his elder brother, John, he assigned the financially far less impressive earldom of Bute. The court of chancery agreed that the will was valid, to the discomfiture of both the disinherited son and the disappointed elder grandson. James Archibald's later incorporation of 'Wortley' into his family name was the least he could do.[18]

The prime concern, at least among long-established landowners, was not, then, the economic exploitation of the estate. It was the legal aspects of its management that took pre-eminence, so as to ensure that it would, in the first instance, provide for as many family contingencies as possible.

Nor was it just a question of provision for younger sons and daughters, but also for surviving relatives (perhaps the landowner's own siblings and, in some cases, parents) and widows. There was always a good chance that a man would remarry: around a quarter of all English peers did so in the eighteenth century, and one in twenty-five married three times. This was all too likely to produce further genealogical complications. There was also a fair chance that women who survived the hazards of child-birth would outlive their husbands. They had to be provided for. In the first 15 years of marriage a wife was twice as likely to die as the husband, but over the eighteenth century as a whole, the life expectancy of the wives of English peers increased from around 36 to 50. A woman's dowry would normally ensure due provision (a jointure) for her widow-hood.[19] This arrangement would normally be built into the legally binding pre-nuptial contract, failure to observe which could unleash the bride's family's lawyers. A landowner more interested in economic innovation than in the preservation of what he had and what his wife brought into the marriage was pursuing a very risky course indeed.

All this meant that, either at marriage or on coming into ownership of the estate, the noble landowner was faced with a number of financial encumbrances. In most states he would have at his disposal his wife's dowry, or portion, yet its purpose was not, in the first instance, to benefit him, but to benefit the offspring of the union. If no offspring survived, or if the wife predeceased the husband, then the dowry, unless specified otherwise in the marriage contract, would revert to her family. One of the purposes of jointure in England was not just to provide for the widow, but to protect the heir, since under common law, widows were entitled to a 'dower' of one-third of the husband's property; coupled with other charges, this could prove financially crippling for the new successor to the estate. Jointure superseded dower. In law, a husband was bound to provide for his wife, even during his own lifetime, though it was normally assumed he would do so out of his current income. Aristocratic marriage contracts (gentry ones far less so) tended to stipu-late a fixed cash income for the wife (in England, this was known as 'pin money') and also for the widow – the jointure which seems by the eight-eenth century to have been settled on average at around 20 per cent of the gross income of the joint estate or, according to other estimates, at around £100 for every £1000 of dowry by 1700. These rates may have increased over the rest of the century – by any reckoning, a hefty pro-vision, even if, in practice, it derived from what the wife herself had brought into the marriage through her dowry. A dowry (unless specified otherwise in the marriage contract) became the absolute property of the husband only where the bride was not an heiress in her own right; if she was, then it remained her property until her death, when it would pass to her children (in default of which it would revert to, or at least be open to, claims from her own relatives). A bride's portion was usually converted into land purchases (which offered some security for its recovery); but this was not always possible, since portions were frequently paid by instalments (and often financed by mortgages by the bride's family). In Poland–Lithuania, custom required that dowries be paid off within three years, but there were cases of frustrated husbands waiting 20, even 50, years for their wives' dues. As an alternative, it was possible to pay 10 per cent interest on a non-delivered dowry or assign lands from the bride's parental estate as security: if unredeemed, it would pass to the bride's husband in perpetuity. It was not supposed to be converted to paying off the husband's debts, or those of his family, although it frequently was. English law, or practice, was much laxer in this respect than in Naples, where extremely strict laws existed to make sure the wife's dowry would pass only to the children, or, in their absence, revert to her family. In practice, in England, and doubtless elsewhere, the bride's portion was often paid to her father-in-law (if he were still alive) while he undertook to provide maintenance for the young couple until he died.[20] In Poland, in law, the husband only administered the wife's dowry on her behalf during her lifetime (including, in this, the lands assigned from his estate for her widow's jointure). But whatever the law said, in practice the husband was generally in a position to do with the dowry as he thought best.

Dowries had to be given. They were a guarantee of the status of the bride, or, if she were not noble, but relied on ennoblement by marriage, they were a compensation for the lack of status. Land was good, cash was better. Where an aspiring male married a woman of higher social status, the jointure was likely to be higher, just as a female of inferior social status, and certainly of non-landed background, had normally to bring a larger dowry than her already aristocratic counterpart. Marrying wealth was acceptable – nobles understood. Liquid capital was always useful, the more so as it was often hard to come by.

If the alternative was the ruin of the ancestral estate, then the bullet of a commoner marriage had to be bitten. In provincial France, a dowry of 40,000 *livres* was increasingly seen as the minimum threshold for a bride of inferior social status to marry into the *robe* nobility (though 60,000 *livres* and above was more frequent). In 1788, Justin, marquis de

Fontanges, scion of one of the most ancient and distinguished families of the Auvergne, may have had his qualms about marrying Marie-Madel-Pauline, only daughter of Jean-Samuel Depont. After all, Jean-Samuel's father, Paul-François, had been a mere commoner shipping magnate. The two-generational process of family ennoblement had begun when Paul-François's father (that is, Jean-Samuel Depont's grandfather and Marie-Madel-Pauline's great-grandfather) had purchased for Paul-François the office of *trésorier de France* in 1721. Jean-Samuel inherited the office in 1744, but he would only secure full, transmissible nobility after 20 years of tenure. He himself had been bought the ennobling, though far more prestigious, office of *conseiller* in the Paris *parlement* in 1748 (conferring full nobility after 20 years). But now, with two enno-bling offices, he could count each year of tenure twice to acquire full enno-blement, requiring only eight calendar years before his nobility was 'complete' in 1756. Nine years later, in 1765, Jean-Samuel became *intendant* of Moulins. So it was a meteoric, though by the same token recent and contrived, rise for the Deponts. But Marie did bring a dowry of 300,000 *livres*, the *rentes* from which brought in 15,000 *livres* a year, 5000 *livres* more than Justin de Fontange's own family's income (and the bride's family also promised to raise an additional 150,000 *livres* to allow the young couple to buy their own estate). This kind of money was enough to overcome any reservations. Without it, the young mar-quis certainly would not have been able to afford to live in Paris.[21] The sort of union where the landowner paid no attention to the bride's circumstances and was ready to accept her without a dowry, as when in 1788 the younger Samuel Whitbread married Elizabeth Grey, daugh-ter of an impoverished Northumberland landowner, was the excep-tion, although the number of such unions may have increased over the century.[22]

Dowries were understood to be a device to repair family fortunes, but they also worked the other way round – such was the price of a kind of financial and social equilibrium. They swallowed up far more of a family's income than any economic 'improvements' because they secured, or reaffirmed, a family's status, but they could be the best possi-ble investment inasmuch as the connection could, if the biological dice rolled favourably, be of immense benefit to the family further down the line. They had to be large, if only because that was the fashion. The Nea-politan restrictions in 1801 on the size of dowries were a well-intentioned waste of time by the Bourbon monarchy.[23] The daughter of a French duke would require around a quarter of a million *livres*.[24] A dowry among comparatively modest provincial French gentry, at around 20,000–80,000 *livres*, could easily swallow up three to four years' income. The less prosperous nobility of Angers might manage at most between 10,000 and 20,000 *livres*. The Florentine noble patriciate's dowries of between 10,000 and 25,000 *scudi* amounted to some five years' income of a moderately wealthy family.[25] This was probably proportionately higher than British dowries, which were closer to those offered by Spanish nobles at all levels: a good year's income. 'Undoubtedly mobilising cash for dowries was the single biggest headache in the lives of most aristocrats of the early modern period.' Thomas William Coke, earl of Leicester, as 'Coke of Norfolk' a self-proclaimed agricultural improver of the first rank, spent a grand total of at least £90,000 on his three daughters' dowries; in any one year, he might have spent a comparatively paltry £2500 and £4500 on his celebrated soil improvements.[26]

Even if dowries were paid by instalments, as annuities, or by a combination of cash, jewellery and land, finding the finance for this had to take priority over any form of infrastructural investment in the estate. Incurring debt was almost inevitable and as soon as one daughter's financial obligations had been met, another's might loom on the horizon. In any case, other members of the family, resident uncles and maiden aunts (even if the latter's spinsterhoods spared the need for more dowries), still had to be provided for. That money was also likely to come in via dowries was a necessary compensation, provided the timing was right. Pity the Petre family: Catherine Walmsley of Dunkenhalgh in Lancashire married the seventh lord in 1712, bringing a handsome dowry of an estate with revenues of £5000. Her husband died one year after the marriage; the widow was inconsiderate enough to live until 1786, creaming off an annual jointure of £2000 that had been rather rashly settled on her, and so sucking some £150,000 out of the family coffers in her lifetime.[27] Dowries seem to have been less of a problem for the old Neapolitan nobility, who since the sixteenth century had used their clan connections to set up endowments to enable them to fund their daughters' dowries. So successful were at least some of these that the majority of Neapolitan aristocratic daughters could be decently married off without biting into the family patrimony.[28] Cash was prized above all. In March 1773, while wringing his hands over the Polish partition, Ignacy Twardowski kept his eye on the Warsaw marriage market, advising his patron, Jerzy Mniszech, to marry off a nephew to the daughter of Antoni Jabłonowski, palatine of Poznań: 'A pleasing lady, refined, with a good dowry and, best of all, it's in ready cash.' Only the richest could guarantee to absorb the vicissitudes of family biology, and that meant walking a tightrope between solvency and debt, hunting for that ever-possible windfall.

The obvious solutions to the problem of younger children who might be a drain on the family resources was either to limit their numbers or to restrict the provision made for them. Restricting provision was easier because it was more controllable. The trend in strict settlements was to put a ceiling on how much of a total portion should be allocated to younger sons and daughters: the more that survived to adulthood, the slenderer their resources would be, or the more dependent they would be on the goodwill of the head of the family. There was some hope for these benighted scions. One was the morbid expectation that the eldest brother might die. Such events were not uncommon. The average life expectancy of a French peer for most of the eighteenth century was, after all, only about 35.[29] What such mortality could mean at a personal level can be seen in the case of the Russell dukes of Bedford: Wriothesley Russell, the second duke, died in 1711 of smallpox, aged 31; the third duke, another Wriothesley, died childless in 1732 aged 24, his health broken by an excess of aristocratic dissipation (at least his death spared the estate the financial disaster his gambling threatened); his rather more proper younger brother, John, managed to reach 61, dying in 1771 – but he lived long enough to see his only son, Francis, die in 1767 at the age of 27, after a fall from a horse while hunting. Francis at least left three sons: his eldest, also Francis, died in 1802 aged 37, felled by a tennis injury; he had not married, allowing a younger brother to scoop the family fortune for a second time (but then the Bedfords, with an income of at least £30,000 per annum, could afford a decent support for younger children). In fact, of younger sons of English peers as many as one in three (mainly second sons) came into substantial estates from either uncles or grandparents or were provided with such by their fathers.[30] Peers were in a position to privilege younger sons, not only by settling some peripheral estate on them, but by setting them up in politics. The number of Commons seats under the direct control of the peerage more than doubled over the eighteenth century, from some 105 in 1715 to around 220 in 1802. The number of sons of English peers sitting in these seats also more than doubled, from 32 in 1713 to 82 in 1796. The House of Commons' resolution in 1701, that the Lords' involvement in the election of MPs amounted to 'a high infringement of the liberties and privileges of the Commons of England', was irrelevant rhetoric.[31]

Further down the scale, younger sons of gentry accounted for around half of the 140 merchants engaged in colonial trades in late eighteenth-century Glasgow. Civic and merchant elites preferred such connections with the local landed gentry to connections with mere up and coming manufacturers.[32] Younger sons were ready to become vicars and estate managers for greater landowners. George Plaxton, younger son of a minor landowner, who ran the estates of the Leveson-Gowers between 1691 and 1720, was indeed both a clergyman and an efficient estate steward.[33] The supervision of large estates in Poland or Hungary would have been impossible without the services of younger sons or poor gentry in general.

But what of those younger children, the great majority, whose families could not or would not afford a decent provision? The founding of independent estates for cadet branches seems to have largely come to an end by the sixteenth century. Suitable occupations were very limited. The general European growth in the size of armies and bureaucracies meant that there was greater scope for suitable employment for younger siblings; and since the acquisition of posts depended less on merit and more on influence and connection, they could, unless of truly impoverished noble stock, expect preferential treatment. The purchase of a decent commission could be so expensive, particularly in France, as to place it beyond the reach of lesser nobles; and even where it was affordable, the recipients continued to rely on handouts from the family to supplement their erratic pay. Very poor nobles might have no choice but to become ordinary line soldiers. Navies offered some alternatives: posts could not be bought in those of either Britain or France, although it does seem that family tradition played a considerable part in influencing the choice of a naval career. The drift of younger sons into the army in Britain was such as to lead early nineteenth-century radicals to claim that the wars of 1688–1815 had been contrived for the benefit of the sons of the aristocracy and gentry. This was demagogic nonsense – the army was a prestigious depository for the landed sector which fortuitously helped mitigate the impact of supernumerary sons. The general expansion of the professions at the same time helps explain the reduction in the number of younger sons of peers and wealthier gentry going into trade compared with the seventeenth century. The fate of the children of younger sons and their children in turn remains something requiring deeper investigation, but it does appear that the law was a much favoured bolt-hole for them.[34]

When examinations were introduced in the Prussian civil service between 1765 and 1770, the results were widely ignored in favour of existing noble clientele networks for at least a generation. There was, at the same time, a marked increase in the number of nobles entering the bureaucracy, particularly the lower posts. Catherine the Great sought to make the Russian provincial bureaucracy more appealing to nobles and massively expanded the number of posts available, from around 16,500 in 1773 to 27,000 by 1795, with a good third of the increase earmarked for nobles.[35] The difficulty with most such posts anywhere was that they were badly paid, and, unless they were very fortunate, those sons of nobles who took them up could not expect to live in the manner to which they might have been accustomed. The Poles found something of a solution when in 1791, in addition to a massive increase in their army, they officially opened all municipal offices to nobles and effectively dropped the *dérogeance* laws; but this simply reflected long-established processes in society and heralded the possibility that the boundary between nobles and commoners would disappear and the whole concept of nobility would become meaningless. Exactly the same fears were voiced in France in the controversies that accompanied the publication of Coyer's *La noblesse commerçante* in 1756.[36] It was the same with occupations as it was with economic opportunities (insofar as it is possible to draw such a distinction): if pushed, many nobles would take whatever was on offer, all the more so as their position gave them a greater say in determining occupational opportunity than any other sector of society. Nobles might well claim that honour was what drove them: at least as often, they demonstrated that it was money and profit.[37]

A widespread commitment to something approaching *de facto* primogeniture could only, of its nature, happen at the expense of younger children. Not only did they have to give up hope of a substantial slice of the family fortune, they also had to accept considerable personal sacrifice. Younger sons and daughters were less likely to marry than their elder siblings, not out of personal inclination but out of social pressure and expectations. Although it is impossible to say just how many younger sons did not assume a career in their own right, it is clear that a substantial number remained as residents on the family estate in some capacity, in receipt of sustenance or an income, perhaps with some kind of administrative role. In the Baltic provinces of Estonia, Livonia and the duchy of Courland, where between one-fifth and one-quarter of nobles' sons and daughters did not marry, the lowest of the low among them (lower even than *Krautjunker*) were the so-called *Krippenreiter* – 'riders from manger to manger'. These were the destitute and the indigent: younger sons, the hopelessly indebted, who sponged off relatives or hung around offering to perform humble managerial tasks.[38] Everywhere, unmarried daughters acted as unpaid teachers and governesses to their nephews and nieces.

Catholic countries were peculiarly well suited to offer welfare facilities to unmarried, poorly endowed younger children. The virtual exclusion of commoners from canonries allowed younger sons to be decently provided for and ensured that they would not produce offspring who would have any claim on the family estate: bastards, after all, enjoyed no such rights. Throughout the eighteenth century, the French episcopate was almost exclusively noble (with a definite trend towards older families tightening their grip on episcopal places). If among the non-episcopal higher clergy (canons, abbots) commoners were still easily in the majority, these places still provided a haven for nobles. Of 439 identifiable younger sons of *parlementaires* in Aix-en-Provence, 118 (over one-quarter) entered the Church (though almost twice as many, 229, went into the army). About a dozen chapters were exclusively reserved for them, but even open chapters began to receive more nobles. Overall, suggests Jean Meyer, by the end of the *Ancien Régime* between 2 and 3 per cent of adult male nobles were probably in ecclesiastical positions, with access to between 15 and 25 per cent of all ecclesiastical revenues.[39]

While much of the income derived from ecclesiastical benefices was spent on ecclesiastical or charitable works, some, usually those at the top, were in a position to redirect considerable sums towards their families. It was possible to tonsure a child at the age of ten, to ensure that revenues began to come into the family coffers. René-Joseph de Gouffier, canon of Paris, was able to lavish 300,000 *livres* on his niece's family at her betrothal to the future duc de Choiseul in 1750.[40] And although the quality of the French senior clergy was far superior to that of the sixteenth century, *abbés* leading a secular lifestyle were sufficiently common to attract attention. Such well-placed noble ecclesiastics might help the family out further by taking in respectable spinster relatives to mind their households for them.[41]

There was a much more pronounced bias in favour of nobles in the chapters of Alsace and Germany, and the lifestyles of many monastic communities was almost secular. The chapters of north-west Germany formed a veritable life-support system for the younger sons of the Catholic Imperial Knights of the region, insisting on long family pedigrees and regarding nobles created by local rulers (as opposed to the emperor himself), *Dienstadel,* as commoners of no social standing. At Mainz, as in all the major cathedral chapters, all great-great-grandparents of would-be candidates had to be of proven 'ancient German knightly origin', a demand which often made it impossible for natives of those territories to break into the chapters. So exclusive were the chapters of Cologne, Bamberg, Würzburg, Hildesheim and Osnabrück (the last two boasted both Catholic and Lutheran canons) that natives of their territories found it more difficult to obtain places on them than noble-born outsiders.[42] Since there were still at least 500 families of Imperial Knights and counts extant in the late eighteenth century, between them ruling about 1600 tiny territories, the chapters furnished a comfortable, and occasionally spectacularly lucrative, occupational niche.[43]

The use of ecclesiastical foundations to cushion noble families continued to a limited extent even in some Protestant territories. In Brandenburg, several foundations designed to provide financial support for widows and unmarried daughters reached back to medieval houses secularised during the Reformation; but similar endowments, *Stiftungen,* continued to be set up by aristocratic families during the sixteenth and seventeenth centuries. Monastic houses and convents served a similar role in Orthodox Russia.[44] In Anglican England, Nathaniel Crew, bishop of Durham, had no qualms early in the century about selling off Church lands to his nephew Sidney Wortley Montagu at bargain basement prices.[45] Otherwise, younger, and even eldest, sons looked to service with more powerful rulers, especially the Habsburgs. The numerous little armies maintained by the empire's rulers served more for ceremonial purposes and to provide employment for such nobles and knights rather than for any practical purpose, as their dismal military performance almost invariably demonstrated.[46] The same twin attractions, the Church and the army, helped cushion the economic consequences of younger sons and daughters in Italy. Here, with few exceptions (Sardinia–Piedmont–Savoy was the most obvious), armies served a predominantly ceremonial role, as trappings for noble and aristocratic families: it could hardly be otherwise, since no individual Italian state could aspire to great power status. Those nobles who sought a serious military career went abroad. Even so, if Sardinia is anything to go by, the Church attracted twice as many nobles as the army – it was, after all, safer.[47]

It was probably the Italians who developed the most remarkable strategies for coping with the problem of younger sons. During the seventeenth century, it had become the accepted norm that in any given family home only one, usually though not invariably the eldest, should marry and continue the family name. In Venice, three or four generations of the same family might live in one *palazzo*, with the third or fourth floor reserved as a *piano nobile* for the currently married and family-heading eldest brother. Younger brothers, unmarried sisters, aunts and uncles not occupied elsewhere had their own rooms or apart-ments in the cavernous structures, although the system was kept within bounds by what seems to have been a deliberate policy of restricting the number of children to one or two. On the other hand, since the sixteenth century about a quarter of aristocratic marriages were childless and almost another fifth produced only one child. Avoiding marriage was a conscious means of cutting down on expenditure. The Venetian variant of the Italian entail, the *fedecommisso*, was unusual in that it did not entail the family property to the eldest son but was assigned to all the sons jointly, although the eldest might receive a larger allowance. The Church, as ever, offered an acceptable career: in 1766, 166 out of approximately 1300 Venetian male nobles (almost 13 per cent) were ecclesiastics. It certainly enabled Venetian families to conserve their wealth, but only at the cost of the gradual biological erosion of the noble patriciate. Given that the nobility, in terms of economic initiative, were but a pallid reflection of the medieval ancestors of whom they were so proud, were reluctant to diversify into new economic ventures and preferred to live off landed rents from the Terrafirma, there seems to have been an almost unconscious collective decision to go for living off existing wealth and redistributing it among an ever diminishing pool of families. Even in the sixteenth century, almost one-fifth of only sons did not marry; in the seventeenth, it was over one-third; during the eight-eenth, almost two-thirds. Although there was a core of families, like the Balbi, the Erizzo, Marin or Riva, that maintained a normal fecundity, producing four or five children in a marriage, they were very much in a minority. The 1300 male nobles of 1775 aged over 25 were down to 1100 by 1797. In the sixteenth century, there had been at least 100 male noble births each year; during the eighteenth century, that figure plunged to little more than 20. The Venetian nobility had found the solution to preserving family wealth by restraints on marriage, children and admit-ting newcomers – but the solution also threatened to bring about their biological extinction.[48]

The detailed arrangements made by the Venetian nobility may have been extreme, but they certainly reflected a wider reality which held good across Italy. By 1690, around only one adult male noble in three married. Many were younger sons, who acted as a reserve for the continuation of the line should the eldest brother choose to adopt an ecclesiastical career. The extensive presence of a Church barely touched by the Reformation and the presence of the papacy itself made such a choice particularly attractive. Such a move, of course, also enabled the brother who climbed far in the ecclesiastical or papal administration to boost his own family's prospects. As for younger daughters, they faced the usual choice of spinsterhood or the nun's veil.[49] Only among long-established aristocratic Neapolitan families did such girls enjoy a (possibly) more comfortable choice: through the creation in the fifteenth and sixteenth centuries of so-called *Monti di marettagi* or *monti delle dotte*, trust funds which seem, overall, to have yielded reasonable enough returns to have allowed all girls who wished to get married.[50] Even the practice of living together under one palatial roof was not uniquely Venetian. Similar solutions could crop up anywhere. Very extended noble families, consisting of a widowed parent and celibate relatives, uncles, aunts, brothers and sisters sharing a property in common, *communiers*, appear also in Franche-Comté and Alsace.[51]

Quite how all this affected family and personal relationships is difficult to say. Throughout the eighteenth century, if not earlier, not only moralists condemned entails as a crime against non-inheriting children. In his unfinished *La scienza della legislazione*, begun in 1780, the Neapolitan reformer Gaetano Filangieri bewailed:

A father who can afford to have only one of his sons rich, wants to have only one son. In the others he sees just so many dead weights for his family. The degree of unhappiness in a family is computed by the number of sons ... So many younger sons deprived of property, and consequently of the right to marry, obliged as many girls to remain single. Deprived of husbands, under pressure from their fathers, these unfortunate creatures are often obliged to shut themselves up in cloisters, where with their bodies they bury forever their posterity.[52]

But then, as the third of 11 children Filangieri would expect to obtain nothing of his very distinguished family's estate – he was reduced to becoming a lawyer. In the day-to-day varying realities of Europe, matters were less simple. Filangieri's indictment was too sweeping. As so many nobles, the rich but, more especially, the not so rich, appreciated, there was a real danger that unrestricted partible inheritance would lead to the fragmentation of their estates. The argument that an unfettered market in land would boost the economy as a whole and stimulate more productive investment was unlikely to appeal to a class whose *raison d'être*, even duty, lay in the preservation of the family name and fortune. Even in Filangieri's Naples it was possible to make provision for younger sons and for them to strike out on their own; and his strictures almost certainly reflect a pre-industrial society, in which land seemed to offer a security that neither position nor paper investments could.

Entailed estates made family relationships much worse than they might otherwise have been. In December 1730, the Russian Senate claimed that Peter the Great's law on entails had provoked

> hatred and quarrels among brothers and drawn-out litigation involving substantial losses and ruin for both sides ... Not only brothers and close relatives but even children beat their fathers to death.[53]

But then, the alternative sources of support and livelihood for Russian nobles were probably more limited than anywhere else in Europe; the 1730 ruling rescinding entails acknowledged that there was no alternative to service for noblemen. The shock of imposed primogeniture in a society unaccustomed to it was bound to lead to a greater degree of disruption and disorientation than elsewhere. For most, the rewards of state service were meagre, and prior to Catherine the Great's reign few civil officials could count on regular receipt of salaries. Nor could every younger son count on the good fortune of Platon Zubov, who amassed his wealth by becoming the ageing Catherine II's toy-boy. On the other hand, the English case demonstrates that fathers and sons could co-operate remarkably sensibly in arrangements for the succession and that, by and large, eldest sons took their responsibilities to their siblings and widowed mothers seriously. Where possible, parents seem to have tried to give their younger sons some start in life, though not at the cost of any serious depletion of the main patrimony. Otherwise, individuals adapted because they had to. In a poor noble family, even being an eldest son was not much consolation: not inheriting might actually enhance the scope of what opportunities were available. Social expectations are a powerful force, and if they placed a premium on younger children settling for a meagre lot, then this may well have been easier to become reconciled to than the twenty-first-century Western mind, with its meritocratic and egalitarian fixations, can readily accept. The demands of a family may have been tyrannical, but the family was the best that the individual could hope for in terms of any security.

7

LIFESTYLES

In February 1698, an ennobled Jean Racine wrote to his son: 'We, good people of family (*bonnes gens de famille*), behave more simply and consider that it is not beneath the dignity of a person of worth (*honnête homme*) to know exactly where he stands financially.'[1] Despite his elevation (via the purchase of the office of *trésorier de France* in 1674), France's great tragedian still thought of himself as a bourgeois, recognising what made 'real' nobles different. A nobleman concerned for his money, wishing to know the condition of his accounts, was scarcely a nobleman at all. According to César-Pierre Richelet's much republished *Dictionnaire Français*, 'to maintain nobility means living nobly, spending in a way commensurate with the nobility of one's birth'.[2] Debt certainly seems to have been more severe among the sword than the robe nobility, another symptom of the latter's inferior status. The best nobles behaved like John, fifth duke of Bedford, one of the richest (and most indebted) men in England, who 'dealt with his financial problems simply by ignoring them', cheerfully leaving £400,000 of unsettled accounts at his death in 1802.[3] Bedford, for all his extravagance, was not (or not just) a wastrel. Unless he lived a lavish lifestyle, there was little point in his being a peer.

'For the landed elite, the tenure and preservation of a country seat was of paramount importance, since it represented the outward and visible symbol of family continuity.'[4] Aristocratic country seats had to be big: they were centres of social and political activity, where dozens, even hundreds, of guests, some of considerable standing, needed to be entertained. In eastern Europe, they served as centres of closely dependent clientele networks, in a way reminiscent of western Europe in the Middle Ages. Jan Klemens Branicki's palace at Białystok boasted a household staff of 170: a large proportion, perhaps even the majority, were petty noblemen, who did not disdain to serve as cooks or butlers. In England or France, the size of domestic staffs tended to be smaller: great nobles did not need to make quite such emphatic assertions of their political power. The fifth duke of Bedford appreciated the importance of keeping open house at Woburn through much of the summer and the need to wine and dine at his own expense the hundreds whom he invited to his showcase agricultural fairs: all this was as much about maintaining the Bedford political interest as anything to do with neighbourliness or progressive farming methods. His open table policy, costing some £20,000 a year, might take a third or more of his income. On top of that, Woburn Abbey had to be refurbished and reconstructed, agricultural improvements and politics proper to be financed, a magnificent ducal state (the fifth duke was a close friend of that other high-liver, George, prince of Wales) maintained: at least as a confirmed bachelor he was spared the burden of providing portions and dowries for his offspring.[5] Lesser country gentlemen, if they felt the need to preserve their electoral interests, were well advised periodically to wine and dine their tenantry.

Where active political participation existed among all levels of the nobility and gentry, not just in Britain but in Poland and Hungary, then great landowners wishing to retain influence and patronage found lavish, mass entertainment, especially at times of elections, to be essential. By 1734, the 'prodigious expense' of electioneering persuaded James Brydges, earl of Carnarvon, to forgo his attempts to preserve his traditional grip on the city of Hereford. Between 1720 and 1742, the Leveson-Gowers spent around £15,000 on consolidating and preserving their grip on the two parliamentary seats of Newcastle-under-Lyme. The electoral interest was maintained only by massive mortgaging and sales of extensive lands inherited in 1711 from the earl of Bath. Electoral expenses between 1742 and 1758 were even higher, as the family sought, successfully but expensively, to extend its influence to more seats in Staffordshire and Shropshire.[6] The duc de Choiseul kept open house at Chanteloup in Touraine after 1770 to thumb his nose at Louis XV for his dismissal from court (though it is unlikely he could have got away with this under his predecessor). Thirty sheep a month, 4000 chickens a year were slaughtered to keep the guests fed. When Choiseul died in 1785, he owed 6 million *livres*, debts almost Bedfordian in scale.[7]

Almost since organised societies had been constructed, rulers and governments had tried to formalise and codify the differences in style and display appropriate to different social groups. Catherine the Great's

Charter to the Towns, promulgated in 1785 as part of her drive to create corporate, estate-type structures in Russia, contained such provision. The very richest merchants, those with a capital worth between 10,000 and 50,000 roubles, were not only exempt, like nobles, from corporal punishment, but were entitled to travel in a coach and pair; merchants with a capital of between 5000 and 10,000 roubles were also exempted from corporal punishment and could travel in a carriage and pair; 'distinguished townsmen' (a heterogeneous mix which included not only the very rich indeed, but very rich nobles resident in towns) could drive around in a coach and four. Yet similar provisions did not exist in the Charter to the Nobility, issued at the same time, even though (or perhaps because) the empress was well aware of the abject poverty in which so many nobles existed; instead, the criteria for merchants reflected what ought to have been taken for granted as the trappings of a noble lifestyle. Catherine's charters were, among other things, an attempt to create the well-regulated 'police state' (*l'État bien policé*) by fixing social and hierarchical differentiation through 'sumptuary' law, decreeing how the population were to dress (determining what types of furs which groups could wear, and banning, for example, the display of gold, silver, silks, velvets to non-nobles) and comport themselves, and even how to construct their houses.

Sumptuary legislation was both very ancient and much reiterated, not least because it had rarely been successful. By the eighteenth century, most governments had largely given up. The last such items of legislation were enacted in England in 1666, in Scotland in 1691, in Venice as late as 1781. Venice's sumptuary officials, the *Provveditori del Pompe*, confined themselves to verbal admonitions against patricians whose dress sense fell foul of the laws. By then, the laws tended to be more concerned with the economic impact of luxury imports rather than the preservation of the social order. They continued to be reiterated in individual German territories, although even in a small, comparatively easily regulated state such as Hesse-Cassel, enforcement in the 1770s proved impracticable. Paradoxically, bourgeois Switzerland was the last western European country to be serious about their implementation, but even here, in 1784, the city council of Bern was warned by its courts that the task was almost impossible. In any case, monarchs and governments themselves muddied the waters. Even an artisan might be entitled to bear some of the status symbols of nobility, most notably carrying a sword, if he were on the roll of the court; and his wife could deck herself out in the finest silks, unlike her less honoured counterparts, who had to make do with more homely materials. In late eighteenth-century Munich, such concessions extended to around 5000 of the city's 38,000 inhabitants (admittedly, the Bavarian court went much further than most in selling such status licences). The decree of the French royal council of 30 October 1767 permitting all nobles (except magistrates) to engage in wholesale commerce also permitted merchants to carry a sword.[8] The English imposed a form of sumptuary law through finance: after 1671, the hunting of game was restricted to those with a freehold income of £100 a year or a leasehold income of £150 a year.[9] The irony of much sumptuary legislation on the continent was that the great bulk of those who considered themselves noble in many countries could scarcely contemplate the costs of dressing even within the upper limits of what was legitimately allowed to commoners. A French nobleman could afford to bury himself in a country retreat in reasonably comfortable circumstances – *aisance* – on an income of between 1000 and 3000 *livres*. In Paris this was nothing.[10]

Since sumptuary legislation was ineffective, there was only one way to demonstrate status: to go for ever richer, more expensive fashions, be it in dress, furnishings or residences. To flaunt wealth was not vulgarity, but an essential sign of power and status. The gulf between the richest and the poorest was immense: to give physical and visual expression to it was to deepen and reinforce it. The villagers and agricultural labourers who lived in the vicinity of the huge palaces at Woburn or Kedleston, Chanteloup or Courances, Puławy or Białystok might as well have lived on another, inferior, planet; and lesser nobles who paid court to the masters of these piles could be nothing other than impressed, awed and kept in their proper place. These monumental expressions of family pride meant nothing unless others were humbled by their sight. Nature was involved too: whether attended by the formal, geometric grounds inspired by Le Nôtre or the more 'natural' landscapes of Capability Brown or Humphrey Repton, these buildings affirmed an almost god-like claim to rule and master the land itself.

For those with real political authority, an impressive country seat was essential. A sample of 120 English country houses erected during the eighteenth century demonstrates not merely, as one might expect, the importance of the wealthy peerage (27 builders were peers) but also of gentry MPs, who accounted for 54 of the new builders. 'The houses were undertaken with a view to success or as a corollary of success in public life. Their distribution is remarkably even throughout the English counties, and it is obvious that a main object was to enhance the owner's position

in the constituency which he might represent at Westminster.' So important was the country house that practising architecture or landscape
gardening was deemed a pastime fully compatible with the status of a
noble or gentleman, the prime example, of course, being the earl of
Burlington.[11] At the beginning of the eighteenth century, few Russian
aristocrats showed any real attachment to their provincial properties.
Under Catherine II, French and English pattern books began to conquer
Russia. The latest French and English fashions in buildings, gardens,
furnishings and dress could be aped across Europe. The great age of
the construction of Russian country houses had begun, reinforcing the
unbridgeable gulf between rulers and ruled.[12] Building, rebuilding was
a crazy, uncontrollable fashion. 'The fury to build is a diabolical thing',
Catherine admitted. 'It devours money, and the more one builds, the
more one wants to build; it is as intoxicating as drink.'[13] And it was a
fashion that crushed and dazzled into submission and subordination.
Even the relatively modest country houses of middling gentry were
far beyond the reach of the great mass of the population, of what the
Hungarian nobility formulaically referred to as the *miserrima plebs*.

By one definition, conspicuous consumption may simply be wasteful
extravagance: but leaving aside the purely economic effects of such
expenditure, in a relatively lightly policed age it was an essential means
both of asserting noble status and of stamping the nobility's authority on
the lesser beings around them. The country house was part of a social
theatre, without which noble, or at least aristocratic, authority could
not be sustained. That theatre, of course, worked its most potent charms
in the countryside, not merely on those who were reminded of their place,
if they needed such reminders, but on its own creators. The great sweeping views which, ideally, went with these houses gave their owners the
impression (occasionally, of course, well-founded) that they owned
everything in sight. The conjuring of Arcadian parks and landscapes
in Britain, dotted with classical and/or gothic follies and statuary, not
only helped to create the landscapes of Italy and ancient Rome in the
minds of their begetters, but also conveniently helped to screen off
the realities of the peasants and tenants whose labour made their world
possible. '[A] close [physical] connection between house and farm was
entirely at variance with the English tradition.'[14] The fact that the construction or reconstruction of a house and grounds might require the
removal of entire villages made the sense of power and command that
went with this theatre even stronger. For those for whom the sunken
ditch of the ha-ha was insufficient obstacle, it was perfectly possible to

wall off the house and grounds with impressive mini-Hadrian's walls whose circumferences ran for several miles.[15]

The illusion of Arcadian separation could be continued within the house: the sixteenth and seventeenth centuries, first in France, then in England, saw the end of 'great chambers' where all the household, servants included, ate communally; smaller dining rooms and parlours introduced a degree of privacy for the landowner's family, while the development of 'backstairs', separate servants' quarters and corridors meant that 'The gentry walking up the stairs no longer met their last night's faeces coming down to them'. The invention of the bell pull in England in the 1760s meant that servants became less of an intrusion in the lives of their masters and mistresses. Without it, some gossiping menial had to be present in almost every room, a convenient, if doubtless unreliable, human appliance.[16] These modernised arrangements discouraged the old use, in England or France, of gentlemen-servants: persons of lower status were cheaper (including women, whose employment in great houses increased after the later seventeenth century). Gentlemen-servants, however, remained plentiful in Poland, Russia or Hungary, where there was no shortage of indigent petty nobles and for whom, as for peasants, domestic service was the closest they could ever hope to get in terms of sharing an aristocratic existence.

Where once private armies and swarms of retainers had been the hallmark of the great lord, that hallmark was ever more sublimated into an overwhelming visual, artistic and architectural dominance, an unearthly aura that ordinary mortals could not match:

> When the Duke of Beaufort dined in state in the salon behind the central frontispiece at Badminton, he was at the hub of a web of converging avenues stretching far into the surrounding countryside, underlining the fact that all the local avenues of power and influence converged on him not just as a great landowner and heir of an ancient family but as Lord Lieutenant and Lord President of Wales.[17]

Much of this was reminiscent of the ceremonies brought to perfection under Louis XIV at Versailles. The truly great men of state would even have their own levées, at which they could gauge their own status by the numbers of persons attending, seeking favours or places and presenting petitions. Just as with the monarch, so the mark of favour and prestige was to be spoken to by the great man in a friendly voice.[18] A few times a year the great rooms, or some of them, of the great house would be thrown open to the local peasantry or tenantry, partly to show that the lord condescended to care for them, partly to drive home their own humble place outside an exalted sphere which they could enter only on sufferance. Even in the downtrodden Baltic provinces, it was customary for the estate serfs to gather around the manor houses on midsummer night, to sing the landlord's praises and decorate him and his family with flowers and greenery; in return, the landlords would ply them with drink and distribute small cash presents.[19] Great aristocrats were indeed 'little kings'.

Up to a point, such impressions might be attenuated in the capital cities. No self-respecting aristocrat would wish to be without some kind of domicile in London or Paris or Vienna. Even in Warsaw, where magnates constructed palaces as quasi-embassies to advertise their political strength, the effect might be dampened by their proximity to each other – although collectively, these edifices left little room for doubt as to who were the elected monarch's rivals. In London, because of its prices and the pressure on accommodation in the more fashionable areas, even the very wealthy might be more happy to settle for (relatively) more modest living quarters. On the other hand, such neighbourliness sparked off fierce competition in fashion and luxury, as owners struggled to outdo each other in the beauty, extravagance and intricacy of furnishings and interiors. Visitors to the *palazzi* of Milan or the *hôtels* of Paris were staggered by what they saw. In the previous ten years, wrote Sébastien Mercier in his great description of Paris in 1780, 'six hundred mansions were built that looked like a fairy land; because imagination does not go beyond a luxury so exquisite'.[20] There was a 'trickle-down' effect: the less well-to-do nobility strove to emulate these constructions, the up-and-coming likewise. The English suburban house and garden are a spluttering vestige of this deferential emulation.

The late eighteenth and early nineteenth centuries saw a massive outpouring of 'villa literature' in England: books and manuals on the design of smaller country residences, appropriate not so much to more modest gentlemen as to up-and-coming merchants and bankers who were not only aping their aristocratic betters, but perhaps even sounding a warning that they could be as good as them by constructing their own mini-country residences, often within commuting distance of towns.[21] But such writings circulated everywhere. For the Russian elite, a house in St Petersburg was a must not only because Peter the Great had forced them to live there, but because their chronic indebtedness made them more dependent on court handouts than any other European aristocracy. Their villas in the environs of the capital were not only a summer retreat but a message to the rulers travelling to their summer residences at Peterhof or Tsarskoe Selo that they were available for both service and, above all, reward. Those who knew they had little or nothing to gain from court connections were more likely to choose residences in the Moscow region.[22] If great landed magnates sought houses in the cities, then urban-based nobles, whether they were Venetian patricians or French *parlementaires*, repaid the compliment by acquiring rural properties that could rarely match the gargantuan estates of great magnates in extent, but still offered agreeable rural illusions.

Those who were lords of the countryside found living in towns at least as, if not more, attractive. There was more company and scope for passing a more interesting and varied life. In Britain, residence in London was absolutely essential for peers, MPs and their hangers-on. The London 'season', which ran from late autumn to late spring, developed in tandem with the trend for parliament to meet over the winter months, a trend itself begun by the need to fit in with the campaigning seasons of the near-continuous wars with France between 1689 and 1712. The pattern equally suited more peaceful pursuits. London living offered a shelter from the grim, freezing, dank isolation of the British winter, particularly for those blessed with huge country piles and unheatable apartments.

The construction and reconstruction of great residences and their furnishing and refurbishment were an even greater drain on aristocratic resources than the dowering of daughters. As a rule of thumb, the construction pure and simple of a great house would account for only a quarter of its final cost: the rest was taken up by the interior fittings, furnishings and adornments (any of which would need renewal every six years or so).[23] Landlords in Poland, Hungary or Russia could cut down on some of the costs by making use of peasant labour for carting materials, quarrying, tree-felling, and so on. Such savings were rapidly cancelled out by the mass import of luxuries – from door-knobs to desks, mirrors to chandeliers from France, the Low Countries, Britain, Germany or Italy. Skilled labour, relatively scarce in eastern Europe, also cost more: landowners met their cost gaps by squeezing their serfs even more harshly.

For those with any measure of means, the library was an increasingly notable feature of noble mansions: only in Russia did it have to wait for the nineteenth century to catch on.[24] On the other hand, Russian nobles were among the most extravagant in maintaining theatre, opera and concert ensembles from among their own household serfs. Since most

Russian towns outside St Petersburg and Moscow lacked such amenities, landowners not in residence in the capitals (and even if in residence, they might bring their troupes with them) organised talented hopefuls from among their serf property into entertainment ensembles which would help while away the tedium of rural existence. Participants were taught to read and write, tutored in singing and acting, even taught foreign languages. They were valuable commodities: in 1800, the heirs of Semen Zorich cleared his million-rouble debt by the sale of the operatic troupe he had formed on his estate at Shklov. They could serve as a handy dowry. The feelings of these exceptional individuals were rarely taken into account.[25] Otherwise, amateur theatricals, in which the nobility and gentry themselves performed, were a widespread mainstay of entertainment across Europe: the eighteenth century was a great believer in the didactic force of the theatre.

If the country house and grounds were one symbol of a ruling local presence, a more spatial, fluid form was the hunt. Hunting had, of course, long been an aristocratic or gentry privilege. A French royal ordinance of 1397 restricting hunting rights to nobles justified the measure by explaining that hunting was 'that exercise in time of peace ... which most closely approaches that of arms', that is, the archetypal function of the nobility. Such restrictions were more prevalent in western Europe, partly because the natural environment had been more visibly impoverished by clearances and agriculture. Commoners were allowed to take game only where pests were involved: wolves, rabbits, or migratory birds (deemed insufficiently 'noble' for gentlemen to hunt). In Germany, too, there was 'high' and 'low' game. 'High' game was reserved (in theory) to territorial rulers – but these were, of course, exceptionally numerous. Non-sovereign nobles found, in law, that they could normally take only 'low' game – hares, foxes, badgers, ducks, partridges.[26] The chief exception in France to the peasants' right to protect their own crops (and an immensely aggravating one at that) was the pigeons that roosted in seigneurial dovecotes, a very visible symbol of seigneurial authority. Outside the Midi, dovecotes were restricted to noble seigneurs; peasants were forbidden to take any action against the birds, which were a serious agricultural nuisance on a par with rabbits. Seigneurial rabbit warrens were another object of peasant loathing. Pigeon meat was much prized as a delicacy, and pigeon-droppings were highly esteemed as manure; but all this was reserved for the seigneur. Non-noble landowners were under the same restrictions as peasants; and the laws governing hunting rights even had their own police force, the officers of 'Eaux et Forêts'. Strict enforcement of the game laws was impossible, though occasional prosecutions for infringement of the regulations by commoners (as opposed to outright poaching) continued to take place. The game laws were one of the most criticised aspects of the *Ancien Régime* in the *cahiers de doléances* of 1789.[27]

The restrictions were far worse in heavily forested Germany, and a constant source of generally unsettled peasant complaint. Peasants were barred from woodlands altogether during nesting and rutting seasons; so too were their livestock; they were often banned from fencing their fields and were, at best, allowed only to scare away marauding animals (deer and wild boar were the worst), without causing them any physical harm. Peasants in Württemberg were forbidden to let their dogs off leashes. In the electorate of Cologne and elsewhere, peasants even had to cut off their cats' ears, to expose their water-sensitive inner ears to the early-morning dew of the fields, woods and meadows so as to discourage their presence. Worse still, given the fondness of German princelings for grand hunts, which so often represented a sadistic, ritualised carnage of everything that could be trapped rather than the military exercises that they were supposedly emulating, peasants were routinely expected to assist with looking after the lords' hounds, and furnish other logistical support. Peasants' residual game rights virtually disappeared during the eighteenth century.[28] In eastern Europe, the wildernesses were more extensive and the quarry more plentiful and spectacular. Polish law banned unauthorised hunting across the property of others, but given the presence of huge estates this was rarely a problem. The English passion for fox-hunting made less progress in eastern Europe than in France, in part because the extensive forests of the area offered a far greater and more spectacular diversity of game: bison, bears, elks, wolves as well as deer or foxes. The organisation of spectacular hunts, including the mass importation of larger game animals to terrain earmarked for the massacre, was a way of impressing fellow-nobles and also reasserting the seigneur's power over the local serfs, who were obliged to turn out en masse as beaters and in other support roles.

Spring was the main hunting season in Russia, with similar sorts of quarry to that in Poland. These great hunts encouraged landowners to collaborate, strengthening the bonds of status and dependency, as men and hounds spent days on the move, from one estate to the next, if necessary sleeping in the open air.[29] Great landowners east and west were equally likely to maintain large packs of hounds. Individual dogs might be worth the price of several serfs: 'to be eaten by dogs' was a proverbial fate for over-extravagant hunt aficionados in Poland.

The English equivalent of these spectacles was, by the 1770s and 1780s, fox-hunting. With the exception of more remote areas such as Exmoor and Dartmoor, there was little big game left in eighteenth-century England. Hare-coursing and game-bird shooting were popular pastimes among the gentry: they of course had the benefit that after the 1670s they were off limits to the lower orders, since hunting game was banned to all with less than £100 per annum of landed income (evasion and poaching were of course widespread). It was above all the wealthy, well-connected Leicestershire squire Hugo Meynell who re-engineered British hunting into the sort of grand social occasion it had been in medieval and Tudor times, and as it still was on much of the continent, by his successful advocacy of the fox-hunt. The fox-hunt, rather like the Ritz Hotel, was open to all social classes (foxes counted as vermin, not game), but it could be enjoyed on a regular basis only by the wealthy. In 1781, Peter Beckford noted that 'Fox-hunting is now become the amusement of gentlemen'.[30] Keeping packs of hounds numbering 40–50 was possible only for the well-to-do. In 1809, the marquis of Tavistock, heir to the duke of Bedford and master of the Oakley Hunt, supposedly spent half his income on his hounds: subscription packs were only just coming in and were still looked down on. Although the spectacle acted, in some degree, as an exercise in social solidarity – tenant farmers, local businessmen occasionally participated, villagers gawped – virtually only the gentry and aristocracy could afford participation on a regular basis during the season (November to March).

The new amusement of fox-hunting, besides affording endless frissons of excitement and even danger, served to remind the local population in no uncertain fashion who was in charge. Gentlemen took it as read that they were free to ride across tenant farmers' lands irrespective of normal property considerations. Any reservations were dispelled in the 1786 *Grundy* vs. *Feltham* judgment, which gave huntsmen virtually a free hand to pursue foxes across others' land. The judgment was reversed in 1809, but tenant farmers and others looking to retain their holdings on reasonable terms would have been very ill-advised to protest against the local hunt, run as it was by the local county establishment. In any case, 'by the *law of honour* no gentleman would prevent his neighbours from taking their accustomed diversion, when the inconvenience would be so trifling to himself'.[31] Those who were not gentlemen did not unduly concern such commentators. So it was elsewhere. The nobles of Courland, much enamoured of the English-style hunt with hounds and on horse-back from the late eighteenth century, were entitled to pursue game into any part of the duchy. Elsewhere in the Baltics, nobles were supposed to confine their hunting activities to their own estates, but it was taken as read that they could range over their neighbours'. The peasantry were simply banned from hunting.[32]

With the effective demise of sumptuary laws over much of Europe, nobility could maintain their status only by ever more ostentatious extravagance and consumption. The eighteenth century, at least in western Europe, saw the arrival of the first consumer revolution: it was incumbent on nobles to out-spend or out-shop the rest. For all their often ravishing extravagance, the fashions of the eighteenth century tended towards simplification, at least by comparison with the seventeenth. The death of Louis XIV put French court culture into suspended anima-tion: under the regency of Philippe d'Orléans, the trend (much influ-enced by England) was for lighter, less bulky clothing to be worn; and when Louis XV returned to Versailles, he lacked his great-grandfather's inclination to regulate court dress, preferring to leave that sort of thing to his mistresses, especially Mme de Pompadour. Simplification of the basic structure of clothing was matched by more sophisticated crafts-manship, embroidery and decoration (the silks and velvets of a formal lady's gown would be only a fraction of the cost of the jewels, braids and spangles that adorned it). And even if the materials were less showy, the cut and quality were expected to be more refined than ever (and preferably executed by a French tailor, just as culinary confections were best created by French cooks). French fashion, often in combina-tion with simpler English styles, had swept through the nobilities of Europe by the second half of the eighteenth century, carried by travel, dolls and, in the 1770s and 1780s, fashion magazines. The simplicity of style that began to catch on in the 1770s in England and the 1780s in France opened up opportunities for parvenus to tailor themselves into a higher social status, leading even Charles James Fox to complain that 'the neglect of dress in people of fashion had contributed much to remove the barriers between them and the vulgar, and to propagate levelling and equalizing notions'.[33] These fashions did not come cheap. Silk was a mainstay material, but rapidly wore out. In England, a decent dress would cost between £10 and £60 – by comparison, a prosperous merchant's house might cost £500. Formal court dresses, which might be worn only once, cost a sizeable fortune. 10,000 *livres*, a good year's income for a prosperous country gentleman, was unremarkable for one of the duchess of Saulx-Tavanes' show-stopping outfits.[34] Even where there was strong attachment to native costume, as among the nobility of Poland and Hungary, the materials remained equally expensive. The maintenance of status required very serious shopping. 'The heavy coach, elegantly curved beneath and riding on steel springs, panelled, carved, and gilded, with blinds fitted to its sliding glass windows, represented both a triumph of technology and an object of display' – and was the near-exclusive prerogative of the super-rich.[35] It was not surprising that nobles were so anxious to avoid taxation: its relatively light burden permitted a level of display that would otherwise have been unattainable.

It was, of course, possible to retire to the country and live well there. Rants against the corruption of large cities and princely courts and the idealisation of a bucolic, simple lifestyle went back at least to ancient Rome. If not motivated by indigence, they might just as easily be motivated by expulsion from the centres of political power. Such considerations apart, the eighteenth century created the material apotheosis of the rural idyll in the *ferme ornée*, the idealised cottage from where shepherds and nymphs issued to enjoy the unsullied pleasures of *fêtes champêtres* of a mythological golden age. Needless to say, this was an option available only to the very wealthy few. William Coxe visited one such pastoral delight at Powązki, belonging to Prince Adam and Princess Izabela Czartoryski, on the northern outskirts of Warsaw, in 1778. He was suitably impressed.

> The house, which stands upon a gentle rise, has the appearance of a cottage, constructed like those of the peasants, with trunks of trees piled upon each other, and thatched with straw: beside the principal building, there are separate cottages for the children and attendants, each with its inclosures and a small garden; this group of structures bears the resemblance of a scattered hamlet. Other buildings, such as summerhouses, pavilions, rustic sheds, and ruins, are dispersed through the grounds; and the stables are constructed in the form of a half-demolished amphitheatre. Several romantic bridges, rudely composed of the trunks and bent branches of trees, contribute to heighten the rusticity of the scenery.
>
> On our arrival we repaired to the principal cottage, where the princess was ready to receive us. We expected the inside to be furnished in the simple style of a peasant's hovel; but were surprized to find every species of elegant magnificence which riches and taste could collect. All the apartments are decorated in the most costly manner; but the

splendour of the bath-room is peculiarly striking; the sides are covered with small square pieces of Dresden porcelain, ornamented with an elegant sprig; and the border and ceiling [sic] are painted in beautiful festoons. The expence of fitting up this apartment must have been prodigious; as each piece of china cost at Dresden three ducats.[36]

Those not quite at the tip of the social pyramid (or those who already possessed gargantuan houses) found an expression for taste and sophistication in the 'villa' – a more compact residence in a rural setting but, in England, often close to London. The precursor of the trend was the earl of Burlington's villa at Chiswick (designed by the earl himself), built in 1725.

While the eighteenth century may be associated with the progress of civility and manners, at table gastronomic blow-outs often ruled the day. Even the meals of 'enlightenment philosophers almost always ended with indigestion' (although to avoid that unpleasantness 'Voltaire purged himself regularly before sitting down to table'). The negotiations for the peace of Utrecht in 1713 apparently saw the perfecting of a new, more delicate cuisine: Napoleon's chef, Antonin Carême, believed diplomats to be especially fine connoisseurs of the table. Perhaps the new dishes that increasingly squeezed out the old crude exercises in gargantuan gluttony appeared more subtle and refined ('You are almost always presented with wicked dishes, that is to say with just those dishes that make you eat even when you have no appetite at all', reported Count Francesco Algarotti from Frederick the Great's francophone court in 1750), but they were still capable of wreaking havoc with the constitution.[37]

Lower down the noble scale, such sophisticated nonsense was eschewed in favour of frequent, outright gourmandising. Poland's mid-eighteenth-century nobility still retains an almost proverbial reputation for its tendency to 'drink, eat and loosen your belt'; Hungarian nobles enjoyed a similar 'fat' time. Not that lack of refinement was an eastern European monopoly. Unrestrained self-indulgence was as much a feature of provincial France – Châteaubriand remembered that at the biennial meetings of the Breton estates, attended in force by the local nobility, the boozing and gourmandising might have come straight from Poland. In Dauphiné in 1780, over a three-month period the seigneur of La Vallette's household and entertainments got through 3800 lb of butchered meats, 478 rabbits, 96 hares, 94 partridges, plus an unknown number of chickens, ducks, geese and turkeys, washed down with unguessable quantities of wine.[38] Such mindless bingeing was all the more likely in more rural areas where there was little in the way of organised alternatives. At least in great cities theatre, opera and concert-going and, at a more mundane level, the sociability of coffee-houses, salons and assemblies and being in the public eye and mixing with respectable, if not necessarily noble, groups may have acted as a spur to reducing boorish behaviour. Periodicals across Europe, taking their lead from Addison and Steele's *Tatler* and *Spectator*, sought to inculcate more considerate manners, not just among nobles but among the more affluent commoners.

Even so, such refinements did not necessarily get in the way of a good time and all that went with it. Gout hit the European nobility in the eighteenth century with a vengeance, leading some to proclaim, with a kind of excruciating pride, that it was a hereditary mark of noble ancestry. Not that the affliction was confined to those groups, but it was so widespread among them that it appeared to be their ailment par excellence. In much the same way, syphilis and gonorrhoea were seen as a 'badge of manliness', not least among well-born males. When in 1771 the fashionable London physician Dr William Cadogan dared to suggest the contrary in his *Dissertation on the gout*, he provoked a furore for challenging the extravagant, dissolute way in which so many peers and gentry lived.[39]

The maladies of the rich required cures: a whole social world was woven around the spas of Europe and their supposedly health-giving thermal and mineral springs. 'Taking the waters' was probably better than most of the concoctions that contemporary medicine devised for chronic diseases, of which gout was but one. A chain of spas, from Carlsbad in Bohemia to Spa itself in the Ardennes, catered to aristocratic ailments and sociability. Carlsbad, the very cynosure of the *Adelsbad*, favoured by Peter the Great, was a must for the aristocracy of central and eastern Europe. Goethe would not allow his wife to accompany him there before 1811, supposedly because she was too frumpy. This might have been less of a problem in Bath, which confirmed itself as England's leading spa in September 1687 when James II and Mary of Modena managed to conceive a son there (though, of course, the achievement helped confirm James's dethronement the following year). Conservatively minded Squire Brambles were soon complaining that 'the wives and daughters of low tradesmen' could 'mingle with the princes and nobles of the land'.[40] Though there was no lack of other watering-places in Britain, the insubordination of rank in an increasingly sleazy Bath helped to build up the popularity of Brighton (sealed by the prince regent's removal there in the late 1780s) and the new bracing 'cure' of swimming in the sea at dawn.

One malady for which there was no cure was gambling. For the court nobility, as if conspicuous display was not enough, gambling was a fevered pastime which gave a frisson to the tedium of the court day. Most of the French monarchs from Louis XIV onwards were great gamblers – their courtiers could hardly not join in, even if they preferred not to. Louis XVI disliked gambling, Marie Antoinette revelled in it, to the alarm of her brother, the Emperor Joseph II. The British government was sufficiently alarmed by the mania for gambling to pass laws in 1739, 1740 and 1745 curtailing the activity, the last banning games of chance altogether. The laws were ignored: casino-owners, if prosecuted, simply paid their fines and carried on as usual.[41] Outside the courts, gambling brought aristocrats and low-lifes together in a strained brotherhood of risk and chance. Georgiana Cavendish, *née* Spencer, the embodiment of the high society fashion statement, who was married to one of the greatest grandees of the realm (and hence, of the world), ran a gambling dive in Devonshire House managed by con-men and card-sharps who cheerfully fleeced their giddy benefactress. Her debts were so large as to be incalculable. She owned up to £61,917 of them in 1790, but she was being disingenuously modest.[42]

The drive to spend and play meant debt across the noble spectrum. Up to a point, a combination of rising rents, grain prices and the difficulties of foreclosing on noble properties could carry the nobles through, but it did little to alleviate the problems, which were often left to successors to cope with. In Russia, Dmitri Miliutin mused sorely on his father's ruinous extravagance at his Titovo estate near Kaluga:

> Hospitality, love of company, and all those habits that accompany a broad nature made him go beyond the limits his material position prescribed . . . the manorial economy was run on a grand scale . . . There was every type of workshop, among them one for carriage making: everything was maintained that was considered necessary for a decent life and for getting credit. The worse one's financial affairs were, the more necessary to cover it up.[43]

The same comment could have been made almost anywhere in Europe.

For it was all too easy for landed nobles to obtain cash or credit. In land they had more tangible and durable assets than almost anyone else.

If they also had impressive arrays of movable property – jewels, paintings, swords, coaches – these served not only as a means of displaying wealth but as devices to raise liquid cash: these articles could be pawned or sold, palaces and town houses could be rented. Inheritances could be sold to meet cash needs. In 1711, the Leveson-Gowers had to sell off family silver to raise ready money.[44] Private individuals might jib at extending credit only *in extremis*: there was always the chance that an indebted noble client would introduce yet more clients looking for credit. The Russian state bank (founded in 1786), the Prussian *Land-schaften*, supposedly set up to help nobles invest in agricultural improvements, were in practice only too ready to finance consumption. It was difficult for tradesmen, or vulnerable monastic or Jewish communities in eastern Europe, to withhold credit from aristocrats, no matter how much they doubted their financial probity. In any case, the great price boom after the Seven Years War seemed to offer the prospect of endless revenue-raising with a modicum of effort or investment. Emperor Paul was so concerned about the extent of indebtedness among the Russian nobility that he agreed, at the suggestion of a Dutch banker on the make, to create a 'Bank of Assistance for the Nobility' which would force the nobles to settle their debts. The punishing schedule of repayments would, however, have proved unsustainable in the majority of cases. The alarm that the scheme sowed contributed greatly to the atmosphere of poisonous loathing amid which the wretched emperor was assassinated. His successor, Alexander, dropped the scheme.[45]

There were more subtle ways in which nobles could differentiate themselves from the common herd. Such codes were expounded in the immensely influential *The characteristicks of men* by Lord Shaftesbury in 1711, then by Addison and Steele's *Spectator*, disseminated in French translation throughout Europe, treasured compendia of behaviour and comportment. A visitor to Venice claimed that 'You could recognise an aristocrat in the depths of his gondola just by watching him raise or lower a window'.[46] It is, of course, impossible to generalise in matters of comportment. For those who thought more deeply about such issues, it seemed increasingly important that nobility or gentility be displayed in manners and behaviour. 'Cleanliness was powerfully associated with gentility' – at least in England. Mere access to water for washing was in itself a mark of superior means.[47] 'Human nature is the same everywhere', wrote the earl of Chesterfield, the most famous exponent of refined aristocratic manners, 'the modes only are different. In the village they are coarse; in the Court they are polite.'[48] It followed that true

gentlemen should distinguish themselves from the vulgar by their manners ('what the French justly call *les manières nobles*),[49] their tastes and
their speech. He spent years bombarding his son with advice to that
effect, advising him to avoid 'low company', 'low in rank, low in parts,
low in manners, and low in merit' as well as the 'genteel vices' of 'the
beau monde'.[50]

> There are some pleasures that degrade a gentleman as much as some
> trades do. Sottish drinking, indiscriminate gluttony, driving coaches,
> rustic sports, such as fox-chases, horse-races, etc., are, in my opinion,
> infinitely below the honest and industrious professions of a tailor and
> a shoemaker, which are said to *déroger*. ... An awkward address, un-
> graceful attitudes and actions ... loudly proclaim low education and
> low company ... do you use yourself to carve, eat, and drink genteelly,
> and with ease? Do you take care to walk, sit, stand, and present your-
> self gracefully? Are you sufficiently upon your guard against awkward
> attitudes, and illiberal, ill-bred, and disgusting habits; such as scratch-
> ing yourself, putting your fingers in your mouth, nose, and ears?[51]

Chesterfield was of course aware that non-nobles could acquire *manières
nobles* as well. It did not worry him in the way it might have worried a
continental nobleman: after all, he and his 160-odd peers in the House
of Lords were the only true nobles in England, the most exclusive club
in the world.

That manners could be acquired by outsiders provided scope for limited social mixing. Balls, assemblies, salons, even masonic societies
enabled the noble and the merely respectable to rub shoulders on neutral
territory – although the further east one went, the feebler the middling
sort and the less likely such mixing was to occur. But even in Warsaw,
after the conferral of limited political rights on townsmen under the
short-lived Constitution of 3 May 1791, it was briefly fashionable for
the nobility to celebrate the new-found solidarity of the nation by attending the same social events as Poland's feeble bourgeoisie (most of whom
were desperate to become ennobled).

Giving a cultural lead, setting the fashion, was, if not necessarily an
intentional means of asserting social dominance by nobles, certainly
a way of distinguishing themselves. The non-Venetian nobility of the
Terrafirma sought to demonstrate that their cities – Piacenza, Brescia,
Padua – were as distinguished as the *Serenissima* through collections
of both artistic creations and natural phenomena – minerals, fossils,

plants – to rival anything that might be found anywhere else in Europe.[52] Maintaining and building up such collections was above all the prerogative of the gentleman. The peculiarities of the Holy Roman Empire, which allowed utterly obscure but well-pedigreed nobles to become territorial rulers, also provided access to funds which permitted an artistic patronage to lift them out of an otherwise impoverished obscurity. How else could Carl Phillip von Greiffenklau, elected prince-bishop of Würzburg, have hoped for apotheosis if not through the frescoes of Domenico Tiepolo in his *Residenz*?[53] The Italian states may no longer have exerted the political influence they had done two centuries previously, but the fashion for Italian opera and art cultivated so assiduously among the more refined gentry of Europe enabled Italian cultural influences to permeate the continent.

Those influences were shown by dozens of cases of (real or fake) antiques and Old Masters which wealthy travellers to Italy brought back with them. Those who had never been sought to create surrogates through the purchase of art and the employment of Italian architects and artists. Of course such cultural activities were hardly an Italian monopoly, but Italians as a group remained dominant at least up to the 1770s, if not beyond. The primarily noble-driven demand for art had already led during the seventeenth century to the establishment of art dealers and agents. Around the turn of the eighteenth century, art auctions, with their attendant catalogues and developing scholarship and expertise, became ensconced in London and Amsterdam, and reached Paris by the 1730s. By the 1770s, if not earlier, paintings were beginning to be seen as a form of useful investment. The mania for art acquisitions worried some governments, including the Spanish, which in 1779 imposed restrictions on the export of paintings, fearful that 'foreigners are buying up in Seville all the canvases that they can acquire of Bartolomé Murillo and other famous painters, and sending them abroad'.[54] And the place to display these acquisitions was, above all, the great house.

The lesser gentry who tried to emulate this kind of establishment on a more modest scale were, by so doing, only flattering the great magnates and rendering an implicit homage to their ascendancy. Those who went too far were punished by debt and penury. 'There cannot be in nature a more contemptible figure than that of a man, who, with five hundred a year, presumes to rival in expence a neighbour who possesses five times that income', snorted Smollett's Squire Bramble – but he was spitting in the wind.[55] One of the reasons why Alsace was a centre of the 'Great

Fear' in 1789 was the belated attempt, especially from the 1730s, by a peripheral nobility to try to catch up with their counterparts deeper inside France in terms of magnificence and consumption. Many, of course, simply could not afford to keep up with the aristocratic Joneses: they had to content themselves with almost Spartan fixtures and furnishings inside their ancestral chateaux, and some noble families had to share their castles and manor-houses, rather like Venetian families, albeit in more straitened circumstances. Those that could get away with it financed the Alsatian château-building boom by borrowing from bankers in Strasbourg and Basel and Alsace's Jewish community. But when, for a small minority, the credit ran out and the bills remained, they had to sell up to merchants and industrialists who, once established in their new country seats, proved as adept at burning themselves out financially as those they had supplanted.[56]

8

AUTHORITY

The Victorian educator Thomas Arnold, on catching his first sight of a passenger steam train, mournfully observed, 'Feudality is gone forever.' During the 1820s, a number of English landlords opposed the building of railways across their estates on the grounds that such developments might well see an influx of 'a rougher kind of man ... who might commit property depredations'. Their kind had voiced similar fears during the late eighteenth-century canal-building booms. These alarms usually melted away before the prospect of obtaining substantial sums of money in return for conceding construction rights.[1] The Russian moralist Prince Mikhail Shcherbatov, in Catherine the Great's reign, deplored the practice of many landowners of despatching peasants from the country estate to earn ready cash in Moscow and St Petersburg to pay their rents, or of leasing, for their own profit, peasant labour to merchants. Shcherbatov, himself guilty on both counts, feared that any attenuation of peasant–landlord links would undermine the natural, noble-run order of society.[2] None the less, those who voiced such concerns were right to be alarmed. The society over which the nobility watched and in which they could feel secure was unchanging, deferential, conscious of its place. 'Ideally, the aristocratic world was static, oligarchic, hierarchical, limited and intimate.'[3]

Broad horizons, cultural and geographic, were for an elite. Outsiders and geographic mobility were potential threats. Even in England, the Law of Settlement and Removal, which dated from 1662 and was revised only in 1795, required those without visible means of support to produce a certificate from their parish of birth if they wanted to find work outside it. That way they could, if necessary, be returned there

without being a burden on another parish's poor rate.[4] It was a requirement remarkably similar to that found in more heavily feudal eastern
Europe, where governments and landowners alike insisted that persons
of low condition should not move around without some form of passport
from higher authority, be that their seigneur or a government official.
When, in November 1789, a reforming Polish parliament created a new
network of commissions of the peace to conduct local administration,
one of their principal tasks was to monitor all 'loose people' – those of
no fixed abode who took it on themselves to travel the country with no
attestation from their seigneurial master. By the same token, it was the
widespread obligation of peasants, serfs, innkeepers and clergy to report
the presence of 'strangers' to the authorities.

It was not just outsiders who threatened to import instability and dis-
order. So too did outside ideas. Indeed, any kinds of ideas were probably
a threat. The ruling orders were well aware that a mental universe which
stressed the immutability of hierarchy and its God-given nature was one
of the strongest, perhaps the strongest, engine of control that they possessed. In their sermons, the clergy repeatedly stressed the importance
of obedience to the powers that be. Among those who thought about
such things, the second half of the eighteenth century saw a lively debate
across much of Europe over what sort of education, if any, the people
(variations on 'the vile multitude' were much in evidence in this discourse) should receive. The great majority of Europe's chattering classes
(not least such luminaries as Voltaire or Diderot) would have agreed
with the English moralist Soame Jenyns who, in 1757, proclaimed that
'Ignorance is a cordial administered by the gracious hand of Providence;
of which [the poor] ought never to be deprived by an ill-judged and
improper education'.[5] The more enlightened conceded that an education limited to reading practical agricultural manuals, the Bible (under
appropriate guidance) and devotional tracts was acceptable. That is to
say, the lower orders would hopefully internalise the need to work harder
and accept the rule of the powers ordained by God. In 1756, Pope Bene-
dict XIV even declared vernacular versions of the Bible – banned by the
Council of Trent – acceptable for Catholics, provided the right kind of
glosses and guidance accompanied that explosive compilation.

Inappropriately guided Bible reading was as much of a problem in
Protestant states. The rulers of Prussia, the Habsburg lands and many
of the German lands made more or less determined efforts to provide
rudimentary levels of education, encased in a carapace of deference and
religious obligation. Much of this effort caused bafflement and irritation

among both peasants and seigneurs. To the former, it was a distraction from the rather more important business of survival; to the latter, it was pointless or dangerous. Russian and Polish landlords were hardly alone in fearing that teaching peasants to write (though many reformers were ready to settle for the ability to read) would only encourage them to forge passports and other documents. The trick was for the 'vile multitude' to accept that there was no alternative: 'We shall find', wrote David Hume in 1741, 'that, as force is always on the side of the governed, the governors have nothing to support them but opinion. 'Tis therefore on opinion only that government is founded: and this maxim extends to the most despotic and most military governments, as well as to the most free and most popular.'[6]

Hume's 'opinion' was much reinforced by the lack of any plausible alternative to hierarchy if society and civilisation were to be preserved. In most cases, peasants themselves seem to have been ready to settle for a benevolent seigneurialism, if only because of the memory of ineffectual and harshly suppressed uprisings in previous centuries. The result was hardly the best of all possible worlds. 'It is impossible on our wretched globe', wrote Voltaire in 1764, 'for men living in society not to be divided into two classes, one of oppressors, the other of the oppressed.'[7] Yet many of the 'oppressed' would probably have agreed. Trying to impose some kind of order on his inchoate revolt of 1773–4, Emelyan Pugachev duplicated the Russian court's ranks and collegiate bodies among his lieutenants; he even gave away serfs to them in reward. One of the serfs who joined his revolt was revealingly frank:

> Who Pugachev was did not trouble us, nor did we even care to know. We rose in order to come out on top and to take the place of those who had tormented us. We wanted to be masters ... Had we won, we would have had our own tsar and occupied whatever rank and station we desired.[8]

How far the lower orders were genuinely interested in politics before the French Revolution is impossible to say. The daily struggle to eke out an existence was far more important. If eighteenth-century England did experience the first consumer revolution, the fact remains that the overwhelming mass of its families were unlikely to have had an income in excess of £20 a year. Their chances of participation in early consumerism were extremely limited; the prospects of any form of wider political representation for them even more so.[9] The crowds that celebrated John Wilkes and 'Liberty' in 1768–9 were largely restricted to the London metropolitan zone. If, in a burgeoning provincial centre like Birmingham, well endowed with libraries, bookshops and newspapers, there was considerable interest in the affair, there was virtually none at all in the rural wilds of Yorkshire, Lincolnshire, Worcestershire or Buckinghamshire.[10] There, of course, the bulk of the population resided. As late as 1831, of the 14,353 parishes of England and Wales, 63 per cent contained fewer than 500 inhabitants. These areas were much easier for the local gentry to control than Wilkes's Middlesex constituency, with its high levels of enfranchisement, literacy and access to the latest political goings-on. The 'intelligent mob' of the great cities was much more difficult to control than a subordinated, isolated, ill-informed rural populace, dependent, at least indirectly, on local gentry and aristocrats for employment, patronage, assistance and relief – if they were lucky. Those with a genuine degree of decent means – better-off tenant farmers – were, if anything, more directly dependent on local landowners and certainly shared an interest with them in ensuring that their social inferiors remained in their proper place. Those who, like Wesley's Methodists, sought to bring a genuine degree of comfort and relief to the poor were also among the most zealous in seeking to preserve the social hierarchy.

It is, of course, true that many foreign travellers to England were much struck by the supposed insolence of the lower orders towards their superiors. In 1743, the 'common people' of Bath flung cabbages at the impossibly haughty Gertrude, duchess of Bedford; four years later her husband, the fourth duke, was apparently horsewhipped by an irate Tory farmer at the Lichfield races.[11] The enclosure by landlords of the English countryside aroused more protest than some authorities have been prepared to recognise, not only in the form of petitions to parliament but also of outright violence; but, over the long term, enclosures went through.[12] For about a week in June 1780, the government lost control of much of London during the Gordon riots against Catholic relief, but in the end, the army restored control: 290 rioters were killed, 25 looters executed, and £100,000 worth of property damaged, 'ten times as much as in Paris throughout the French Revolution'. The events gave 'a terrible warning of what might happen if concessions were made to the popular voice'. Hierarchy was to be reaffirmed, for the only alternative seemed 'democracy', that is, mob rule.[13]

The mob, the 'vile multitude', had few realistic alternatives but to accept the status quo. In England, there was more than one gentry or landed family to every parish, at least two in Kent. There was simply no escape from gentry and aristocratic domination. In Warwickshire and Worcestershire it was possible to see from one country house to another. True, as the eighteenth century progressed, long-established families tended to view the key offices of local government, those of sheriff and Justice of the Peace, as something of a burdensome chore best left to newcomers or, if held, to be held primarily as a dignified, prestige position, the real work to be done by others. That was beside the point: there was never any shortage of newcomers of acceptable background ready and willing to take up these offices just in order to prove that they, too, could break into 'county' society, win acceptability and join in the rule over others. As for states which had a numerous petty nobility, be it Portugal or Spain, Poland or Hungary, for all the divisions within those nobilities, the poorest gentleman prided himself on his affinity with the greatest magnates: anything, rather than associate directly with the lowest forms of commoner life. The shared interest in keeping social 'inferiors' in their proper place was preserved.

The organs of authority and justice were often the same: the courts. And the first courts that most rural dwellers encountered were those belonging to or run by the nobility and the gentry. There was little in the way of any separation of the powers, even in England, despite Montesquieu's praise of that principle in his encomiums on the constitution. The gentleman-lord of the manor directly appointed the bailiff, the chief official of the manorial court. The court dealt with the most petty offences and problems of rural life and the day-to-day running of the village. It functioned in the lord of the manor's name and allowed his principal tenants to maintain village discipline. Likewise, committees of tenant farmers made up the chief organ of parish government, the vestry. Complaints and appeals from these bodies went to individual magistrates, the Justices of the Peace, at petty or quarter sessions. JPs were either landed gentry or drawn from groups associated with them: clergy, lawyers, professionals, better-off tradesmen seeking to establish themselves as gentry. Only the burgeoning towns of the industrial revolution were to open an escape route from these interlocking meshes of landowner influence, and even that was to take years. But in the boom period of the later eighteenth century, the citizens of these towns were more concerned with making money than with acquiring a direct political voice; the growing towns presented landowners and their tenants with markets for the products of their estates. An uneasy symbiosis persisted until the slump that followed the Napoleonic wars.[14]

Deference prevailed, then, even in economically innovatory England. Elsewhere, the manorial courts were very much more vigorous, even if they were increasingly being made to share their authority with the state. The range of labour duties and tributes in kind that were imposed on the rural population (including the inhabitants of what affected to regard themselves as towns) in much of Europe kept the peasantry in a permanent reminder of their state of subordination. Any remissness in discharging labour duties, payment of cash rents or presenting of tribute in kind was liable to elicit a summons before the seigneurial court. Peasants who had to perform (or hire others to perform for them) several days' labour services per week may have had every interest in not discharging them properly, but they were in no position to mount an effective challenge to the system that produced such demands. The boundary between 'free' peasants and 'unfree' serfs is elastic and unclear. The real burdens that were imposed could be as severe for supposedly free rural labourers in Sussex or sharecroppers in southern France and northern Italy as for unfree peasants in Pomerania, Poland or Russia. The mere fact of such impositions served only to reinforce the peasants' dependency. Not surprisingly, to landowners in the German-speaking lands such peasants were literally their 'subjects', *Untertanen* in Germany and the Habsburg lands, *poddani* in Poland. In the Baltic territories, peasants who met nobles on the public highway were obliged to dismount from their carts or horses, remove their hats and step off the road.[15] Such signs of respect and obeisance were expected across Europe.

The key task of landowners was to persuade peasants that subordination and the duties associated with it were natural and inescapable. Village assemblies, drawn mainly from more substantial adult males, helped regulate the day-to-day management of relations between peasant and landlord, in much the same way as manorial courts did in England. In southern Italy, these organs of parish government had often compounded with the local seigneur in order to lease his jurisdictional rights in return for cash payments – an agreed acceptance of seigneurial authority. The Neapolitan fiefs were, indeed, often run on the seigneurs' behalf by notionally unsalaried officials elected by the villagers (and townspeople) themselves. Rather like English tenant farmers, or French *fermiers-généraux*, such individuals, almost invariably drawn from the better-off villagers, found that they had a shared interest in the maintenance of the system, from which they benefited as much as, perhaps even more than, the landowner. Provided landowners did not try to pile on excessive pressure for unrealistically high revenues, the system could function without breaking down. But it was all too easy for seigneurs, bred and clad in the mantle of judicial power and command, to fail to appreciate where the lines should be drawn. In 1700, the ever hard-up James, fourth duke of Hamilton, took over the Lancashire and Cheshire estates of a mother-in-law who had been all too long a-dying and tried to squeeze more out of the tenants to alleviate his desperate finances: little good it did him. Cattle on his home farms were killed or mutilated and the perpetrators could not be found.[16] It was a warning to a pushy land-owner, but hardly a threat to the social order.

The inevitability of the hierarchic status quo was immensely bolstered by the ruling groups' ability to co-opt people from among their social inferiors to collaborate with those ruling groups. These people could be either those with aspirations to join the ruling groups, or individuals who were prepared to ally, or could be made to ally, with the authority of the ruling order, be it the state or the *seigneurie*. Thus the collection of most forms of direct taxation devolved, at the very lowest level, onto villagers or townspeople either elected by their fellows or appointed by higher authority (be it seigneur or an officer of state) in order to gather in those moneys: whether it was the *taille* in France or the soul-tax in Russia, the principle was the same. Such collectors were almost invari-ably drawn from the well-to-do among the commonalty, since they would be expected to make good any shortfalls from their own pockets. Ultimately, the state would expect the seigneur to ensure taxes were col-lected. A share of the proceeds would be expected to go, officially or unofficially, to the collector, to cover his own expenses; alternatively, he might be relieved of some, or all, of the obligations to which he would normally be subject. Either way, he would have a material interest in the maintenance of the system, be it tax payments to the state or dues collected on behalf of the seigneur. A comment made in 1881 by a Rus-sian observer could just as easily have been made a century earlier anywhere in Europe: 'Every peasant, if the circumstances are favour-able, will exploit everyone else in the most splendid fashion; it is all the same whether it be a peasant or a lord, he will squeeze the juice out of him, he will exploit his need.'[17] Dividing greatly eased the task of ruling.

This did not, of course, extend merely to the administration of cash dues or taxation. The allocation of labour services in eastern Europe was one of the tasks of councils of village elders (in Russian parlance, 'old and wise peasants'). At the extreme, a trusted peasant could well find himself virtually running the estate as the owner's manager – this was common in Russia. Some at least, in return for co-operation with, or policing on behalf of, the *seigneurie*, could expect total or partial relief of their services, which would, however, not be 'lost' to the lord but redistributed among other villagers. The village elders in Russia had a further means of maintaining their own dominant status and keeping in check any challenges to their authority: they might well be entitled to choose or have some say in which villager should be taken into the army by the dreaded *branka*, the conscript levy. The existence of swarms of poor nobles in eastern Europe especially gave a further element of stability to this system: at the very least, it provided the powers that be with a pool of manpower that was anxious to maintain its status but was in economic terms on a par with the peasantry. They in effect furnished a ready-made supply of civilian NCOs to help direct and control the mass of the peasant population.

All of this, however, was predicated on one thing: that the *seigneurie* should not push its demands so far as to make them insupportable to all. Studies from Poland show that landowners could often call upon poor peasants to support them against more powerful and exploitative village elders; or that the latter, at odds with their landlords, were prepared to use physical force to coerce poorer peasants and labourers to maintain a front of solidarity. What is remarkable is how ready peasant communities were to contest seigneurial jurisdiction where any opportunity, no matter how tenuous, seemed to exist to do so. When Tsar Peter III proclaimed the 'emancipation' of his nobility from their obligation to serve the state in February 1762, a burst of localised revolts followed among peasants who were convinced that since nobles no longer needed to serve the state, peasants were no longer required to work for nobles.[18] The peasant revolt that shook much of Transylvania in late 1784 was propelled by the misguided belief that the Habsburg Joseph II, at odds with the Hungarian nobility over his reforms, must have wanted the peasantry to rise up against them.[19] The widespread peasant refusals to discharge labour services across much of the Habsburg monarchy in 1790 was based on the equally mistaken notion that the emperor's most recent reforms of 1789–90 involved their abolition. It was the same in Poland in the immediate aftermath of the May 1791 constitution, which was widely misinterpreted as giving the peasants much more than it actually did (which was very little). The summoning of parish and *bailliage* assemblies in spring 1789 to draft *cahiers de doléances* for consideration by the forthcoming Estates-General in France was taken by many peasants to mean that the dues of which they complained were in the process of being abolished.[20]

Most Polish and Russian peasants were in the particularly invidious position of having no alternative to which they could represent their grievances. They were stuck with seigneurial authority. In January

1765, Catherine the Great reaffirmed long-standing decrees forbidding peasants from appealing against their landowners directly to the sovereign, a prohibition originally imposed to prevent the ruler from being swamped with petitions from an aggrieved population; at the same time, she allowed landowners to send recalcitrant serfs to Siberia.[21] Polish serfs had been forbidden to appeal to royal from seigneurial justice since 1518; it is clear, however, that where opportunities for such appeals could be created, most notably on crown estates leased out to nobles, serfs did take advantage of the fact that, strictly speaking, their landowner was the crown itself; and during the reign of Poland's last, reform-minded king, their grievances were likely to receive a sympathetic hearing. By contrast, the peasantry of Mecklenburg, among the worst oppressed and most dispossessed in Europe, were simply helpless before the demands of their landlords.

For peasants, the real opponent was not so much landlordism as the sheer economic fragility of their position. Only a minority had enough land to produce enough food for themselves and their families. Nature, with its erratic weather and harvests, was a far more dangerous enemy than landlords; and any form of dearth or shortages was liable to trigger off riots, usually short-lived and, as often as not, terminated simply by the appearance of military units. A spate of such disorders hit Britain in 1756 and 1757. The 1757 riots in Richmond were quelled by the appearance of local gentry, backed by some 900 armed followers and servants: gentry paternalism had its iron fist.[22] In 1766, another wave of hunger riots washed over the country, as it did over Hungary and Bohemia, France and Spain. King Charles III and his ministers had briefly to flee Madrid.

Whether the rural poor in much of Britain were any better off than their counterparts on the continent is an impossible question to answer – but what helped to give point to anti-landlord feeling on the continent, in a manner not generally found in Britain, was the proliferation of various tributes, dues, special payments, rents and labour obligations found in varying permutations across the European mainland. For those living on the margins, such impositions aggravated their already nearintolerable circumstances. Of course, in many instances they simply suffered without protest. The 1770s, with their wet weather and dearths, were a grim time for much of the European peasantry. In 1772, the fantastically wealthy Prokofii Demidov scandalised (and possibly inconvenienced) Dresden society by buying up all available food in the city and redistributing it among the local poor, instead of leaving them to suffer in silence.[23] Maria Theresa and Joseph II both blamed landlord indifference for making the plight of their hunger-stricken peasantry much worse amid the near-famine conditions of the mid-1760s and early 1770s. They (Joseph particularly) may have despised their nobles, but they could see no alternative to them as a force for government. Their failings would have to be rectified by regulation.

Those governments strong enough to do so insisted on at least a token assurance that seigneurial courts should take their task seriously. From the 1750s, Habsburg officials were specifically charged (admittedly with limited effect) with the enforcement of the ever-increasing volume of decrees designed to offer peasants protection against seigneurial abuses. In 1772, formal procedures were laid down allowing peasants to appeal from seigneurial courts (such measures came as a particular shock to Polish proprietors whose estates passed that year under Habsburg rule in the First Partition). After 1784, seigneurs were made liable for their officials' abuses. Three years later, Joseph II insisted that the seigneurial courts should be presided over by a legally qualified official, or a justiciar be attached to patrimonial courts, to ensure their proper running. The effectiveness of such measures varied, but there is no doubt of their unpopularity among landowners.[24] For where peasants did have access to state justice, they made determined use of it, expensive though the procedures often were (though in the Habsburg lands it was seigneurs who were expected to pay the peasants' costs). The Recess of 1653 in Brandenburg did not end peasants' right to appeal to the ruler's courts: it banned 'frivolous' appeals. By the time that conditions for a broad seigneurial squeeze on the peasantry were in place after the Seven Years War (thanks mainly to population growth, which made labour more available and therefore cheaper), peasants had learned sufficiently to take advantage of access to state courts for a royal proclamation to reiterate in 1787 the 1653 injunction against 'frivolous' appeals and to complain that they were clogging up the courts. Litigation between seigneur and community could drag on for years, convincing at least some landlords that a shift to a straightforward commercial relationship with their tenants might be preferable to the complex of feudal services.[25] The reaffirmation of seigneurial authority by the *Allgemeines Landrecht* in 1794 marked the beginning of a rearguard action by the nobility.

It would be wrong to assume that seigneurial courts were simply an institution of landlord oppression. In France, only around a quarter of cases heard by them dealt with seigneurial rights. The seigneurial courts provided an invaluable forum for the settlement of the interminable disputes, often of a very minor character, that were a staple of village life: field boundaries, succession disputes, insults, minor affrays. Around half of those heard in a sample of Breton courts were not even originated by the *seigneurie* or its officials but by local villagers. Many were, indeed, settled very rapidly out of court. Nor were the courts staffed purely by seigneurial hangers-on, although the judicial personnel were usually appointed at the seigneur's pleasure.[26] The leading villa-gers as well as the seigneurial bailiff might make up the court in eastern Europe, although this could lead to its own problems, as the village elite sought to exploit its position to its own advantage. On the other hand, it facilitated the policy of divide and rule. Well-run seigneurial courts, properly staffed by trained judicial personnel, were extremely expensive for the seigneur, but they were what the peasants wanted – as long as they were not utilised in order to increase the range of exactions to which they were subjected; and if the cost was a drain on the *seigneurie*, it should also be seen as part of the public responsibility of the nobility and gentry, just as much as in England the unpaid services of Justices of the Peace and sheriffs were. Those nobles who, in France, were too poor or insufficiently concerned to provide seigneurial justice were also those who might expect the greatest insolence and even acts of violence from their peasants.[27] But then even the wealthiest nobles, if their peasants were determined enough to resist what they viewed as unjust impositions, might find themselves confronted by peasant litigiousness, with appeals to royal courts, or outright refusal to perform the duties demanded, or both. Sometimes it was easier to give way graciously, as Étienne-François, comte de Stainville, the future duc de Choiseul, did on his Burgundian estate in 1750, finally agreeing that the two days' annual harvest labour owed by his reluctant peasantry should be commuted for a nominal annual payment.[28] But for every noble prepared to give way, there were several others, like Louis, marquis de Mailly, in Picardy, who was determined to extract his dues in full, rejecting his steward's repre-sentations of his peasants' poverty with the argument that 'the peasant is like an obdurate horse: first, give him a sound thrashing, then he'll do what you want'.[29]

Peasants had a sense of 'moral economy'. This went beyond periodic riots against grain speculators and subsequent sales of the liberated bread at a 'just price'. Peasant moral economy manifested itself in a feel-ing that traditional obligations (not always clearly defined, sometimes entirely in the realms of a wholly fictitious previous 'golden age') were admissible and, in return for genuine services from the *seigneurie*, perhaps even desirable. In practice, it amounted to a sense of live and let live, and mutual accommodation with the landowner, and what each party could get away with. By the eighteenth century, Polish peasants took it as read that any increase on old norms, especially labour dues, was wrong and should either not be performed at all, or performed badly. This extended to other measures. When Andrzej Zamoyski, a Polish reforming landlord, sought to encourage his peasants in the 1760s and 1770s to build up banks of surplus grain against years of dearth, he encountered widespread opposition, on the grounds that since he was the landowner, it was his responsibility to take such precautions, and that encouraging the peasants to fend for themselves was just a fresh imposition.

The sense of traditional norms, which often seems to have spilled into a notion of basic liberty, could be so far violated as to burst into revolt. The cossacks of the Polish Ukraine and of large swathes of Russian borderlands enjoyed, since the sixteenth century, a wide range of immunities, especially from personal labour services. Polish landlords' violations of these in the mid-seventeenth century provoked revolts that brought their precious Commonwealth to its knees; and renewed landlord pressure in 1768 provoked one of the greatest uprisings of the century. What was tolerated and tolerable in the more settled lands further west was anything but in the wilder terrain of the Ukraine. The same sort of factors, outraging long-established traditions and modes of existence on the south-eastern peripheries of European Russia (though the bulk of the pressure came from the tightening grip of the central state), brought about the immense Pugachev Uprising of 1773–5. The unfettered sale of firearms in Roussillon was a source of some dismay to French ministers, but local officials warned that any attempt to restrict this ancient privilege would spark off revolt.[30]

The most sophisticated, and to seigneurs most damaging, interpretations of this moral economy were to be found in France on the eve of the Revolution. Peasants who might once have accepted seigneurial privileges in principle were increasingly questioning them in the changed conditions of the eighteenth century; and they were particularly hostile to seigneurial efforts to convert their privileges and monopoly rights into cash cows to support an increasingly luxurious lifestyle. In Burgundy, peasants complained that former obligations to maintain the fabric of seigneurial châteaux, which had made sense in the troubled seventeenth century, made none at all in the late eighteenth and were simply being abused by resident nobles to embellish their houses on the cheap. Encouraged by lawyers who increasingly saw in serf–seigneurial litigation a fruitful field of profit, peasants ever more aggressively went to law to challenge seigneurial rights. The pattern was spreading ominously across France. Even in Provence, which for much of the eighteenth century had a reputation for being something of a quiet area of peasant–seigneurial relations, there are glimpses of chronic animosity, which were to turn it into one of the major epicentres of peasant revolt in the spring of 1789.[31]

It was in the second half of the eighteenth century that pressures for conspicuous consumption increased among the French nobility, as indeed did the government's fiscal demands on it. The obvious answer to these pressures was to squeeze more out of the peasantry, far beyond the limits that prudence ought to have dictated. For when the peasant revolts of 1788–9 did come, it was remarkable how far they united every sector of peasant society against the *seigneurie*, be it represented by nobles, clergy or well-to-do great bourgeoisie. Yet what was equally remarkable about those revolts was that not a single nobleman was killed. Apart from the plunder of granaries and wine cellars, only to be expected by peasants on the verge of starvation, the main damage was to the symbols of seigneurial authority: the destruction of archives and documents and the laying waste of châteaux and gardens. The peasants had learned from experience that killings would bring about harsh military retribution.[32]

This was not the case everywhere. Three revolts, all in eastern Europe – the *Koliszczyzna* revolt in the Polish Ukraine in 1768, the Pugachev Rising in Russia of 1773–5 and the Horea revolt in Transylvania in 1784 – demonstrated what the ferocity of an aggrieved peasantry could do. Yet all were conditioned by peculiar, if similar, factors: they all erupted on the territorial peripheries, and they were aggravated by ethnic, linguistic and religious antagonisms between local nobles and the majority of the population. The peasantry of the Polish Ukraine were largely Orthodox and readily identified themselves with a Cossack notion of freedom, owing service to none. The nobility were widely perceived as alien, either Polish or polonised, and predominantly Roman Catholic; mutual, traditional antagonisms, punctuated by more or less savage insurrections, reached back almost 200 years. Strains were aggravated by the imposition of higher labour services in an area in which, in the wake of serious conflicts at the beginning of the eighteenth century and the 1730s, they had been kept at low or token levels. Rivalries between Orthodox and Uniate (Greek Catholic) clergy stoked up the temperature, which was brought to boiling point by illusory hopes among the Orthodox of Russian military support, at a time when

Russian political involvement in Poland reached new heights in the mid-1760s. For some three months, from May to July 1768, the Poles lost control of wide swathes of their Ukrainian lands. Many of the insurgents felt they were simply carrying out the orders of the person they hoped would be their real ruler, Catherine II. How many perished is incalculable: the 'traditional' estimate, of 10,000–12,000 nobles and Jews slaughtered in the bloodbath in the town of Uman, has been more recently revised to a still chilling estimate of around 2000.[33] It was mainly Russian troops who suppressed the rising in the course of July and August, though much of the work of reprisal, involving hundreds of hangings, was conducted by Polish soldiers. One of the leaders, Ivan Gonta, was slowly flayed alive before being hacked to pieces.

Pugachev's great uprising of 1773–4, geographically far more extensive than the *Koliszczyzna*, shared many elements with it. The Cossacks of the Yaik (Ural) river plain, on the borderlands of European and Asiatic Russia, believed they had been settled to guard their lands 'to live as free men' for all time. Instead, they were being brought ever more into the regimented life of Russian military units by a government which was increasingly tightening its grip on a once marginal frontier zone. The manpower requisitions of the war begun with Turkey in October 1768 added fresh burdens. A conservative strand of Orthodoxy, so-called Old Belief, which had developed in the wake of efforts to modernise ritual, liturgy and ecclesiastical texts since the 1660s, was strong in the area. The whole region south of the Ural mountains was a tinder-box, seething with the grievances not only of Cossacks, but even more so of semi-nomadic Muslim tribes, Kalmyks, Kazakhs, Tatars, and especially Bashkirs, who had seen their lands taken over by military garrisons and Russian settlers, their environment devastated, and an alien religion imposed. When Pugachev roused the Yaik Cossacks in the autumn of 1773, they flocked to him en masse, sensing their last chance to shake off Russian rule. A huge area of eastern European Russia fell into the hands of the rebels, though they succeeded in sacking only one major town, Kazan. For all its huge territorial extent, the insurrection, like almost all such, crumbled as soon as sufficient numbers of regular troops were sent to contain the situation. Significantly, Pugachev, though he took the town of Kazan, was unable to make headway against its citadel, where a disciplined military force held out. Extensive peasant involvement came only in the later phases of the revolt, in the summer of 1774, when some 3 million people, around 12 per cent of the population, mainly in eastern European Russia, were involved on Pugachev's side.

At least 3000 people were massacred by the insurgents, a good half of them nobles and their families. It seems to have been the case that the relaxations of state service introduced under Peter III and preserved *de facto* by Catherine encouraged a much tighter control over their peasantry by landlords who now were more likely to reside full-time on their estates, but who could not afford to live in the capitals: only three noble victims owned more than 300 serfs; most owned fewer than 50. The extent of the rising caused panic in Moscow and St Petersburg, where a visiting Denis Diderot felt the tension all the more, as no-one at court was prepared to talk openly about the unfolding catastrophe. He even speculated that Catherine might not keep her throne.[34] Yet there was no real chance of this as long as the empress did what she was very good at doing, holding her nerve. Once enough regular troops had been assembled in late August 1774, the revolt was doomed, although it spluttered along fitfully until November. Pugachev, betrayed by his own supporters, was executed in January 1775, in a kinder way than Gonta had been in Poland: Catherine ordered he should be beheaded before his body was quartered and displayed in different districts of Moscow. But even after the suppression of this revolt, minor riots and insurgencies continued for the rest of Catherine's reign and throughout her son's. Napoleon's 1812 invasion led to some serf uprisings – Russian officials dreaded the consequences of any edict he might issue emancipating the serfs, but it never came. In the wake of Pugachev, Catherine had embarked on carefully limited reforms aimed at entrusting greater control over the countryside directly to the gentry through new judicial and police organs, but the jitters that Napoleon's invasion caused showed just how concerned Russian elites were by the fragility of their situation.

Many of the same factors were at work in the revolt led by Nicola-Vasilii Urs (known as Horea) and Ion Oaiga (or Cloşca) in 1784 in Transylvania. A largely Rumanian peasantry was being squeezed by a minority of Hungarian nobles, many little better off than the peasants themselves, and who accounted for almost a tenth of the principality's population of around 1.5 million. The Rumanian peasants were Orthodox, the nobles mainly Protestant or Catholic. The area of the revolt, which was concentrated in southern Transylvania, had long been notorious for violence and brigandage – just like the 'wild plains' of the Polish Ukraine. The nobles, trying vainly to keep up with their better-off brethren elsewhere in the Habsburg monarchy, were ratcheting up *Robot*, or labour dues. Joseph II was hoping to create a frontier defence force for the region. The peasantry got it into their heads (persuaded by Horea's simplistic analysis of the situation) that the emperor was hostile to the nobility (which in many ways he was) and was therefore on their side (which was hardly the case) and would grant freedom from serf dues to those who joined the proposed frontier militia. Peasants began to volunteer en masse. The local nobility were obstructive, fearing a loss of dues and labour services. Local officials panicked. The upshot was a revolt by about 5000 peasants in October and November 1784. Hundreds of noble families were butchered – the slaughter was on a level with that of the *Koliszczyzna* and Pugachev's revolt – but by December, regular troops had restored order. Almost 40 ringleaders were executed. The antagonisms that the revolt showed up have never entirely been effaced.[35]

The alternative to violence was running away, and there is no doubt that where serfdom predominated, the 'vagabondage' of serfs was a major problem for landlords. Mass decampings, where the inhabitants of entire villages simply fled, were rare and confined to frontier areas. The border zones of Prussia, Poland, Austria and Russia buzzed with complaints by landlords. The Russian ambassador Jakob Sievers, during the final phase of negotiations for the Second Partition of Poland, wrote to his daughter with some satisfaction that his Polish opposite number, Vice-Chancellor Joachim Chreptowicz, was the very man to whose estates 'some hundred and fifty of my Belorussian peasants had fled'. Polish historians have guessed that up to 10 per cent of serfs who should have been legally bound to the soil may have been on the move, illegally, at any one time.[36] This is surely an exaggerated view. It was not at all easy for peasants simply to abscond, particularly if it involved taking their families with them. Relatives and neighbours were reluctant to abet flight because it might mean punishment and almost certainly increased obligations for those left behind. Innkeepers were often under instructions to report the movements of all strangers, and, increasingly, authorities demanded the production of some form of passport by vagrants. The landlords of Estonia and Livonia had a reputation as being some of the most exacting in Europe, but their peasants had few easy destinations to which they might run: in Russia, the very few nobles who showed any serious interest in agricultural reform held up the estates of their Baltic counterparts as a model. Landlords, even in territories where serfdom predominated, in any case accepted that at least some of their serfs would spend considerable periods of time away from the estate performing seasonal tasks (cartage, river haulage, periodic industrial work, or just selling their own and others' produce) in order to supplement their incomes (and the landlords'). Some, of course, did not return; most did.

All the eastern European revolts were far bloodier than the Great Fear in France in 1789 was to be, and they achieved far less: if anything, they made the condition of the peasantry worse. On the other hand, if the Great Fear also contributed to the formal overthrow of feudalism in France in August 1789, it was only able to do so because orderly, routine government was crumbling under a very different array of pressures. Only with the physical arrival of something that really looked like democracy was a practical alternative to age-old hierarchy available. Hitherto tolerable because they had so far seemed theoretical or hopelessly idealistic, calls such as Rousseau's or Voltaire's for equality and the abolition of privileges were no longer admissible after the Revolution. Across Europe, censorship was tightened and social reform was put on ice. Edmund Burke was more conscious than most (or, at least, his consciousness developed earlier) of what 'democracy' could mean for the ruling order without which he believed society could not exist: hence the venom of his *Reflections on the revolution in France* in November 1790. Tom Paine's response, the two parts of the *Rights of man* (February 1791– February 1792) had to be banned (as a seditious libel, in July 1792) not just because he articulated that alternative vision while lambasting the hereditary principle in both monarchy and aristocracy, but because the *Rights of man* sold in thousands (200,000 copies by 1793, according to one estimate) and was being disconcertingly often celebrated in public and private gatherings. Dr Johnson's poser, 'What is it but opinion, by which we have a respect for authority, that prevents us, who are the rabble, from rising up and pulling down you, who are gentlemen from your place, and saying "We will be gentlemen in our turn"?',[37] was acquiring an uncomfortable topicality.

9

NOBLEWOMEN

For noble and aristocratic males, the prime function of women was to continue their family name: this required in the first instance the production of male heirs, whose arrival and survival would ensure the transmission, and accumulation, of family property in the husband's line. What legal rights women enjoyed were largely predicated on that assumption and, if anything, were increasingly regulated to conform with it. As wealth had become, in practice, a more important criterion of noble status than military prowess, the rights of women had to be more closely circumscribed, so that they could not pose a threat to the well-being of the lineage. Women were of course a threat to men and had been ever since Eve had led Adam astray (an event which most educated persons believed had occurred only 5000 or 6000 years previously). More than anyone else, Aristotle had complemented the religious, biblically ordained subordination of women with a scientific platform, demonstrating them to be a biologically and psychologically inferior form of men. He and Scripture formed a potent combination. Without superior (male) guidance, women were only too prone to giddiness, extravagance and folly and might undermine the achievements of their better halves.

Not everyone agreed. In 1675, Hannah Woolley, in her *Gentlewomans companion*, cocked a snook at these pretensions, arguing that 'Mans Soul cannot boast of a more sublime Original than ours':

> Vain man is apt to think we were meerly intended for the Worlds propagation, and to keep its humane inhabitants sweet and clean; but ... had we the same Literature, he would find our brains as fruitful as our bodies. Hence I am induced to believe, we are debarred from the

159

knowledge of humane learning, lest our pregnant Wits should rival the towring conceits of our insulting Lords and Masters.[1]

A few males were prepared to endorse such impertinences, but impertinences they were, more likely to persuade most men of precisely the opposite: of the dangers of not keeping women firmly in their place. Woolley wrote at a time when memories and legends of women supposedly empowered during the chaos of the British civil wars were still strong. In the real world of the eighteenth century, they could scarcely hope to appear on a par with men (save, of course, if they were dealing with males of inferior social status), not least because, as Hannah Woolley had observed, they scarcely ever received a comparable education.

Those who demanded equal education for women were few and largely unheard; those who demanded anything approaching equal rights were fewer still. That most civilised of males, Baron Montesquieu, accepted the inevitability of a double standard. The family, after all, was 'a sort of property' (belonging to the husband). Adultery, whether committed by women or men, was, he agreed, the same misdemeanour. Yet it was right that civil society should treat it more harshly in women than men

because the violation of modesty presupposes in women a renunciation of all virtues, because a woman in violating the laws of marriage leaves her state of natural dependency ... besides, the bastard children of a wife belong necessarily to the husband and are the husband's burden, whereas the bastard children of a husband neither belong to his wife nor are her burden.[2]

Rousseau agreed. 'Every faithless husband ... is an unjust and barbaric man; but a faithless wife goes further, she dissolves the family and breaks the ties of nature; by giving her husband children which are not his, she betrays them all, joining perfidy to infidelity.' If husbands could not be sure of the paternity of their children, how could they love them? Society itself would be in danger.[3] Wives and mothers who were undisciplined (independent) might all too easily undermine and destroy that which it was their prime duty to preserve and propagate. Fathers and husbands could of course (and did) do likewise, but insofar as this consideration entered any calculations, it was taken for granted that they had a vested interest in the preservation of their name.

The consequences of such misdemeanours were always harsher for women than for men. In seventeenth-century France, an adulterous wife was subject to public whipping and, on receipt of a *lettre de cachet* from the crown, two years' incarceration in a convent. The eighteenth century saw the whipping dropped, but the convent remained. If the aggrieved husband did not take his wife back after two years, she could remain in the convent for the rest of her life, legally dead, her property shared out between her relatives and the convent. A deceived husband suffered nothing (save a reputation for being a cuckold); even if he killed his straying wife *in flagrante*, he could take his pardon for granted.[4] In Orthodox Russia, a marriage was automatically dissolved if a wife entered, or was forced into, a nunnery (as Peter the Great did with his first wife, Evdokia, in 1698; she was still alive when he married Marta Skavronskaia in 1712). On the other hand, Peter did rescind (though not very effectively at first) the old Muscovite law enjoining the burying alive up to their necks of adulterous wives. Lesser noblewomen were presumably just as likely to suffer this fate as peasants.[5]

In law, the final responsibility for the family lay everywhere with the husband. It could be said that in a very real sense the wife was his property. The point was enshrined in the English legal principle of coverture, as explained by William Blackstone: 'the husband and wife are one person in law, and that person is the husband'.[6] Only widows would normally regain some degree of independence. The male head of the family extended his protection to that family, whose members, in return, owed him almost unquestioning submission and obedience. The man conferred his status on the woman he married, scarcely ever the reverse (one notable exception was Venice, where the offspring of a patrician who married a commoner would lose his noble status – although such unions were extremely rare in the city).[7]

Paradoxically, perhaps, this meant that ennoblement was far easier for women than for men. But this simply reflected the very lack of women's rights. Unlike social-climbing males, they were not a threat to the integrity of established elites. All other things being equal, nobles preferred to marry within their own sphere but, if needs must, non-noble females would do – provided they brought with them generous dowries. Marrying wealth was acceptable – nobles understood. If the alternative was the ruin of the ancestral estate, then the bullet of a commoner marriage had to be bitten. No-one looked askance at the £20,000 that Elizabeth Fazakerley brought to Granville Leveson-Gower (heir to the Gower barony) in 1744, even if she was a Lancashire merchant's daughter. The money helped out with the growing costs of election expenses and the rebuilding of Trentham Hall. Elizabeth had the good taste to die two years later, leaving Granville (made an earl in 1746) free to marry the rather more blue-blooded Louisa, daughter of the duke of Bridgewater (Granville had to be content with a £10,000 dowry this time).[8] But this was exceptional. British peers normally married the daughters of other peers because most peers were wealthy: a cash dowry of £25,000 seems to have been the average over the eighteenth century. True, between 1740 and 1759 marriages of peers and their sons with the daughters of wealthy bankers and merchants reached a peak of 9 per cent (12 in all!), but then they declined to around half those levels between 1760 and 1800, accounting for just 18 out of 640 marriages in that later period. If peers' sons did not marry peers' daughters, they were most likely to marry into the wealthy gentry.[9]

Though comparable data from France is hard to come by, French dukes and peers seem to have been more likely to succumb to the charms, pecuniary or otherwise, of the daughters of great financiers. These girls were, after all, at least as well educated and brought up as anything the older nobility could manage – it was not just their money that made the women of the Crozat family desirable trophy wives. Lower down the noble scale there seems to have been more resistance to marriage with commoners, but then there was comparatively little shortage of well-pedigreed females. But even the notoriously proud Andlau family in Alsace did not disdain rich plebeian brides. The great Italian nobility were notorious for their reluctance to marry outside their own milieu, but even this varied from region to region. The marriage of a son of the illustrious Milanese house of Stampa to the daughter of a rich merchant caused a scandal, but even among the self-consciously exclusive Venetian patriciate around 11 per cent of all marriages (210 of a total of 1741) between 1699 and 1795 were contracted with the daughters of wealthy commoners.[10]

Distinctly less acceptable were marriages between high-ranking nobles and very lowly commoners. Henri de Boulainvilliers, one of the most ardent exponents of the virtues of ancient race and ancestry, was never able to get over his father's second marriage to a servant girl; and Charles-Hugues de Lionne, youngest son of Louis XIV's minister, disgraced the family name by marrying the daughter of an Alsatian innkeeper in 1709. Nobles were ready to apply to the king for a *lettre de cachet* to incarcerate those guilty of such indecent and dishonouring intentions, although in the second half of the eighteenth century, the monarchy was increasingly reluctant to issue such *lettres* in purely family matters. Inequality of estate was not considered sufficient grounds on which to do so.[11] In England, the elopement in 1716 of young Lord Tankerville with a butcher's daughter was perhaps the most scandalous of a series of incidents which led to the passing of the Act against Clandestine Marriages in 1753 (perhaps fittingly, Tankerville died of a stroke the same year).[12] Peter the Great's eventual marriage to a semi-literate Lithuanian peasant woman, Marta Skavronskaia, which paved the way to her accession to the tsarist throne, was not so much an exception that proved the rule as a demonstration of the despotic powers of tsardom. When, in 1801, Count Nikolai Sheremetev, one of the wealthiest men in Russia, married one of his own serfs, the couple were ostracised.[13] Likewise, it was supposedly extremely uncommon for noblewomen to marry beneath themselves, since to do so might mean assuming the husband's commoner status (which would also affect the offspring of such a union). On the other hand, given the opportunities for informal ennoblement across much of Europe, it may well have enabled enterprising commoners to assume the wife's status.

The brutal, mercenary aspect of marriage is adumbrated in a pair of short poems published by an unknown Livonian noblewoman in a Baltic German periodical in 1781:

> Money covers all Shortcomings
> Ten thousand Thaler have significant value!
> If the girl is dumb,
> If she has property,
> Then even if she is blind and stupid,
> None the less, she will be desired for a wife.

> The Best Choice
> A girl whom luck has endowed with riches
> Has everything even if she lacks reason and virtue:
> A swarm of fools will be busily engaged
> For her hand, which they choose only for money.[14]

The one country where noblewomen did marry commoners en masse was Sweden. The reason was simple: there was a dearth of eligible nobles, because of the blood-letting wars of the later seventeenth and early eighteenth centuries. Any penalties arising from the practice seem not to have been applied. Such marriages, it is true, were very rare among the great titled Swedish nobles, but it was a different story among the untitled: in the 1680s, one-third of over 500 noble brides took commoner husbands; in 1710–19, the figure was some 490 of over 830 brides – almost two-thirds. The figures dipped in the following decade, but seem to have run at about one-third of all marriages involving noble brides for the rest of the century (the trend continued into and strengthened during the nine-teenth century). Noblewomen were as adept as the men at adapting to circumstances. It is true that it was more usual for brides who came from ennobled families, or families from a civil service rather than an estab-lished landed background, to contract such marriages, but the entire process contributed in the long term to a significant devaluation of the notion of nobility in the eyes of Swedish society at large.[15]

Yet marriages between very poor nobles and commoners or peasants may have been more common than contemporaries liked to admit. Prussian nobles were, in principle, forbidden to marry below their status, yet after 1750, about a quarter of all marriages of Brandenburg nobles were with non-noble women. As early as 1739, a royal ordinance faced facts when it permitted 'an impoverished nobleman to assist his family through an unequal marriage with a person of low, but respectable, birth and exceptional wealth'. The power of money over lineage could receive no clearer recognition. In May 1763, on the other hand, Freder-ick the Great issued an ordinance banning his overwhelmingly noble officers from keeping 'the company of low-born people or townsfolk', part of his drive to maintain the exclusivity of the nobility. How far it deterred younger officers from marrying non-noble women is probably unquantifiable.[16]

Whatever their social origins, women were wise to be at least seen to know their place. To have rebelled would have made life very difficult, perhaps impossible. Even Jane Austen's Elizabeth Bennett accepted that fact of life. It followed from their subordination that there was no need for women to receive the sort of upbringing that males could expect. John Locke's *Some thoughts concerning education* were directed at that of the young gentleman; what he had to say about that of daughters amounted to little more than occasional asides. Across the Channel, in 1686, three years before Locke published his work, Louis XIV and his ex-mistress Madame de Maintenon founded the Maison Royale de Saint Louis à Saint-Cyr, a convent school, with a generous endowment of 8 million *livres*, which yielded, a century later, a steady aristocratic income of some 400,000 *livres* a year. This was more than enough to cover the costs of the education of the 260 or so 'young ladies of the poor nobility' who graced its apartments at any one time. The whole purpose of this school lay in turning out good wives and mothers: they would write beautifully, enunciate clearly, calculate household accounts correctly. They would be pious and submissive − a submission they would demonstrate above all by knowing when to be silent. A wholesome fare of moral homilies, proverbs, maxims and devotional literature, never reaching beyond the likes of Jacques-Bénigne Bossuet and François de Sales, would underpin the ten years or more they might spend in this school, almost totally isolated from the distracting influences of their own families. The clearest statement of what these girls were there for came in the shape of a 3000 *livre* dowry that each would receive from the school on entering marriage.[17] Almost 80 years later, in May 1764, that most emancipated of women, Catherine the Great of Russia, founded the Smol'nyi Institute for Noble Girls in St Petersburg: she enriched the curriculum with foreign languages, dancing and music, but Scripture and catechism remained at the core. Like Mme de Maintenon's establishment, like so many *pensions* and convents across Europe, the chief purpose of the Smol'nyi was the production of good wives and mothers.[18] Women's was the realm of the practical, the dutiful and the decorative, not that of abstruse scientific or metaphysical inquiry.[19]

Not that deliberate intellectual suffocation always worked. Take the by any reckoning very exceptional Claudine-Alexandrine Guérin de Tencin, the unregenerate fifth child of a wealthy *robe* noble from Grenoble. Her father put her in a convent at the age of eight, intending her for the religious life. The day after being made to take her vows in November 1698, she escaped with the help of an infatuated clergyman. Though she was brought back to the convent, the episode at least convinced the authorities she was not cut out for a nun's habit and the vows were formally quashed. In 1712, she made her way to Paris: mischievous, rebellious and vivacious, her collection of lovers included the regent, Philippe d'Orléans, who encouraged her to set up one of the great salons of enlightened France. Her regular visitors included Fontenelle, Marivaux, Montesquieu and Voltaire. Her more fleeting sexual encounters included an artilleryman, the chevalier Destouches, by whom she had an illegitimate son in 1717. She promptly abandoned him to the care of his father: almost as unconventional as Claudine-Alexandrine, he took responsibility for the child, at least to the extent of ensuring it was well fostered by a respectable glazier's family. It was perhaps entirely fitting that the baby should grow up to become the great mathematician, *encyclopédiste* and subversive Jean Le Ronde d'Alembert. His mother's conquests included an equally rebellious, though plebeian (not that it bothered Mme de Tencin), Marie-Thérèse Rodet (whose pious grand-mother had vainly brought her up in the belief that 'knowledge is superfluous in a woman'), the future Mme Geoffrin, who was to bring the Enlightenment salon to a peak of sophistication, taking over on her mentor's death.[20]

'Salons' varied in quality: in 1771 the abbé Galiani complained wist-fully of the tedium of those of Naples compared with those of Paris. None the less, they were an inevitable concomitant of the spread of manners and politeness. Such social forms were a new way of stressing social dis-tinction, and could serve as an instrument of distancing from uncouth gentry backwoodsmen while conferring a limited social recognition on approved commoners. The etiquette that hostesses and female guests were expected to demonstrate in them could be as demanding as any-thing found at court.[21] Yet they were symptomatic of a development, or at least a widening appreciation, in some social circles across Europe of a new role for women as worthwhile social beings in their own right, who could be intellectual and social companions, not merely agents of procreation and property transmission. In itself this was nothing new – at the very highest court circles there had always been well-educated women who had to be treated by men as equals. And grim though Mme de Maintenon's school at Saint-Cyr might appear today, its founder appreciated that women were not powerless and passive. Those who left its classrooms were supposed to reform and purify a degenerate France through their example and morality. For Rousseau, women should use their nature, especially their natural *douceur*, or 'sweetness', to offset the injustices of bad menfolk and to guide and direct the good. After all, politeness, *politesse*, came more readily to women than to men: 'Man will say what he knows; woman will say what pleases'. Women ought to use these capacities to encourage their menfolk to higher achievements, and by the same token to improve society as a whole (shades of Mme de Main-tenon) – after all, no man actually wished to be despised by women.[22]

Again, these arguments were hardly new: they had long circulated in conduct books in France and elsewhere. In the early eighteenth century in England, they had been formulated by Addison and Steele's *Spectator*, a staple guide to new social conduct not only in England but, in numerous translations and renditions, across the continent. Rousseau in his *Émile* (1762) added his own twists. His Sophie, Émile's bride, had received the following education (by the age of 15), mainly at the hands of her parents, modest but virtuous country nobles: basic religious knowledge (though not from a catechism) – so that there would be no question of her being a bigot or *dévôte* (it would be up to her husband to initiate her into more sophisticated religious mysteries); she could sing, dance and play the harpsichord to an agreeable level; she could sew and embroider, run a household and its budget, and appreciate wholesome, simple food. Her serious reading was confined to François Barrême's teach-yourself *Arithmétique*[23](!) and Fénélon's *Télémaque* (she ached for a similar prodigy as husband). Edifying family conversation had moulded 'an intellect pleasing without being brilliant, solid without being profound', in a character which united the temperament of an Italian, the sensitivity of an Englishwoman and the pride of a Spaniard. This object of Rousseau's fantasisings was not a threat: she knew that 'Woman is made to give way to man and to endure even his injustices' – quite unlike the learned, witty female, the sort who presided over literary salons, disdainful of 'all the duties of woman', 'the scourge of her husband, her children, her servants and all the world'.[24]

In fact, the *salonnières* of whom Rousseau so disapproved were not all that different from his Sophie. They were rather more aggressive and self-confident (something he could not abide, especially if they also happened to patronise or even be kind to him), but essentially their role was a supportive one for the men. At best, women were useful for smoothing out men's rough surfaces, their cursing, brawling, drinking and nose-picking ('Hottentots, not men, when assembled together', was one long-suffering wife's verdict),[25] if only in female company. Their capacity to offer such support was more likely to be found in some milieux than others. Urbanisation, commercialisation, or perhaps, more properly, consumerisation, in Britain and France helped create social and physical spaces in which women could and even had to play a part. This was far less the case, or extended much less further down the noble scale, in less commercialised and urbanised societies, although even in provincial Russia, Catherine the Great ordered her governors in 1776 to establish theatres, which would 'bring people together, for the spread of social life and politesse'.[26] Men, after all, wanted an active social life: conversation was the key. And with the advent of the coffee-house and the assembly room and the pleasure garden, public spaces became available at which all who could pass themselves off as genteel or polite could mingle. The Squire Brambles of the world affected to be much anguished by such socially undiscriminating venues, but in reality they were drawn to them almost as much as their racier young relations.

The place that individual women carved out for themselves, or even had thrust upon them, remained just that – a matter of individuals. The extent to which there was any *de facto*, as opposed to *de jure*, widening of women's rights remains a matter for debate. The eighteenth century saw only one truly spectacular shift in women's roles, in a very narrow social segment: in Russia, as a result of Peter the Great's reforms, the wives and daughters of great aristocrats were almost literally removed from the closet, the *terem*, in which in the old Muscovite state they had been kept in almost seraglio-like seclusion, and thrust into a public limelight. That, however, did nothing to alter their basic *raison d'être* as purveyors of heirs and transmitters of estates to their menfolk. The French Revolution may have widened women's property rights and brought some easing in divorce; but it maintained their basic subordination to men by excluding them from the newly conferred franchise, placing them on a par with children, minors and convicted felons. Many European aristocrats deeply loathed Napoleon: but few of them would have taken issue with the Napoleonic Code's neat formulation: 'The husband owes his wife protection; the wife owes her husband obedience.'

No wives, no matter what their station, could expect to escape the toils of childbirth. Yet despite some dreadful horror stories, it is by no means certain that giving birth was more dangerous to women than any form of illness (admittedly, that may not necessarily have come as much consolation). Between the mid-sixteenth and mid-twentieth centuries, fewer than one in five female British aristocratic wives died in childbirth. Of 121 such women giving birth between 1700 and 1749, 7 (5.7 per cent) died; of 225 giving birth between 1750 and 1799, 18 (8 per cent) died. Although wider statistics are impossible to find, there is no reason to suppose that the incidence of death in childbirth was any different among other social groups. It may, indeed, have been the case that the rise in childbirth deaths among aristocratic wives stemmed from the growing fashion, especially after the 1730s, to employ male doctors to help delivery with the fashionable forceps, rather than relying on the traditional skills of uneducated midwives (after 1800, deaths in childbirth dropped to 4.3 per cent – perhaps male doctors had come to acquire the necessary skills and expertise).[27] But given the wide range of factors that could impinge on childbirth, it would be rash to try to read too much into them.

In one area, more progressive male doctors and other 'experts' gave a lead to women: the eighteenth century saw a veritable cult of breast-feeding in the literature, notably extolled in England by William Cadogan's *Essay upon nursing and the management of children*, first published in

1748, which ran to numerous editions. Though far better received than the same author's *Dissertation on the gout* of 1771, for all its popularity it seems to have done little to wean upper-class women in any appreciable numbers off the practice of wet-nursing. Rousseau extolled the virtues of breast-feeding in his *Émile*, which did, apparently, lead to something of a breast-feeding mania among aristocratic French women in the 1780s (granted, they did not produce many children). The marquise de Bombelles insisted on breast-feeding her son at court. Some of these women, at least, may have gone in for the practice as a token gesture towards the fashions of the day.[28] When, in 1783, the duchess of Devonshire chose to breast-feed her daughter (a duty, it has to be said, that she at least took very seriously), it was deemed so unusual as to elicit (favourable) comment in the popular press.[29] But wet-nursing was convenient, traditional and a major rural service industry, especially in the vicinity of larger towns. If fashionable theories began to contribute to the gradual erosion of the practice, then the view that ignorant, irresponsible, drunken and possibly diseased peasant women might pass on their vices and infections to genteel children played at least as great a role.[30]

Beneath the rhetoric of obligation and subordination, in private wives could be, and often had to be, partners. Looking after the running of a household which ran to a home farm, or perhaps a significant town house, a domestic staff of several servants, dealing with tradesmen, ensuring the presence of home comforts, was taken as read to be primarily the preserve of the wife. Keys and a small memorandum-book symbolised the lady of the house's authority. In Russia, the traditional women's wing of the noble household was under the direct jurisdiction of the lady – perhaps this was good managerial practice for her role in running the property as a whole, which, given the liability of all nobles to military and state service for much of the eighteenth century, she was all too likely to be called on to perform.[31] She too, or a spinster relative, was expected to provide some kind of basic education for the children, even if only at the level of reading, writing and religion. 'Keeping house' could mean responsibility for a very wide range of essential domestic management: finding and keeping servants, ensuring their work was satisfactory, dealing with local tradesmen, settling local accounts, ensuring that the house was maintained and furnished in a way commensurate with the family's status. Indeed, the desire to find a trusted partner who would relieve them of some of the burden of such duties was cited by many bachelors or widowed lords and gentlemen as an entirely normal reason for finding a wife. Conversely, wives whose husbands did not trust them with domestic management might find themselves demoralised and undervalued: it was a standard grievance among women petitioning for separate maintenance before ecclesiastical courts.[32] In the final analysis, however, no matter how trusting or affectionate the relationship between the spouses, only the husband's death could change the wife's legal dependency.

In England, the medieval practice of dower entitled a widow to life tenure of one-third of all property owned by her late husband at any time (including land that might have passed to others). Dower, however, abolished only in 1925, represented a disruptive nuisance (at the least) in an age of frequent property transfers. Lord Eldon warned in 1805 that its application 'would affect the titles to a large proportion of the estates in the country'.[33] But the threat had long been neutralised via binding, contractual arrangements (including marriage contracts and strict settlements) which, while usually providing some form of safeguard for the woman, ensured that her rights did not threaten the process of landed property accumulation. Thus jointure (originally 'a formal grant of land to husband and wife in joint tenancy and for the life of the survivor')[34] replaced dower: a stipulated income from the husband's estate (including the lands she herself had brought in as part of her dowry), or even from stipulated portions of the estate. Sir John Habakkuk suggests that 'ratios of 20 to 25 per cent [of jointure to estate income] seem to have been common', but the reality depended on a massive array of circumstances: a debt-laden aristocrat might be prepared to offer a much higher jointure in order to assure himself of a wealthy heiress. Susan Staves is inclined to take a less charitable view, suggesting £1500 as an aristocratic widow's average jointure and those of gentry widows as ranging from around £500 to as little as £15.[35] Whether widows necessarily always received these entitlements is another matter: their allocation was an obvious area in which hard-pressed (or just improvident) heirs might wish to economise. Occasionally, provision was made for the jointure itself to lapse if the widow remarried. Such a stipulation led the king of Poland's sister, Elżbieta Poniatowska, to keep her marriage to Stanisław Mokronowski a secret (an open one) after the death of her aged but fabulously wealthy first husband, Jan Klemens Branicki. Pre-nuptial agreements might also entitle the wife to 'pin money' (the term came into use in the 1690s) or its equivalent, her own spending allowance during the marriage: otherwise, the provision of necessities was the legal obligation of the husband, as the wife's legal guardian and virtual owner. Georgiana, duchess of Devonshire, enjoyed a quite exceptional pin money of £4000 a year from the fifth duke – but it was nothing like enough to cover her fabulous gambling debts.[36]

The basic system of jointures, pin money and husbandly 'protection' for the wife appeared in various guises across Europe. The constraints of law and custom could always be circumvented by private agreement. Lawyers across the continent devised elaborate devices to facilitate such circumventions – a procedure which, of course, both increased the likelihood of litigation among disgruntled or grasping relatives and also ensured that lawyers were never short of work and remuneration. It was understood that wealth and influence should be shored up with more wealth and influence and connection. The safeguards that were put in place in pre-nuptial agreements were primarily safeguards for property, not for the person of the wife: if no heirs were produced by the marriage, then the wife's dowry lands would revert to her family, and would not remain in the hands of the husband or his family. She could not, of course, sell, alienate or mortgage them on her own account, or even her husband's – any such transaction would normally require the approval of her relatives. But even here, provision would be made for a jointure and for the estate to descend to the children. Even if a wife's dowry property was not strictly the husband's, he could count on the right to administer the dowry property unless specified otherwise in the marriage contract. In England, women who sought to make their own arrangements to protect their property from the possible depredations of a future husband were liable to have such arrangements overturned in the courts and declared fraudulent, unless the prospective husband had given them his prior approval.[37] Where the dowry was in cash, the defences against a needy or feckless husband were much less secure and might, indeed, be non-existent. Frederick, Lord 'Bully' Bolingbroke, ran through the huge dowry of his wife, Diana Spencer, without adverse legal repercussions. He did, however, impoverish and destroy himself by his degenerate lifestyle, which ended in paralysis of the brain and committal to the madhouse.[38] A wealthy, parvenu family giving their daughter to an illustrious but indigent one would, of course, understand, or expect the husband to use the money to pay off obligations, acquire more land or modernise the ancestral seat. In the final analysis, the ability of a woman to secure the provisions laid down in a contract depended more than anything else on the goodwill of all parties involved.

Surprisingly, perhaps, it was in Russia that, in theory at least, noblewomen secured the greatest rights to the administration of their property – for in June 1753, the Senate ruled that wives were entitled to dispose of property that they had brought into the marriage as part of their dowry, and, indeed, to administer it themselves if they so wished. In practice, dowry properties continued to be administered by males: either the woman's husband, a relative or, if she were a widow, by a son. Indeed, it was, until the mid-eighteenth century, normal for the dowry land to be given by the wife's family directly to her spouse. But, increasingly, dowry agreements began to be made between the bride's parents and the bride herself (or, if she were illiterate, her male represen-tative), rather than with the groom. This development was as pragmatic as any other relating to inheritance and land law for Europe's elites. In the factional in-fighting that marked the Russian political scene, Russian nobles of any standing, especially in the first half of the century, were liable to imprisonment, exile or death and confiscation of estates.[39] The preservation of women's separate property offered at least some kind of buffer to the offspring of husbands caught up in these political misfortunes. Not only nobles (chronically indebted) but merchants and manufacturers came to appreciate the benefits of transferring property to their wives as a defence against debt and bankruptcy. The technique could backfire, as it did for Nikita Gavrilov, who found in 1809 that he was unable to recover from his wife (the marriage had broken down) property that he had bought in her name over 20 years previously. Such transactions were only open to a tiny minority of Russian women: most dowries were likely to consist of a few serfs. If a husband ordered her to sell them off, there was little the wife could do, despite old laws stipulating that they could not be forced or beaten into such sales. 'Moderate correc-tion' was permissible in all societies, subject to the somewhat elastic proviso that the woman's life should not be threatened. An English judge ruled in 1782 that a husband could legally beat his wife 'so long as the stick was no thicker than his thumb'.[40]

The Russian case was not wildly extreme: such was the variation of law and custom, even within a single country, that the wife might be able to retain some real measure of control over her property. In much of south-ern France, the law recognised *paraphernaux*: non-dowry property over which the wife could exercise full control without reference to the hus-band. Technically, too, the dowry would revert to a widow, though it was always to pass on to any children who had come of age. Its adminis-tration then remained, technically, in the hands of the widow – although in Normandy, a male relative of the deceased husband had to approve her decisions. On the other hand, in Naples, where dowries were predominantly conferred in cash, widows had full control over dowry management – though the need to safeguard the family interest meant that dowry sums could not normally be used for anything other than the purchase of land or government annuities. Widows were a formidable force in the world of Neapolitan finances.[41]

The transmission of property and pedigree took precedence over the feelings of the women themselves. Their views on their future husbands were often the least consideration to be taken into account in the construction of marriage alliances. Unfettered freedom of choice existed for virtually no-one, nor was it thought that it should. 'The marriages of these girls were made ... in a world of haggling, of parental decisions and compulsions, where family financial policy was the primary concern.'[42] Peter the Great decreed that no woman should be forced into marriage: his *ukazy* of 1700, 1702 and 1722 were as pointless as any number of ecclesiastical injunctions of any denomination stressing that marriage was a voluntary union by both parties. The stress on finance is perhaps a little too crass. Pedigree and connection were deemed at least as important, if only because it was expected that wealth would inevitably accompany a great family name: but it is true that great wealth could compensate for a girl's lack of status, just as great wealth could cleanse of common status and ennoble. In 1688, mere ennoblement was not enough to secure the Portuguese financiers the Pintos social acceptance into the highest circles of the old Neapolitan aristocracy: but the marriage of Teresa Pinto to Giuseppe Caracciolo, eighth marquis of Brienza, did the trick: the price-tag was Teresa's dowry of 50,000 ducats in ready cash, a quarter of the value of the marquis's estates.[43]

In this search for connections, there was little room for sentiment. In 1712, Mary Pierrepont tearfully remonstrated with her father, Lord Dorchester (whose own marriage had been arranged by his mother), over his plans to marry her off to the repellent Clotworthy Skeffington, heir to the Irish lordship of Massereene: 'my Aversion to the Man propos'd was too great to be overcome, that I should be miserable beyond all things could be imagin'd, but I was in his hands, and he might dispose of me as he thought fit. – He was perfectly satisfy'd with this Answer, and proceeded as if I had given a willing consent.'[44] Lord Dorchester was rather less satisfied, after shelling out £400 on his own wedding suit, when Mary eloped with Edward Wortley Montagu. The fact that Montagu was not some impecunious cad, but nephew to the earl of Sandwich and heir to a huge fortune built on Northumberland and Durham coal, helped bring about a reconciliation a year later. But the option of elopement, for all the worry it caused many parents, was hardly one taken commonly. Girls did as they were told, if only for the sake of their reputation. True, a wayward daughter might be prepared to marry a social inferior, but it was a grave insult to family honour and could well lead to her being cut off from all contact. When, in 1765, the 38-year-old widow Elizabeth Parker, of comfortable Lancashire gentry background, eloped to Gretna Green with a wool merchant 18 years her junior, her family simply disowned her. The beatings and whippings that her drink-prone swain took to administering did nothing to ease her wretched existence.[45] That grim patriarch Franciszek Salezy Potocki, 'the little king of the Polish Ukraine', took a rather harsher line when, in 1772, Gertruda Komorowska, daughter of a perfectly respectable middle-ranking nobleman (though no match for one of the Potocki clan), committed the error of yielding to his smitten son's importunings of marriage: he had her drowned. For every Claudine-Alexandrine de Tencin, there must have been any number of daughters like Clara de Lantery in Spain who took two husbands in the space of five years at her father's behest because 'she had no desire but to do the will of her father'.[46]

   This is not to say that girls were always denied any choice: more urbanised and 'polite' societies developed mechanisms that allowed young people some scope in the choice of partner: salons, assemblies, balls, resorts. These were not, of course, places of indiscriminate social gathering, rather they were venues where large numbers of persons of similar social background could gather. The acquaintances made would be safe, interactions would be chaperoned and public: they were known marriage marts. These are the gathering places of Jane Austen's England – but here, too, 'the length of a man's rent-roll remained the ultimate aphrodisiac'.[47] Sentimental novels and romances and a new cult of the loving family all helped to make it, in principle, desirable that girls should, at the very least, be allowed some say in whom they married. Some moralists felt such profane literature should not be available to young women, for it might only encourage the vice of female masturbation or, at least, make girls even more frivolous and empty-headed than they already were.[48] But the idea of marriage for love rather than as a purely business proposition, and the accompanying view that children should have greater latitude in the choice of a spouse, made some progress over the century – most of all perhaps in England, least of all in Russia, where until the reforms of Peter the Great it was unusual for the offspring of the higher aristocracy to meet each other for more than a few hours before their invariably arranged matches. Any softening of this subordination of the individual to the ambitions and demands of family made very slow progress indeed in Russia.[49]

Where such 'freedoms' existed, a deluge of conduct manuals warned prospective brides against the dangers of impetuosity. If 'noblewomen of the later eighteenth century were clearly fascinated by the idea of marrying for love', they could not simply surrender to it.[50] Reason (calculation) had to bridle passion (romantic love). It was not just a question of material comforts: how could a woman judge whether a personable suitor would turn into a domineering bully or a syphilitic philanderer? Once the knot was tied, there was no going back: in England between 1670 and 1857 there were only 325 divorces (fewer than two a year), confined mainly to the gentry and peerage; and the overwhelming bulk of those were secured by men against their wives, not by wives against their husbands. It was scarcely easier in other countries: the option of a slight 'irregularity' in the marriage ceremony, which could leave scope for canonical annulment, occasionally practised in Poland and perhaps in other Catholic countries, was limited to a very few. The best that unhappy partners might hope for was separation, although, unless the deeds were carefully worded, the wife might still find that the husband (or his relatives) exercised considerable powers over her. These powers could even extend from beyond the grave: in parts of France, a widow who failed to mourn her husband with due reverence could be sued by his family and lose any monies she had inherited from him.[51]

The daily reality of marriage was something that law could regulate only at best in part. Marital happiness is an elusive quality in any society. It is clear that some unions were blissfully happy, just as others were desperately wretched, with all gradations in between. As ever, those at the very top of the aristocratic tree were able to evolve strategies to allow them to cope with the repercussions of having undesirable spouses forced upon them. 'Open' marriages, where both sides understood each other's extra-marital affairs, were one solution. In the 1760s, Adam Kazimierz Czartoryski allegedly extended his understanding (and *politesse*) to escorting his wife, Izabela, to the Russian ambassador's Warsaw residence in the evenings and collecting her in the mornings. This was perhaps going a little far, but the principle was hardly confined to the Polish–Lithuanian Commonwealth. It was rumoured that the almost invariably unmarried younger brothers of Venetian patricians could expect to enjoy the shared sexual favours of their elder brothers' wives.[52] The

London Magazine in 1780 condemned adultery as 'the fashionable vice' of the aristocracy. French scandal sheets enjoyed an equal field day, seeing in the spread of syphilis among the great aristocracy and royal family the corruption and pollution of the body politic.[53] The provincial nobles of Poland revelled in tales of the Babylonian degeneracy of the Warsaw court.

The curious institution of cicisbeism in some countries, notably Spain, Italy and even Austria, formalised the position of a wife's protector: the cicisbeo had the task of escorting and seeing to the wants and needs of the wife while the husband was busy elsewhere. The term, and the practice, were found in British aristocratic circles. Such a cicisbeo was, in theory, a kind of male chaperone: he might be a relative of the wife or husband or an impecunious family friend. Italian marriage contracts might even specify his duties and remuneration. Inevitably, there was considerable speculation that cicisbei also serviced their charges sexually: doubtless this happened, but it would be wrong to portray such events as the prime purpose of the institution. Venetian ladies, liberated in the early eighteenth century from the anachronistic fashion statements of exaggeratedly high platform shoes, were as likely to find their cicisbei a hindrance to any affairs they might wish to pursue.[54]

Not all women married: dowries were for eldest daughters, one shining match was enough in a family. Even the wealthiest family might feel its resources strained by dowering more daughters, although the very limited information available about the demography of younger children makes any kind of generalisation difficult. English families took care to provide an income for daughters – in theory: but often it would become payable only when the daughter left home to be married (and then it would constitute her dowry, the interest serving as her income). In these circumstances it was to the advantage of the head of the family, be it the girl's father or her elder brother, to keep at least some at home for as long as possible.[55] If one made a brilliant marriage, unless the family was very rich indeed her sisters might well have to content themselves with lesser marriages, since the favoured sister had used up the cash reserves: but this would at least tie the family in to lesser gentry and strengthen useful local connections. 'At the level of the [English] parish ... the image of a profound cultural gulf yawning between the local elites of land and trade bears little resemblance to the teeming interactions of the marriage market and the dining-room.'[56] The high Neapolitan aristocracy seem to have been unusual in that they had, since the Middle Ages, developed investment banks (rather as did

Neapolitan commoners), *monti di maretaggio*, which were specifically designed to produce dowries: while this did not absolve the family from the need to dig deep into their pockets to find cash for at least one daughter, it did facilitate the marrying off of others, especially since they did not object to their marriage to nobles of lesser standing.[57] Venetian families preferred to marry off one daughter, just as they preferred to marry off only one son.

Younger daughters accepted being bundled off to the numerous nunneries, many of which were extremely lax in their daily discipline, allowing their inmates a full social life, sexily tailored habits and assignations; on the other hand, there were also nunneries in Venice that were known for their moral rigour. The devotions and piety, no matter how conventional, of nobles and gentry in Catholic Europe were such as to promote the cloister as a way of life in its own right for females. After all, in Anglican England holy orders were deemed perfectly acceptable for younger sons of even the most affluent gentry. Nuns were expected to bring in dowries, which, at the least, generated an annuity to assure the beneficiary of some home comforts. In general, these were much smaller than the dowries of their married sisters, although even here, the more fashionable the convent, the greater the dowry.[58] Of the 80,000 nuns in France in 1789, around 1 in 20 (4000) were of noble stock, approximating to around the same proportion of adult females among the *noblesse*.[59] Well over half, perhaps as many as three-quarters, of the 3000 or so nuns in Polish and Lithuanian convents were of noble extraction, although by the mid-century there had been a marked fall in the number of novices from magnate families. Many daughters settled for spinsterhood, living in the main family home as dependants, informal tutors or governesses and chaperones. Given the unhappy nature of many marriages, spinsterhood must have seemed something of a relief to many of these singletons. Equally, given the exploitative and bullying nature of so many families, many enforced spinsters must have yearned for the imagined bliss of married life.

It is, perhaps, all too easy to look on women as passive, helpless victims of a gender-oppressive (even internalised gender-oppressive) social, cultural and legal system. Human beings are not automata; systems and rules exist to be circumvented. Women may have been legal subordinates, but their status, connections and the bloody-minded determination of those endowed with it enabled them to play a real part in the world, beyond the confines of family domesticity. Given the close intertwining of the political and the domestic worlds for the noble elite, even a domestic role such as framing marriage alliances could entail major political factors. The achievements of those at the top of the tree, an Elizabeth Farnese, a Maria Theresa or a Catherine the Great, may have done nothing for the advancement of their sex, but they demonstrated, for better or for worse, that they could cope as well as any male with what the eighteenth century threw at them. The most determined simply had to do the best within the constraints of what the social structures and conventions allowed. So it was, all the way down the scale. Elizabeth Montagu ran not only one of the most famous salons in London after 1750 but, after her husband's death in 1775, the family estates and coal mines, increasing their revenues from £7000 to £10,000 per annum. The extraordinary Catherine Vorontsova, Princess Dashkova by marriage, piloted her husband's massively indebted estates to solvency after his death in 1765[60] and enhanced her astonishing curriculum vitae in 1783 when Catherine the Great appointed her director of her Academy of Letters. In Poland, Izabela Branicka, like Elizabeth Montagu, had a reputation for the combination of intellect and management. Her near-contemporary Katarzyna Kossakowska, *née* Potocka, was known not only as a behind-the-scenes fixer and arranger of aristocratic unions but as a political harridan before whom the nobility of much of southern Poland quailed.[61]

The proliferation of assembly rooms in later eighteenth-century Britain and the expansion of musical and theatrical activities allowed women to play a part in their administration, sometimes even taking the lead: theatre and concerts were an area in which women born or married into the aristocracy or the wealthier and more refined gentry could influence and direct, not just serve as fashion icons. But even in this role, the wives and mistresses of great aristocrats lent themselves to the shoring up of the social order. The theatre and the opera were not merely the arena of spectacle on stage: they were also the occasion for men, but even more so women, to display themselves in their finery, to re-emphasise the gulf between their world and the rest, even as they were gawped on. In France or England, the newspapers and scandal sheets brought the latest gossip about these celebrities of the *ton* or of 'Society' to scandalised readers lower down the scale, who could never read enough about what was missing in their own lives.[62]

Given that one of the *raisons d'être* of noble wives was to act as a household and domestic manager, it is not surprising that so many did not fit the stereotypes of submissive subordinates; and that despite the formal constraints, individual noblewomen (crowned heads aside) could make a significant impact on the political scene. A noblewoman who was an estate manager in her own right was everywhere automatically a political figure. Any landed estate was not just an economic enterprise – it was a centre of local employment and hence of political patronage and influence. Sarah, duchess of Marlborough, was important not just because she was married to one of the major political and military figures of the age and had direct access to the queen; even without all that, and after her husband's death, she was important because of the influence she commanded through her ownership of extensive properties in the parliamentary borough of St Albans. In the electoral constituencies of the Polish–Lithuanian Commonwealth, widowed, divorced (and, for that matter, married) female nobles administering extensive landed estates automatically commanded the respect and service of nobles great and small who looked to their 'interest' for alliances or for employment and advancement. It was commonplace for Polish magnates to secure royal agreement to allow the reversion of crown properties awarded to the husband for service to the state to revert to their widows; such properties might command not only substantial revenues but extensive rights of patronage and appointment in the local administration and judiciary. Well-born women were expected to use their influence on behalf of family and friends in elections, although when Georgiana, duchess of Devonshire, publicly (and successfully) canvassed on behalf of Charles James Fox in the raucous and crowded Westminster election of 1784, such was the vituperation this unwonted spectacle elicited from many quarters that she never repeated the exercise. It may be that the comparatively open, fluid patterns and wider accessibility of the British and Polish political systems did permit more overt female participation in politics than elsewhere (one distinguished Polish historian was sufficiently impressed by women's roles in eighteenth-century political life to produce a work entitled *When women ruled us*).[63] Women were certainly spectators of parliamentary debates in both countries (at least until they were barred from the public gallery of the House of Commons in 1778).[64] But the case of Georgiana rather proved the point: in terms of received opinion, female involvement in politics was unnatural. The kind of opprobrium heaped on her in England was mirrored in that thrown at Marie Antoinette and her friends (who included Georgiana) in France. And those women who had high hopes of the Revolution in that country for the advancement of their sex were to be sadly disappointed.

In the final analysis, for aristocrats and gentry marriage was and had to be a business. Presumably this caused less difficulty within established landed families not hell-bent on social climbing. Partners were and in most cases had to be sought within circles of friends and families. Perhaps the highly structured forms of English politics, where friendship and patronage were increasingly more important than kinship, allowed prospective brides and grooms a wider say in their future partners. Where kinship networks were more important, as in Naples, Poland or Russia, then girls in particular had to bow readily to family wishes. The best that could be hoped for was not to have to marry someone too repugnant. The 18-year-old Izabela Poniatowska would have been less than human to have found her marriage in 1748 to the 59-year-old Jan Klemens Branicki anything other than distasteful. Still, she did her duty – in vain, since political friendship between Branicki and his in-laws did not materialise. But she could count herself lucky: not only was she able to seek solace in the more youthful Andrzej Mokronowski, her husband's aide-de-camp, she also inhabited an aristocratic milieu very understanding of such liaisons. Such behaviour for the daughters of middling and lesser gentry was almost intolerable. They had to resign themselves to fate and duty.

EPILOGUE

THE EUROPEAN NOBILITY AND THE FRENCH REVOLUTION

On 21 April (Old Style) 1785, her 56th birthday, Empress Catherine II of Russia promulgated a charter 'on the Rights, Freedoms and Privileges of the well-born Russian nobility'. Though pulling together much in the way of already existing decrees and laws on Russia's *dvorianstvo*, the charter gave the nobility what it had hitherto lacked: a clearly defined corporate structure, accompanied by a body of privileges which put it on something approaching a comparable footing with nobilities elsewhere in Europe. A sixfold division was established for nobles. Those ennobled over the past century, be it by personal grant of the ruler or through military and bureaucratic service, comprised in effect the three categories of those who had made their way up the Table of Ranks instituted by Peter the Great in 1722. The three remaining categories, however, constituted a more exclusive, aristocratic grouping: they were made up of those descended from noble families originating outside Russia, those in receipt of titles of prince, count or baron, and those whose nobility went back for over a century. The charter went on to lay down procedures for registration, entry and loss of status. Peter III's 1762 edict emancipating the nobles from compulsory service to the state was finally confirmed. They were free to travel abroad, even to enter foreign service; they were free from corporal punishment; and they could be tried for crimes only by a jury of fellow-nobles. They finally received their properties in full ownership and free disposal. They would run their own affairs at local level through noble associations, *sobrania*, electing local officials, keeping registration records, looking after noble affairs, in a manner comparable to the assemblies to be found in so many other parts of Europe.

If the new organisation of the nobility bore the marks of a systematic, rational approach, at its core it remained conservative: nobility was

> an hereditary distinction derived from the quality and virtue of out-standing men of former times who distinguished themselves by their deeds and who, having thereby made their service worthy of honour, acquired the title of nobility for their posterity.[1]

The reference to deeds, even ancestral deeds, was misleading. Catherine's charter was regressive even by comparison with Peter's approach, since ownership of land, rather than service, was taken to be the predominant distinguishing characteristic of nobles: only those who owned land could participate actively in the *sobrania* or stand for elected office. The state kept a watchful eye on them: the marshals of the *sobrania* were salaried by the state, and all elected officials and judicial verdicts in the local courts remained subject to confirmation by local governors. Catherine was reconciling Russian tradition and centralism with what might have been regarded as 'best practice' in the way Europe's nobilities were organised.

Only four years after the promulgation of the charter, the principles it represented received a punishing blow. On 17 June 1789, nearly 600 deputies of the French Third Estate renounced their membership of the Estates-General, which had been meeting at Versailles since 5 May. Instead, they had decided that they were no longer part of that gathering, but formed a national representation in their own right. They were a National Assembly, which alone could legislate for the kingdom,

> first, because its members are the only representatives properly and publicly known and accredited; secondly, because they have been sent here by practically the whole nation; and thirdly, because there can be only one single indissoluble body of representatives. No deputy, in whatever Order he may have been chosen, has any right to exercise his functions apart from the present assembly.[2]

Three days later, locked out of the great hall at Versailles by royal order, the deputies made their way to a nearby indoor tennis court and swore an oath that they would not disperse until they had given France a new, reformed constitution. 'The step that the Commons have taken', appreciated Arthur Young, 'is in fact an assumption of all authority in the Kingdom.' Louis XVI was adamant that the society of orders should remain unscathed. He was ready for some concessions, but not for the end of the social world he knew. At the *séance royale* of 23 June, what had once been the Third Estate defiantly stood its ground. The renegade nobleman the marquis de Mirabeau defiantly challenged royal ministers to disperse the assembly at bayonet point. Louis XVI did not have the stomach for such work. Over the next few weeks, the majority of the deputies of the clergy and nobility drifted over to the assembly.[3]

As if this was not enough, on the night of 4 August this new assembly proceeded to demolish the old regime and its governing principles. It formally declared the abolition of the 'feudal system'. Exclusive seigneurial hunting rights disappeared. Manorial courts were abolished. Seigneurial impositions deriving from any form of serfdom were scrapped without compensation, although all other such impositions (rents, fees, payments, tithes) would only be abolished subject to indemnification of their owners. The sale of offices was forbidden. All forms of fiscal and pecuniary privilege were overthrown. 'All citizens, without distinction of birth' were declared 'eligible to any office or dignity, whether ecclesiastical, civil, or military'. No form of occupation would henceforth be deemed demeaning. Of course there were qualifications and reservations in the decree, but this was the end of the *Ancien Régime* in France. The bonfire of feudal vanities was codified and formally promulgated on 11 August. Just over a fortnight later, on 27 August, the Declaration of the Rights of Man and Citizen made clear that the new principles of legal equality and equity would form the foundation of a new France and a new society.[4]

Had this happened in some minor German principality it would, no doubt, have elicited much patronising interest and would have remained at little more than the level of an enlightened curiosity. That was certainly to be the fate of the incomparably less radical Polish constitution (or, as some had it, 'revolution') of 3 May 1791. But this took place in the most powerful nation in Europe, possessed of 28 million inhabitants. Quite why the privileged members and landowning bourgeois – 'bourgeois living nobly' – of the National Assembly allowed themselves to do this remains a matter of debate. Their admirers are ready to ascribe it to a collective, enlightened enthusiasm; those who are inclined to the view that the politicians of the past were no more or less idealistic than those of the present might point to the garbled, terrifying reports of widespread peasant insurrection, 'the Great Fear', that reached Versailles and propelled seigneurial landlords to make concessions before their properties were destroyed and perhaps their very lives lost.[5]

If this overturning of the old order had sustained its relatively bloodless course, Europe might still have accommodated itself to the Revolution. There was, after all, no shortage of those in Britain who felt that the French had simply embarked on a rather more excitably Gallic version of the Glorious Revolution of 1688. If France was in turmoil, its neighbours, especially in England and Germany, could feel safe, smug and secure.[6] But the process of the overthrow of the nobility, the keystone of the social order across the continent, was well under way in Europe's most important state. Already in January 1789, in his brilliant *Qu'est-ce que le Tiers État?* (*What is the Third Estate?*), the abbé Emmanuel-Joseph Sieyès had compared the nobility to 'a malignant disease which preys upon and tortures the body of a sick man', a parasitic, predatory minority of oppressors. The Revolution turned more violent, more bloody, more horrifying and more radical and the nobility were its most prominent victims and scapegoats. On 19 June 1790, all titles of hereditary nobility were abolished. The nobility were eradicated as a legal entity: coats-of-arms, servants' liveries, distinctive pews in church, all the trappings, the *particule*, the 'de' followed by the name of the *seigneurie*, belonged to the past. The marquis de Ferrières, a noble deputy from Poitou, was appalled at this demolition of his world:

> The assembly looked like a gang of drunken men in a shop full of delicate furniture, breaking and smashing at will everything that came to hand ... Soon the ancient French constitution, crumbling noisily under redoubled blows from this gang of wild men, was seen with astonishment to consist of nothing but a shapeless mound of ruins and fragments.[7]

Just to make sure, on 30 July 1791 all the ancient orders of chivalry were abolished. On 21 September 1792, France ceased to be a monarchy and became a republic, though Louis XVI was not executed until 21 January the following year. Many nobles, or those who had once been nobles, had fled abroad: some 20,000 by May 1792 (of whom around one in ten were to die abroad). The Revolution took appropriate counter-measures. In August, parents of *émigrés* were forbidden to leave their municipalities. A decree of 23 October of that year forbade *émigrés* from returning, on pain of death; any who had fled abroad but had since returned were, the following month, given 15 days to leave France. Nobles were increasingly demonised as the source of all France's ills, so much so that there were those who advocated renaming the now clearly offensive 'Grenoble' as a politically correct 'Grelibre'. In March 1793, *émigrés* were declared stripped of all civil and family rights: they had become legally dead; those accused of being *émigrés* were regarded as guilty until proven innocent. In April, (ex-)nobles were barred from holding passports; by September, all (ex-)nobles were confined to their places of domicile, while all who had not been active supporters of the Revolution were declared liable to arrest. And so it went on. The law of 29 November 1797, or 9 *frimaire* of the year VI, deprived all former nobles, including their children, of all political rights. Besides the 20,000 or so nobles who fled France, between 1792 and 1799 alone some 3000 were killed. Another 20,000 were arrested. The Terror as a whole may have claimed 40,000 lives − as ever, the nobility remained a prominent minority.[8]

Nor were these events a spectacle that Europe was allowed to watch passively, even had it wished to do so. On 20 March 1792, the French declared war on Austria, knowing that this would inevitably drag in its ally, Prussia. On 20 September, their forces hurled back the Prussian army at Valmy and proceeded to chase it back across the Rhine. On 19 November, the republic promised its assistance to all oppressed peoples − which, by revolutionary definition, meant any non-privileged inhabitant of anywhere in Europe (or, for that matter, the world). For good measure, the republic went on to declare war against Britain and the Dutch Republic the following February.

The resilience and adaptability of the nobility of the *Ancien Régime* has already been remarked on. This continued during the revolutionary years. Up to 8 per cent of French nobles turned *émigré*; another 2 or 3 per cent may have lost their lives directly as a result of the Revolution. All this adds up to a significant minority, but a minority nevertheless.[9] Most nobles, mainly those of more modest means, stayed put, living quietly on their estates, tightening their belts at the ending of all fiscal exemptions and the imposition of new taxes and contributions. With the loss of feudal dues, their real incomes may have halved. But some could find compensation: they were often able to purchase confiscated ecclesiastical land and even able to pay for it in the inflationary *assignats* issued by the new regime. Ironically, these *assignats* often came from compensation payments to holders of venal (including once-ennobling) offices, most of which were abolished by October 1791.[10]

Many (although it is impossible to quantify how many) joined the Revolution and flourished: 'a sizeable minority of nobles remained at the cutting edge of radicalism through both the Terror and the Directory'.[11] The attitude of the revolutionary governments to nobles was, frankly, inconsistent. Mere *anoblis* were not regarded as true nobles. Those who co-operated with the Revolution and jettisoned the memories of their pedigrees could take their chances under the new order as much as anyone else. After all, Barère and Saint-Just were thought to have been noble, even if they were not. Some 40 such *ci-devant nobles*, or former nobles, sat in the National Convention of September 1792–October 1795. Without noble (or rather, former noble) officers (Napoleon was one) the revolutionary army could not have achieved what it did. In the course of 1793 and 1794, the number of ex-noble officers slumped to under 900, but, despite all the ideological purges, it picked up during 1795 to exceed 1000, including some 100 general officers.[12] Among the more surprising men to have thrown in his lot with the Revolution was Louis-Nicolas-Hyacinthe Chérin, former court genealogist, son and (briefly, from 1787 to 1791) successor to the ennobled Bernard Chérin, who had served both Louis XV and Louis XVI in that capacity (Louis-Nicolas even praised in print the 1791 abolition of nobility and the loss of his own job).[13] He rose to become chief of staff of the joint armies of the Danube and Switzerland, dying of wounds during the siege of Zürich in June 1799.

Yet to conservative revolutionaries – and these included Sieyès himself – democratic rule had never been what they wanted: full political rights and political participation were for property owners. The excesses of the Revolution confirmed their views. Napoleon's *coup d'état* of 10 November 1799 was meant to save the Revolution from itself: the law of 14 December could announce to the world that 'the Revolution, grounded on the principles on which it began, IS OVER'. Real power, of course, passed to First Consul Bonaparte. And he it was who began the process of reconstituting a nobility. In this new dispensation, lineage did not cease to count, but it had to serve the state. Before 1799 was out, Bonaparte allowed select *émigré* nobles to return – not as nobles, but as 'individuals', including such great names as the marquis de La Fayette and the duc de la Rochefoucauld.[14] Most *émigrés* were amnestied on 30 October 1802; those who were prepared to pay court to the first consul began to find that they could get at least some confiscated estates back.

On 19 May 1802, to the consternation of die-hard revolutionaries, Bonaparte created the Légion d'Honneur (Legion of Honour), a new and supposedly meritocratic order of chivalry. Its beneficiaries were graded in hierarchies and often additionally rewarded with grants of land and pensions. By 1815, he had created about 30,000 *chevaliers*. It all smacked of putting the clock back, not least because of the large-scale rallying of the old aristocracy to the new regime. True, Bonaparte's judicial murder of the duc d'Enghien on 21 March 1804 scandalised the old European aristocracy. It was, said Tsar Alexander I's minister Prince Adam Czartoryski, an insult 'against the whole association of European states and even against humanity itself'.[15] But the scandal made little practical difference. In December 1804, Napoleon crowned himself emperor. What sort of emperor could there be without a court and all its trappings? A stream of new titles poured out on Napoleon's family and helpmates: kings, princes, dukes. In 1806, 22 imperial ducal fiefs were created. In May 1807, Napoleon created Marshal François-Joseph Lefebvre duke of Danzig, the first such hereditary creation outside his own immediate family. For a man who was the son of a miller and who had been a sergeant in 1788, it was a career trajectory unthinkable under Bourbon rule. His wife, now first duchess of the empire, had been a laundress. As for the old Bourbon aristocracy, 'they hurled themselves into my antechambers', said Napoleon of the many who sought his favours. Over a fifth of the 3263 imperial nobles (including 29 dukes, 500 counts and 1468 barons) he created between 1808 and 1814 were drawn from the old nobility.[16] They numbered such great names as Praslin, Luynes, Rohan, Colbert, Ségur.

Napoleon appreciated the value of these *hochets*, 'baubles', in driving and attaching men and women to his rule. He knew that the award of titles was a means of distinguishing men – of appealing to their vanity and their desire to be above others, a sign that they stood close to the centre of power. The decree of 1 May 1808 formalised the new nobility. There would henceforth be five titles: prince, duke, count, baron and *chevalier*. That same month Napoleon made Sieyès, already a *grand officier* of the Légion d'Honneur, a count of the empire. 'Have you seen Sieyès? Have you seen Sieyès? *Qu'est-ce que le Tiers État?*' whooped another delighted *chevalier* of the Légion.[17]

This was not, however, a return to the old regime.

> The French Revolution's essential achievement, which was never reversed, was not the destruction of the nobility as such ... but the destruction of the société d'ordres, which removed from the nobles, and from the members of a great variety of other groups, the particular social and economic privileges guaranteed them by law.[18]

This was a nobility that paid taxes, that enjoyed no seigneurial privileges, whose titles were, with some exceptions, purely titular (thus Marshal Lefebvre had no authority at all over his 'duchy' of Danzig) and overwhelmingly a reward for service, primarily military, but also civil. More successful soldiers might expect to be named princes or dukes; ministers or senators, counts; senior members of the judiciary, barons. This nobility might have enjoyed high salaries and generous landed endowments; but the old panoply of jurisdictions, dues and tributes was gone. In the early stages of the Revolution, there had indeed been plenty of voices that had been ready to accept a non-privileged nobility of merit.[19] The emperor was sufficiently conscious of old revolutionary sensibilities to restrict the new duchy-fiefdoms to Italy, without extending them to France proper. Their recipients received no jurisdictional powers over their inhabitants and most of the new dukes did not even reside in them. Though the holders enjoyed lucrative endowments and properties, these were rarely if ever situated within the new creations. Napoleon was determined that this should be an entirely dependent, and therefore co-operative, nobility. The new titles of nobility, right down to the level of *chevalier*, were not, however, entirely without privilege: their holders could transmit the title and their estate by strict entail and male primogeniture (which had otherwise been abolished by the Revolution and the Napoleonic Code), but only if they could guarantee levels of revenue appropriate to their rank (in the case of *chevaliers*, at least 3000 francs a year). 'I make something of a monarchy, in creating heredity, but I remain in the Revolution, because my nobility is not at all exclusive.' Napoleon was ever the pragmatist.

The constitutional charter of 4 June 1814, promulgated by Louis XVIII on his restoration, preserved the 'new' nobility while allowing the 'old' to resume their titles in full. This was more than just words, for the substance on which so many of the 'new' nobility depended for their incomes (and a significant proportion of the old), the so-called 'national lands', the properties confiscated from the Catholic Church by the Revolution, were guaranteed to their holders as 'inviolable'. Napoleon's brief adventure of 1815 did nothing substantially to alter this: only those few of his creations who rallied to him were penalised. Over the century, new and old nobilities gradually fused. The privileges of the old order of nobility remained in abeyance. Frenchmen would remain 'equal before the law, whatever may be their titles and ranks', and would continue to 'contribute without distinction, in proportion to their fortunes, towards the expenses of the state'.

The revolutionary and Napoleonic experiences demonstrated that the old nobility could survive in France. It was the same elsewhere. Few areas were as subject to as thorough and continuous French rule as the old kingdom of Sardinia–Piedmont, which was formally incorporated into the French republic after 1801. All noble titles, distinctions and privileges had been banned under French military occupation since December 1798. But the great majority of nobles held on to their lands and could continue to rely on the deference of the bourgeoisie. They did well out of the purchase of confiscated ecclesiastical lands and were very content to be counted among the new imperial nobility.[20] The French invaders simply preferred to work with the local ruling establishments of the parts of Europe they dominated – it was so much easier. Nor did nobles have to worry too much about the export of revolutionary principles under Napoleon. Where in central and eastern Europe serfdom was abolished in law, the reality of servile labour dues remained.

None of this is to suggest that the nobilities and gentry of Europe could look with equanimity on what was going on in France. No ruling order proved more adept at preserving and, if anything, strengthening its position than Britain's. Yet the events in France genuinely alarmed, even terrified, the great majority of the aristocracy and gentry, not least because 'Jacobin' rhetoric seemed to have a wide popular appeal. Tom Paine easily outsold Edmund Burke. There seemed to be a plethora of subversive 'Corresponding Societies' across the country. Some 100,000 people supposedly attended a rally in St George's Fields on the outskirts of London in June 1795, demanding peace and political reform. Rallies in Islington in October and November drew similar numbers. On 29 October, George III was mobbed in his carriage on the way to the House of Lords, gasping out on arrival, 'My Lord, I, I, I've been shot at!'[21] Only 15 years earlier, a mob had savaged London during the Gordon riots.

The ruling order could cope. To keep itself in power, it was prepared to violate the liberties it so proudly asserted belonged to every free-born Englishman and true Briton. Habeas corpus was suspended in May 1794; in December 1795, assemblies of more than 50 persons were banned without a magistrate's licence and it became a treasonable offence to incite hatred or contempt of king, government or constitution. More to the point, the ruling establishment proved itself adept at exploiting the French threat against radicals and would-be revolutionaries. The smashing up of Joseph Priestley's Birmingham home by a riot of loyal 'Church and King' subjects in July 1791, some 18 months before war with France, was only one of many such incidents. And once war with France had begun, very few were prepared publicly to support the Revolution. The ruling order in Great Britain emerged from the wars with France stronger than ever.

The threat to the survival of the *ancien régime* outside France only hit home in those territories that the French revolutionary armies actually conquered. But the French liberators were so often their own worst enemies. Where the 'liberation' of the oppressed peoples of Europe did take place – northern Italy, the Rhineland, the Low Countries (and, according to Napoleon, Egypt) – the overwhelming majority of the population manifested little gratitude for the military brutality, forced contributions, fiscal oppression and contempt for ancient and familiar customs that accompanied the new, revolutionary order. Napoleon's taming of the Revolution after 1799 served to provide a further springboard for a new military adventurism. His anti-democratic credentials offered little by way of consolation to the elites of Austria or Prussia or Russia. On the other hand, there were aspects of the transformation in France that offered plenty of attractions to governments, not least reactionary and repressive ones, outside it. The Revolution had, by abolishing privilege, cleared the decks for a professionalised, responsive state machine. There were those who could see the benefits of this. The Prussian minister Karl August von Struensee acknowledged as much to the French *chargé d'affaires* in 1799: 'the salutary revolution [of the abolition of privilege] you have made from below will come about gradually in Prussia from above'.[22] The brutality of the French experiment was not to be emulated, but monarchs could see that the abolition of privilege was a way of ending the reigns of 'little kings' and harnessing them more effectively than ever to their service.

Yet the Revolution had made the issue of democracy a serious item on the political agenda across Europe. 'The shadow of 1789 lay on Europe's nineteenth-century aristocracy.'[23] If it could happen in France, surely it could happen anywhere. At more or less the same time, the industrial revolution proved at least as potent a threat to the position of the aristocracy and landed classes. The demands of industry and the towns for the products of aristocratic estates also helped to boost aristocratic and landed incomes; so, too, did the expansion of towns for those who were fortunate enough to own what rapid urbanisation demanded. The sheer extent of landholdings and wealth among the European landed classes meant that if they were to be dislodged from their position at the top of society, it would almost certainly be a prolonged process. In the 1870s, around 600 British peers owned a good fifth of the land of England and Wales and around a tenth of all national income. Four-fifths of all the land in the United Kingdom was owned by fewer than 7000 people.[24] But this was precisely the decade in which their position began to be eroded on a large scale by forces beyond their control. That position, and the position of other landed aristocracies, ultimately rested on an unchanging, predominantly agrarian and uneducated society. Once large-scale industrialisation, and with it urbanisation, took hold, they were bound to be eased off their perches. The growth of education, the emergence of a professional middle class and the ambitions of politicians looking to extend their own power bases meant that landed aristocrats became more of a hindrance than a help, an embarrassment rather an asset, in running a country. The arrival of cheap American grain under-cut their economic base; the development of industry meant that new, plutocratic, industrialising wealth began to assert its claims and rights. Old, landed wealth was simply incapable of matching it; the democratic franchise had to be extended. Where it was not, the alternative was vio-lent revolution.

In the late nineteenth and twentieth centuries, the aristocracy became almost an irrelevance. There was no need to harness them to state service because amid growing democratic conditions there was no need for nobles or aristocrats. The aristocracy could draw on its still impressive material advantages and reinvent itself by adopting the professionalised outlook of the middle class, or by trading on its still considerable air of prestige and pedigree to act as a kind of ornament to civic and industrial activity – the plumage of Tom Paine's dying bird. As for the poor re-lations, they were degraded into a discontented intelligentsia or simply sank out of sight. But as a practical, utilitarian group that ruled and commanded society, its day was passing, even if slowly.[25] That demise was prefigured by the events and processes of the closing years of the eighteenth century.

NOTES

Preface

1. Those who wish to get a closer sense of the debates could do worse than consult R. Mousnier, *Social hierarchies* (London: Croom Helm, 1973; orig. French edn, Paris, 1969); and, more recently, the essays in *Social orders and social classes in Europe since 1500: studies in social stratification*, ed. M. L. Bush (Harlow: Longman, 1992).

Chapter 1: Nobility in the Eighteenth Century: An Introductory Survey

1. Articles 'Noble (*Jurisprud.*)' and 'Noblesse (*Jurisprud.*)' in the *Encyclopédie ou Dictionnaire raisonné des sciences, des arts, et des métiers, par une société de gens de lettres*, ed. Denis Diderot and Jean le Rond d'Alembert, 17 vols. (Paris, 1751–65), vol. 11 (1765), pp. 163, 167–81.
2. R. E. Jones, 'The Charter to the Nobility: a legislative landmark?', *Canadian–American Slavic Studies*, 23/1 (1989), pp. 2–3.
3. C. Donati, 'The Italian nobilities in the seventeenth and eighteenth centuries', in *The European nobilities in the seventeenth and eighteenth centuries*, ed. H. M. Scott (Harlow: Longman, 1995), vol. 2, pp. 237–68. The quotation is from Giovanni Botero, ibid., p. 239.
4. P. Higonnet, ' "Aristocrate," "Aristocratie": language and politics in the French Revolution', in *The French Revolution, 1789–1989: two hundred years of rethinking*, ed. S. Petrey (special issue of *The eighteenth century: theory and interpretation*, 1989), pp. 47–66.
5. L. Stone and J. C. F. Stone, *An open elite?: England, 1540–1880* (Oxford: Clarendon, 1984), p. 14; N. Landau, *The Justices of the Peace, 1679–1760* (Berkeley: University of California Press, 1984), pp. 152–60.
6. J. V. Beckett, *The aristocracy in England, 1660–1914* (Oxford: Blackwell, 1986), p. 34; figures from G. E. Mingay, *English landed society in the eighteenth century* (London: Routledge & Kegan Paul, 1970), pp. 19–26.
7. P. Jenkins, *The making of a ruling class: the Glamorgan gentry, 1640–1790* (Cambridge: Cambridge University Press, 1983), p. 16.

8. Article 'États' in the *Encyclopédie*, vol. 6 (1756), p. 26.

9. F. L. Carsten, 'La noblesse de Brandebourg et de Prusse du XVIe au XVIIIe siècles: ordre, caste ou classe sociale?', in *Problèmes de stratification sociale: actes du Colloque International, 1966*, ed. R. Mousnier (Paris: PUF, 1968), pp. 168–9.

10. J. M. Sallmann, 'Les biens communaux et la "réaction seigneuriale" en Artois', *Revue du Nord*, 57 (1976), pp. 210–11.

11. Work on such bodies in the eighteenth century is very limited. See the classic work by S. and B. Webb, *English local government*, vol. 2/1, *The manor and the borough* (London: Cass, 1963 edn), chs. 1–3; for an illuminating case study, see J. V. Beckett, *A history of Laxton: England's last open-field village* (Oxford: Blackwell, 1989), ch. 2.

12. C. de Saussure, quoted in Stone and Stone, *An open elite?*, p. 299.

13. Charles Louis de Secondat, baron de Montesquieu, *The spirit of the laws*, trans. and ed. A. M. Cohler, B. C. Miller and H. S. Stone (Cambridge: Cambridge University Press, 1989). See esp. Book III, chs. 6–7, Book IV, ch. 2, Book V, ch. 9.

14. Beckett, *Aristocracy in England*, pp. 25, 34–5.

15. N. Ravitch, 'The social origins of French and English bishops in the eighteenth century', *Historical Journal*, 8 (1965), pp. 309–25.

16. S. Carlsson, 'The dissolution of the Swedish estates (1700–1865)', *Journal of European Economic History*, 1/3 (1972), esp. pp. 604–8.

17. J. Cannon, *Aristocratic century: the peerage of eighteenth-century England* (Cambridge: Cambridge University Press, 1984), pp. 13–20; J. C. Davis, *The decline of the Venetian nobility as a ruling class* (Baltimore: Johns Hopkins, 1962), pp. 54–8.

18. E. Burke, *Reflections on the Revolution in France*, ed. C. C. O'Brien (Harmondsworth: Penguin, 1969), pp. 194–5.

19. Article 'Honneur' in the *Encyclopédie*, vol. 8 (1765), pp. 288–90.

20. For a full account, see R. Pomeau, *D'Arouet à Voltaire, 1694–1734* (Oxford: Taylor Foundation, 1985) (*Voltaire en son temps*, vol. 1), pp. 203–9.

21. U. Frevert, *Men of honour: a social and cultural history of the duel* (Cambridge: Polity, 1995), pp. 20–1.

22. I. de Madariaga, 'Penal policy in the age of Catherine II', in I. de Madariaga, *Politics and culture in eighteenth-century Russia* (Harlow: Longman, 1998), p. 116.

23. F. McLynn, *Crime and punishment in eighteenth-century England* (London: Routledge, 1989), pp. 149, 150–1, 265, 266.

24. K. J. V. Jespersen, 'The rise and fall of the Danish nobility, 1600–1800', in *European nobilities*, ed. Scott, vol. 2, pp. 45, 56–64.

24. J. L. Price, 'The Dutch nobility in the seventeenth and eighteenth centuries', in ibid., pp. 84–8.

26. J.-D. Bredin, *Sieyès: la clé de la révolution française* (Paris: Fallois, 1988), pp. 104–22; G. Chaussinand-Nogaret, *The French nobility in the eighteenth century: from feudalism to Enlightenment*, trans. W. Doyle (Cambridge: Cambridge University Press, 1985; French original, 1976); cf. J. Meyer, 'La noblesse française au XVIIIe siècle: aperçu des problèmes', *Acta Poloniae Historica*, vol. 36 (1977), esp. pp. 7–21. This article contains, among other things,

a trenchant critique of some of Chaussinand-Nogaret's estimates. See also V. R. Gruder, *The royal provincial intendants: a governing elite in eighteenth-century France* (Ithaca, NY: Cornell University Press, 1968), pp. 176–7; R. Butler, *Choiseul*, vol. 1 (Oxford: Oxford University Press, 1980), pp. 250–1. Disagreements among historians of this calibre are a measure of the confusion surrounding such elementary information.

27. W. G. Monteiro, 'Noblesse et aristocratie en Portugal sous l'Ancien Régime (XVIIe – début du XIXe siècles)', *Revue d'Histoire Moderne et Contemporaine*, 46/1 (1999), pp. 185–210.

28. Montesquieu, 'Mes pensées', *Oeuvres complètes*, ed. G. Vedel and D. Oster (Paris: Éditions du Seuil, 1964), p. 1034.

29. *Letters of Lord Chesterfield to his son* (London: Dent, 1929), p. 95. Letters of 28 Feb and 6 July (Old Style) 1749, pp. 95, 96, 109.

30. R. Butterwick, *Poland's last king and English culture: Stanisław August Poniatowski, 1732–1798* (Oxford: Clarendon, 1998), pp. 102–23.

31. E. Pelzer, *Der elsässische Adel im Spätfeudalismus* (Munich: Oldenbourg, 1990), pp. 181–5.

32. C. Duhamelle, 'Les noblesses du Saint-Empire du milieu du XVIe au milieu du XVIIIe siècle', *Revue d'Histoire Moderne et Contemporaine*, 46/1 (1999), pp. 146–70.

33. W. Doyle, *The parlement of Bordeaux and the end of the Old Regime, 1771–1790* (London: Benn, 1974), p. 19.

34. J. A. Lynch, *Bourbon Spain, 1700–1808* (Oxford: Blackwell, 1989), pp. 60, 66.

35. K. Maxwell, *Pombal: paradox of the Enlightenment* (Cambridge: Cambridge University Press, 1995), pp. 78–86.

36. Lynch, *Bourbon Spain*, pp. 62–6.

37. Carlsson, 'The dissolution of the Swedish estates', pp. 574–624.

Chapter 2: Ennoblement

1. Quoted in T. Esper, 'The *odnodvortsy* and the Russian nobility', *Slavonic and East European Review*, 45 (1967), p. 131.

2. G. Holmes, *British politics in the age of Anne* (London: Hambledon, 1987 edn), pp. 395–6.

3. Robert Walpole, quoted in Clyve Jones, ' "Venice Preserv'd; or A Plot Discovered": the political and social context of the Peerage Bill of 1719', in *A pillar of the constitution: the House of Lords in British politics, 1640–1784*, ed. C. Jones (London: Hambledon, 1989), pp. 79–112, here p. 103.

4. W. J. Callahan, *Honor, commerce and industry in eighteenth-century Spain* (Clifton, NJ: A. M. Kelley, 1972), pp. 28–9.

5. Davis, *Venetian nobility*, pp. 96–7, 118–23.

6. Donati, 'Italian nobilities', in *European nobilities*, ed. Scott, vol. 1, pp. 246–7.

7. For more detail on this extraordinary phenomenon, see J. Goldberg, 'Die getauften Juden in Polen–Litauen im 16.–18. Jahrhundert', *Jahrbücher für Geschichte Osteuropas*, NF, 30 (1982), pp. 54–99.

8. A. F. Upton, 'The Swedish nobility, 1600–1772', in *European nobilities*, ed. Scott, vol. 2, p. 30; Donati, 'Italian nobilities', in ibid., vol. 1, pp. 237–68 is an heroic attempt to portray the bewildering complexities found in almost every region of Italy. Price undertakes a similar task for the almost equally confusing situation in the United Provinces in 'Dutch nobility', in ibid., vol. 1, pp. 82–113. See also J. M. Roberts, 'Lombardy', in *The European nobility in the eighteenth century*, ed. A. Goodwin (London: Black, 1967), pp. 64–7.

9. Davis, *Venetian nobility*, p. 117; J. Georgelin, *Venise au siècle des Lumières* (Paris: Mouton, 1978), pp. 620, 627, 646–8.

10. I. A. A. Thompson, 'The nobility in Spain, 1600–1800', in *European nobilities*, ed. Scott, vol. 1, pp. 219–21.

11. C. B. A. Behrens, *Society, government and the Enlightenment: the experiences of eighteenth-century France and Prussia* (London: Thames & Hudson, 1985), p. 50; *Allgemeines Landrecht für die Preussischen Staaten von 1794*, ed. H. Hattenheuer (Neuwied: Luchterhand, 1996 edn), p. 541.

12. H. Carré, *La noblesse de France et l'opinion publique au XVIIIe siècle* (Paris: Honoré Champion, 1920; Geneva, Slatkine reprint, 1977), p. 12.

13. The foregoing is based on R. Mousnier, *The institutions of France under the absolute monarchy, 1589–1789*. Vol. 1, *Society and the state* (Chicago: Chicago University Press, 1979), pp. 482–3; R. Forster, *The nobility of Toulouse in the eighteenth century* (Baltimore: Johns Hopkins, 1960), p. 208; Y. Durand, *Vivre au pays au XVIIIe siècle* (Paris: PUF, 1984), p. 131; K. Böse, 'Amt und sozialer Aufstieg: die Familie Guillaume de Chavaudon', in *Ämterkäuflichkeit: Aspekte sozialer Mobilität im europäischen Vergleich*, ed. K. Malettke (Berlin: Colloquium, 1980), pp. 53–8; G. V. Taylor, 'Types of capitalism in eighteenth-century France', *English Historical Review*, 79 (1964), pp. 480–1; W. Doyle, *Venality: the sale of offices in eighteenth-century France* (Oxford: Clarendon, 1996), p. 157.

14. M. Cubells, *La Provence des Lumières: les parlementaires d'Aix au 18ème siècle* (Paris: Maloine, 1984), p. 204.

15. Carré, *La noblesse*, pp. 12–13; P. Higonnet, *Class, ideology and the rights of nobles during the French Revolution* (Oxford: Clarendon, 1981), pp. 140, 209–10.

16. C. B. A. Behrens, 'Government and society', in *Cambridge economic history of Europe*, vol. 5, ed. E. E. Rich and C. H. Wilson (Cambridge: Cambridge University Press, 1977), pp. 564–5.

17. See the comments by W. Doyle, 'The price of offices in pre-revolutionary France', *Historical Journal*, 27 (1984), pp. 832–3.

18. Böse, 'Amt und sozialer Aufstieg', pp. 53–8.

19. Doyle, *Venality*, pp. 11, 31. This is now the standard treatment of the subject.

20. R. G. Wilson, 'The Denisons and Milneses: eighteenth-century merchant landowners', in *Land and industry: the landed estate and the industrial revolution*, ed. J. T. Ward and R. G. Wilson (Newton Abbot: David & Charles, 1971), pp. 145–72.

21. Gruder, *The royal provincial intendants*, pp. 120–2.

22. D. Bien, 'Manufacturing nobles: the chancelleries in France to 1789', *Journal of Modern History*, 61 (1989), pp. 445–86, here p. 463.

23. Doyle, *Venality*, pp. 122, 163–6.
24. Chaussinand-Nogaret, *The French nobility in the eighteenth century*, p. 34; C. B. A. Behrens, 'Nobles, privileges and taxes in France at the end of the Ancien Régime', *Economic History Review*, 2nd ser., 15 (1962–3), pp. 456–7.
25. Bien, 'Manufacturing nobles', pp. 469–71. Most of these posts were in any case suppressed in 1715 and then offered for re-sale at a more 'normal' price of 20,000 *livres*.
26. Quoted in Callahan, *Honor, commerce and industry*, p. 10.
27. See the comments in M. Reinhard, 'Élite et noblesse dans la seconde moitié du XVIIIe siècle', *Revue d'Histoire Moderne et Contemporaine*, 3 (1965), pp. 14–25.
28. G. Richard, *Noblesse d'affaires au XVIIIe siècle* (Paris: Colin, 1974), pp. 87–8.
29. See the contributions of F. Tomás y Valiente, 'Les ventes des offices publics en Castille'; I. Mieck, 'Vénalité des offices et mobilité sociale en Castille comme problème de la recherche historique'; J. Böer, 'Aspekte der Ämterkäuflichkeit in Valladolid (Altkastilien) im 18. Jahrhundert', all in *Ämterkäuflichkeit*, ed. Malettke, pp. 89–114, 115–21, 122–4.
30. Cubells, *Provence*, pp. 53–6, 63; Doyle, 'Price of offices', p. 837.
31. Carré, *La noblesse*, pp. 42–4; J.-P. Brancourt, 'Un théoricien de la société au XVIII siècle: le chevalier d'Arcq', *Revue Historique*, 250 (1973), pp. 337–62, here 338–9; B. R. Kroener, 'Militärischer Professionalismus und soziale Karriere: der französische Adel in den europäischen Kriegen, 1740–1763', in *Europa im Zeitalter Friedrichs des Grossen: Wirtschaft, Gesellschaft, Kriege*, ed. B. Kroener (Munich: Oldenbourg, 1989), p. 106; D. Bien, 'La réaction aristocratique avant 1789: l'exemple de l'armée', *Annales, ESC*, 29 (1974), pp. 29–35.
32. Figures based on P. M. G. Dickson, *Finance and government under Maria Theresa, 1740–1780* (Oxford: Clarendon, 1992), vol. 1, pp. 79–82. The data especially for Charles VI and Maria Theresa are incomplete; here they refer only to non-titled ennoblements.
33. Carlsson, 'Dissolution', pp. 574–624.
34. Thompson, 'The nobility in Spain', pp. 220–1.
35. C. Duffy, *The army of Frederick the Great* (Newton Abbot: David & Charles, 1974), pp. 27–8.
36. I am unaware of any complete translation of the Table of Ranks into English. For the Russian text, see *Polnoe Sobranie Zakonov Rossiiskoi Imperii* (St Petersburg, 1826–1913), no. 3890.
37. W. M. Pintner, 'The evolution of civil officialdom, 1755–1855', in *Russian officialdom: the bureaucratization of Russian society from the seventeenth to the twentieth century*, ed. W. M. Pintner and D. K. Rowney (London: Macmillan, 1980), pp. 190–226.
38. Reinhard, 'Élite et noblesse', pp. 14–15.
39. Callahan, *Honor, commerce and industry*, pp. 17–18, 34–6.
40. J. M. Hittle, *The service city: state and townsmen in Russia, 1600–1800* (Cambridge, MA: Harvard University Press, 1979), pp. 198–9, 216–23.
41. Behrens, *Society, government and the Enlightenment*, p. 64; *Allgemeines Landrecht*, pp. 350, 352, 458, 460, 544–8.
42. Quoted in Doyle, *Venality*, p. 64. See also ibid., pp. 72–3, 104–5, 134–6, 147.

43. D. Bien, 'La réaction aristocratique', pp. 23–48, 505–34.
44. A. Goodwin, 'The social structure and economic and political attitudes of the French nobility in the eighteenth century', *XIIe Congrès International des Sciences Historiques, 1965. Rapports*, vol. 1 (Horn, Vienna: Ferdinand Burger, 1966), p. 358.
45. J. Egret, 'L'aristocratie parlementaire française à la fin de l'Ancien Régime', *Revue Historique*, 208 (1952), pp. 5–6, 11; Bien, 'Réaction aristocratique', pp. 526–8.
46. Higonnet, *Class, ideology and the rights of nobles*, pp. 52–3.

Chapter 3: The Nobility and the State

1. Quoted in J. S. Shaw, *The management of Scottish society, 1707–1764: power, nobles, lawyers, Edinburgh agents and English influences* (Edinburgh: John Donald, 1983), p. 2.
2. Carré, *La noblesse*, pp. 22–8; Goodwin, 'Social structure', p. 358. For the most accessible survey of European court life, see *The princely courts of Europe: ritual, politics and culture under the Ancien Régime, 1500–1700*, ed. J. Adamson (London: Weidenfeld & Nicolson, 1999).
3. R. Forster, *The house of Saulx-Tavanes: Versailles and Burgundy* (Baltimore: Johns Hopkins, 1971), pp. 10–20, 41–51.
4. T. M. Barker, 'Military nobility: the Daun family and the evolution of the Austrian officer corps', in his *Army, aristocracy, monarchy: essays on war, society, and government in Austria, 1618–1780* (New York: Columbia University Press, 1982), pp. 128–46.
5. Esper, 'The *odnodvortsy* and the Russian nobility', pp. 124–34.
6. For these figures, see J. P. Le Donne, *Absolutism and ruling class: the formation of the Russian political order, 1700–1825* (New York: Oxford University Press, 1991), p. 22, who warns that accurate data before 1782 are very scant. On the other hand, C. B. Stevens, *Soldiers on the steppe: army reform and social change in early modern Russia* (DeKalb, N. Illinois University Press: 1995), pp. 18–19, estimates there were 200,000 *po otechestvu* (hereditary) servitors in the provinces alone: if so, the Table of Ranks must have led to a massive reduction in the numbers of those for whom equivalence with 'nobles' might be claimed.
7. Price, 'Dutch nobility', in *European nobilities*, ed. Scott, vol. 1, pp. 82–113.
8. Upton, 'The Swedish nobility', in ibid., vol. 2, p. 32.
9. C. W. Ingrao, *The Hessian mercenary state: ideas, institutions, and reform under Frederick II, 1760–1785* (Cambridge: Cambridge University Press, 1987), pp. 39–44, 59; K. Vetter, 'Die Stände im absolutistischen Preussen', *Zeitschrift für Geschichtswissenschaft*, 24 (1976), pp. 1290–306.
10. U. Dann, *Hanover and Great Britain, 1740–1760: diplomacy and survival* (Leicester: Leicester University Press, 1991), p. 4.
11. Z. E. Kohut, 'The Ukrainian elite in the eighteenth century and its integration into the Russian nobility', in *The nobility in Russia and eastern Europe*,

ed. I. Banac and P. Bushkovitch (New Haven, CN: Yale University Press, 1983), pp. 65–97.

12. See the comments of B. Meehan-Waters, 'Social and career characteristics of the administrative elite, 1689–1761', in *Russian officialdom*, ed. Pintner and Rowney, esp. pp. 85–6.

13. J. Casey, *Early modern Spain: a social history* (London: Routledge, 1999), pp. 111–37.

14. Davis, *Venetian nobility*, pp. 47–72; Georgelin, *Venise au siècle des Lumières*, pp. 651–66.

15. Quoted in Dickson, *Finance and government under Maria Theresa*, vol. 1, p. 391.

16. C. Brooks, 'Public finance and political stability: the administration of the Land tax, 1688–1720', *Historical Journal*, 17 (1974), pp. 281–300; Landau, *Justices of the Peace*, pp. 27–33. D. E. Ginter's *A measure of wealth: the English land tax in historical analysis* (London: Hambledon, 1992) is a forbidding critical look at the problems of interpreting the data, but it is permeated by perceptive comments on the strength of local influence and tradition. The best general treatment of English fiscality is J. Brewer, *The sinews of power: war, money and the English state, 1688–1783* (London: Unwin Hyman, 1989).

17. M. Marion, *Dictionnaire des institutions de la France aux XVIIe et XVIIIe siècles* (Paris: Picard, 1972; reprint of 1927 edn), pp. 69–71.

18. R. Bonney, ' "Le secret de leurs familles": the fiscal and social limits of Louis XIV's *Dixième*', *French History*, 7/4 (1993), pp. 383–416.

19. P. M. Jones, *Reform and Revolution in France: the politics of transition, 1774–1791* (Cambridge: Cambridge University Press, 1995), p. 64.

20. Forster, *The house of Saulx-Tavanes*, pp. 104–5; K. Norberg, 'The French fiscal crisis of 1788 and the financial origins of the revolution of 1789', in *Fiscal crises, liberty, and representative government, 1450–1789*, ed. P. T. Hoffman and K. Norberg (Stanford, CA: Stanford University Press, 1994), p. 265; M. Kwass, 'A kingdom of taxpayers: state formation, privilege, and political culture in eighteenth-century France', *Journal of Modern History*, 70/2 (1998), pp. 295–339.

21. I. G. Toth, 'Le monde de la petite noblesse hongroise au XVIIIe siècle', *Revue d'Histoire Moderne et Contemporaine*, 46/1 (1999), pp. 171–84.

22. Kwass, 'A kingdom of taxpayers', pp. 317–18.

23. R. J. P. Kain and E. Baigent, *The cadastral survey in the service of the state: a history of property mapping* (Chicago: Chicago University Press, 1992), here esp. pp. 182–95, 212–24.

24. R. Herr, *Rural change and royal finances in Spain at the end of the Old Regime* (Berkeley: University of California Press, 1989), pp. 7–10.

25. The exemptions could also apply to others, not just nobles. G. T. Matthews, *The royal general farms in eighteenth-century France* (New York: Columbia University Press, 1958), pp. 145–65.

26. Behrens, *Society, government and the Enlightenment*, p. 462.

27. Kwass, 'A kingdom of taxpayers', pp. 321–3.

28. R. Gates-Coon, *The landed estates of the Esterházy princes: Hungary during the reforms of Maria Theresa and Joseph II* (Baltimore: Johns Hopkins University Press, 1994), p. 9; P. Jenkins, *The making of a ruling class: the Glamorgan gentry, 1640–1790* (Cambridge: Cambridge University Press, 1983), p. 82.

29. O. Büsch, *Militärsystem und Sozialleben im alten Preussen* (Berlin: Colloquium, 1962), p. 104.
30. R. L. Daniels, 'V. N. Tatishchev and the succession crisis of 1730', *Slavonic and East European Review*, 49 (1971), pp. 551–2.
31. Quoted in Higonnet, *Class, ideology and the rights of nobles*, p. 49.
32. Quoted in Doyle, *Venality*, p. 122.
33. Quoted in F. A. J. Szabo, *Kaunitz and enlightened absolutism, 1753–1780* (Cambridge: Cambridge University Press, 1994), p. 158.

Chapter 4: Education

1. See Kroener, 'Militärischer Professionalismus und soziale Karriere', pp. 99–100.
2. Article 'Histoire' in *Encyclopédie*, vol. 8 (1765), pp. 222–3.
3. John Locke, *Some thoughts concerning education*, ed. J. W. and J. S. Yolton (Oxford: Clarendon, 1989), p. 217.
4. C. Hibberd, *The Grand Tour* (London: Weidenfeld, 1969), pp. 55–6.
5. Locke, *Some thoughts concerning education*, p. 215.
6. G. Hanlon, *The twilight of a military tradition: Italian aristocrats and European conflicts, 1560–1800* (London: UCL, 1998), p. 344; M. Motley, *Becoming a French aristocrat: the education of the court nobility, 1580–1715* (Princeton, NJ: Princeton University Press, 1990), p. 150.
7. M. V. Wallbank, 'Eighteenth-century public schools and the education of the governing elite', *History of Education*, 8 (1979), pp. 1–19.
8. Locke, *Some thoughts concerning education*, p. 208.
9. Ibid., pp. 235, 261.
10. See Butler, *Choiseul*, vol. 1, pp. 133–41.
11. M. Grandière, 'L'éducation en France à la fin du XVIIIe siècle: quelques aspects d'un nouveau cadre éducatif, les "maisons d'éducation", 1760–1790', *Revue d'Histoire Moderne et Contemporaine*, 33 (1986), pp. 440–62.
12. H. Vautrin, *La Pologne du XVIIIe siècle vue par un précepteur français*, ed. M. Cholewo-Flandrin (Paris: Calmann-Levy, 1966).
13. Quoted in Wallbank, 'Eighteenth-century public schools', p. 4.
14. Cannon, *Aristocratic century*, pp. 39–44.
15. Ibid., p. 54; Wallbank, 'Eighteenth-century public schools', pp. 7–10.
16. Cannon, *Aristocratic century*, pp. 44–54.
17. Doyle, *The parlement of Bordeaux*, p. 24; Cubells, *Provence*, pp. 250–2.
18. On the *Ritterakademien* of Prussia, see R. Dorwart, *The Prussian welfare state before 1740* (Cambridge, MA: Harvard University Press, 1971), pp. 202–5, 207.
19. C. McClelland, *State, society and university in Germany, 1700–1914* (Cambridge: Cambridge University Press, 1980), pp. 27–57.
20. The comment is less applicable to the Ukraine or to the Baltic provinces. See M. J. Okenfuss, *The rise and fall of Latin humanism in early-modern Russia: pagan authors, Ukrainians, and the resiliency of Muscovy* (Leiden: Brill, 1995). For the quotation from Lomonosov, see p. 169.

21. W. W. Hagen, 'Seventeenth-century crisis in Brandenburg: the Thirty
     Years' War, the destabilization of serfdom, and the rise of absolutism',
     American Historical Review, 94/2 (1989), p. 334.
22. M. Hochedlinger, 'Mars ennobled: the ascent of the military and the crea-
     tion of a military nobility in mid-eighteenth-century Austria', *German
     History*, 17/2 (1999), pp. 141–76.
23. Carré, *La noblesse*, pp. 154–60, 207; J. Chagniot, 'L'art de guerre', in *His-
     toire militaire de la France*, ed. J. Delmas (Paris: PUF, 1992), vol. 2, pp. 68–75.
     On the erratic quality of Prussian schooling, see C. Duffy, *The army of Fred-
     erick the Great* (Newton Abbot: David & Charles, 1974), pp. 28–31.
24. J. P. Le Donne, 'Local politics in Catherine's Russia: the Gorokhov case',
     Cahiers du Monde Russe et Soviétique, 27/2 (1986), pp. 153–71, here pp. 154–5.
25. J. Cracraft, *The Church reform of Peter the Great* (London: Macmillan, 1971),
     pp. 93–4, 272–3; L. Hughes, *Russia in the age of Peter the Great* (New Haven,
     CN: Yale University Press, 1998), pp. 174–5, 300–9; Okenfuss, *Rise and fall*,
     passim. See also ch. 4 of Marc Raeff's classic work, *The origins of the Russian
     intelligentsia: the eighteenth-century nobility* (New York: Harcourt, Brace and
     World, 1966).
26. The comte de Preux to his sister, commenting on his income of 10,000–
     12,000 *livres*. Quoted in R. Forster, 'The French provincial noble: a reap-
     praisal', *American Historical Review*, 68 (1963), p. 691.
27. Hibberd, *The Grand Tour* (London: Weidenfeld, 1969), pp. 24–5, 44;
     A. Young, *Travels in France and Italy* (London: Dent, 1976), p. 27.
28. Hibberd, *The Grand Tour*, p. 10.
29. P. M. Jones, 'Living the Enlightenment and the French Revolution: James
     Watt, Matthew Boulton, and their sons', *Historical Journal*, 42/1 (1999),
     pp. 162–3.

Chapter 5: Resources

1. Quoted in J. Casey, *Early modern Spain: a social history* (London: Routledge,
    1999), p. 144; and R. M. Berdahl, *The politics of the Prussian nobility: the devel-
    opment of a conservative ideology, 1770–1848* (Princeton: Princeton University
    Press, 1988), p. 84. Cf. Büsch, *Militärsystem*, p. 135.
2. B. H. Slicher van Bath, 'Eighteenth-century agriculture on the continent of
    Europe: evolution or revolution?', *Agricultural History*, 42 (1968), p. 174;
    idem, 'Agriculture in the vital revolution', in *The Cambridge economic history
    of Europe*, vol. 5, ed. Rich and Wilson, pp. 69–70. For an accessible intro-
    duction to this vexed and complex question, see D. H. Fischer, *The great
    wave: price revolutions and the rhythm of history* (Oxford: Oxford University
    Press, 1996), pp. 102–10, 120–56.
3. G.E. Mingay, 'Thrumpton: a Nottinghamshire estate in the eighteenth
    century', *Transactions of the Thoroton Society*, 61 (1957), pp. 50–6.
4. F. C. Mougel, 'La fortune des princes de Bourbon-Conty: revenus et ges-
    tion, 1655–1791', *Revue d'Histoire Moderne et Contemporaine*, 18 (1971),
    pp. 30–49.

5. T. Astarita, *The continuity of feudal power: the Caracciolo di Brienza in Spanish Naples* (Cambridge: Cambridge University Press, 1992), pp. 82–7, 107.

6. W. Kula, *An economic theory of the feudal system: towards a model of the Polish economy, 1500–1800* (London: NLB, 1976), pp. 119–33. See also J. Blum, *The end of the old order in rural Europe* (Princeton, NJ: Princeton University Press, 1978), pp. 241–4.

7. B. N. Mironov, 'Consequences of the price revolution in eighteenth-century Russia', *Economic History Review*, 2nd ser., 45/3 (1992), pp. 457–78.

8. G. S. Ford, 'The Prussian peasantry before 1807', *American Historical Review*, 24/3 (1919), pp. 360–4, 368; H. Harnisch, 'Peasants and markets: the background to the agrarian reforms in feudal Prussia east of the Elbe, 1760–1807', in *The German peasantry: conflict and community in rural society from the eighteenth to the twentieth centuries*, ed. R. J. Evans and W. R. Lee (London: Croom Helm, 1986), pp. 41–3; Ingrao, *The Hessian mercenary state*, pp. 69–70.

9. W. W. Hagen, 'The Junkers' faithless servants: peasant insubordination and the breakdown of serfdom in Brandenburg–Prussia, 1763–1811', in *The German peasantry*, ed. Evans and Lee, pp. 71–101. Cf. Harnisch, 'Peasants and markets', in ibid., p. 48.

10. D. Brown, 'Reassessing the influence of the aristocratic improver: the example of the fifth duke of Bedford (1765–1802)', *Agricultural History Review*, 47/2 (1999), p. 194.

11. J. V. Beckett, 'Landownership and estate management', in *The agrarian history of England and Wales*, vol. 6 (1750–1850), ed. J. Thirsk (Cambridge: Cambridge University Press, 1989), pp. 590–1; J. R. Wordie, *Estate management in eighteenth-century England: the building of the Leveson-Gower fortune* (London: Royal Historical Society, 1982), p. 185.

12. P. M. Jones, *Reform and revolution in France: the politics of transition, 1774–1791* (Cambridge: Cambridge University Press, 1995), pp. 83–8.

13. A. Donovan, *Antoine Lavoisier: science, administration, and revolution* (Oxford: Blackwell, 1993), pp. 203–4.

14. R. Carr, 'Spain', in *The European nobility in the eighteenth century*, ed. Goodwin, pp. 50–1; R. Herr, *Rural change and royal finances in Spain at the end of the Old Regime* (Berkeley: University of California Press, 1989), pp. 27–9, 38–41.

15. Beckett, 'Landownership and estate management', pp. 598–608.

16. Slicher van Bath, 'Eighteenth-century agriculture', pp. 169–79; L. Żytkowicz, 'Grain yields in Poland, Bohemia, Hungary and Slovakia in the 16th to 18th centuries', *Acta Poloniae Historica*, 24 (1971), pp. 51–72.

17. Harnisch, 'Peasants and markets', pp. 47–8.

18. M. Confino, *Domaines et seigneurs en Russie vers la fin du XVIIIe siècle* (Paris: Institut d'Études Slaves, 1963), pp. 51–2.

19. Quoted in ibid., p. 95.

20. Butler, *Choiseul*, vol. 1, p. 958.

21. Forster, *The house of Saulx-Tavanes*, pp. 55–128.

22. Confino, *Domaines et seigneurs*, pp. 48–51, 71–3.

23. H. L. Root, 'Challenging the seigneurie: community and contention on the eve of the French Revolution', *Journal of Modern History*, 57/4 (1985), pp. 652–81.

24. Quoted in G. Zeller, 'Une notion de caractère historico-social: la dérogeance', *Cahiers Internationaux de Sociologie*, n.s., 22 (1957), pp. 40–74, here p. 53.

25. J. P. Le Donne, 'Indirect taxes in Catherine's Russia, II. The liquor monopoly', *Jahrbücher für Geschichte Osteuropas*, 24/2 (1976), pp. 173–207; A. Kahan, *The plow, the hammer and the knout: an economic history of eighteenth-century Russia* (Chicago: Chicago University Press, 1985), pp. 320–3.

26. Pelzer, *Der elsässische Adel im Spätfeudalismus*, pp. 119–25, 157–72.

27. A.-G. Boucher d'Argis, 'Noblesse verrière', in the *Encyclopédie*, vol. 11, pp. 179–80.

28. Ibid., vol. 11, p. 171; Carré, *La noblesse*, pp. 21–2; Zeller, ' Une notion de caractère historico-social', pp. 40–74.

29. A.-G. Boucher d'Argis, 'États', in *Encyclopédie*, vol. 6 (1756), pp. 20–8.

30. R. Forster, *Merchants, landlords, magistrates: the Depont family in eighteenth-century France* (Baltimore: Johns Hopkins, 1980), pp. 4–14.

31. G. Richard, *Noblesse d'affaires au XVIIIᵉ siècle* (Paris: Colin, 1974), pp. 39–44, 199–201.

32. T. J. Raybould, 'The development and organization of Lord Dudley's mineral estates, 1774–1845', *Economic History Review*, 2nd ser., 21 (1968), pp. 529–44; *idem*, 'Aristocratic landowners and the industrial revolution: the Black Country experience, c. 1760–c. 1840', *Midland History*, 9 (1984), pp. 59–86; Beckett, 'Landownership and estate management', p. 579.

33. M. Roberts, 'Sweden', in *The European nobility in the eighteenth century*, ed. Goodwin, pp. 142–3.

34. Richard, *Noblesse d'affaires*, pp. 147–79.

35. Ibid., pp. 121–84.

36. Callahan, *Honor, commerce and industry*, pp. 18–26.

37. F. Sheppard, 'The Grosvenor estates, 1677–1977', *History Today* (Nov. 1977), pp. 726–33; D. Cannadine, *Lords and landlords: the aristocracy and the towns, 1774–1967* (Leicester: Leicester University Press, 1980), pp. 85–92.

38. G. E. Mingay, *English landed society in the eighteenth century* (London: Routledge & Kegan Paul, 1970), pp. 196–9; Wordie, *Estate management*, pp. 143–4. For a detailed account, see H. Malet, *Bridgewater: the canal duke, 1736–1803* (Manchester: Manchester University Press, 1977).

39. Richard, *Noblesse d'affaires*, pp. 72–119.

40. Jenkins, *The making of a ruling class*, p. 57.

41. J. B. Collins, *The state in early modern France* (Cambridge: Cambridge University Press, 1995), p. 237.

42. G. Blakiston, *Woburn and the Russells* (London: Constable, 1980), pp. 128–9.

43. J. H. Brown, 'The free economic society and the nobility, 1765–96: some observations', *Canadian–American Slavic Studies*, 14/3 (1980), pp. 427–35.

44. Forster, *The nobility of Toulouse*, pp. 106–16; *idem*, *Merchants, landlords, magistrates*, pp. 23, 72.

45. R. E. Giesey, 'Rules of inheritance and strategies of mobility in prerevolutionary France', *American Historical Review*, 82 (1977), pp. 271–89; cf. Böse, 'Amt und sozialer Aufstieg', pp. 53–8.

46. Giesey, 'Rules of inheritance', pp. 279–80.
47. Forster, *Merchants, landlords, magistrates*, pp. 152–8.
48. H. Glassl, *Das österreichisches Einrichtungswerk in Galizien (1772–1790)* (Wiesbaden: Harrassowitz, 1975), p. 96.
49. Beckett, 'Landownership and estate management', pp. 635–7.
50. D. Sugarman and R. Warrington, 'Land law, citizenship and the invention of "Englishness": the strange world of the equity of redemption', in *Early modern conceptions of property*, ed. J. Brewer and S. Staves (London: Routledge, 1995), pp. 111–43.
51. Ibid., p. 117.
52. C. Clay, 'Marriage, inheritance and the rise of large estates in England, 1660–1815', *Economic History Review*, 2nd ser., 21 (1968), p. 513.
53. Herr, *Rural change*, pp. 1–3, 45–6.
54. Hagen, 'The Junkers' faithless servants', p. 79; Büsch, *Militärsystem*, pp. 104–9, 150–5.
55. Blum, *The end of the old order*, pp. 168–70; E. Melton, 'The Prussian Junkers, 1600–1786', in *European nobilities*, ed. Scott, vol. 2, p. 103.
56. Berdahl, *The politics of the Prussian nobility*, pp. 83–4.
57. L. Namier, *The structure of politics at the accession of George III* (London: Macmillan – now Palgrave Macmillan, 1973), pp. 221–5.
58. R. E. McGrew, 'The politics of absolutism: Paul I and the Bank of Assistance for the Nobility', in *Paul I: a reassessment of his life and reign*, ed. H. Ragsdale (Pittsburgh: Pittsburgh University Press, 1979), p. 105.
59. Ibid., pp. 104–24; Kahan, *The plow, the hammer and the knout*, pp. 311–15; Le Donne, *Absolutism and ruling class*, pp. 247–9.
60. A. Kahan, 'The costs of "westernization" in Russia: the gentry and the economy in the eighteenth century', *Slavic Review*, 25 (1966), pp. 40–66.
61. R. E. Jones, *The emancipation of the Russian nobility, 1762–1785* (Princeton, NJ: Princeton University Press, 1973), pp. 19–27.
62. For the full ramifications, see ibid., *passim*; R. E. McGrew, *Paul I of Russia, 1754–1801* (Oxford: Clarendon, 1992), pp. 223–4. For some individual cases of noble hardship, see C. S. Nash, 'Students and nobles: the Society for the Education of Noble Girls as a charitable institution', in *Russia and the world of the eighteenth century*, ed. R. P. Bartlett, A. G. Cross and K. Rasmussen (Columbus, OH: Slavica, 1988), pp. 262–3.
63. Carsten, 'La noblesse de Brandebourg et de Prusse', pp. 163–4; Büsch, *Militärsystem*, pp. 2, 83, 95, 110–33.
64. See J. Meyer, 'Un problème mal posé: la noblesse pauvre. L'exemple breton au XVIIe [sc. XVIIIe] siècle', *Revue d'Histoire Moderne et Contemporaine*, 18 (1971), pp. 161–88.
65. Berdahl, *The politics of the Prussian nobility*, pp. 21–2; Melton, 'The Prussian Junkers, 1600–1786', p. 104.
66. Namier, *The structure of politics*, pp. 221–5.
67. Callahan, *Honor, commerce and industry*, p. 13 n. 55; Jespersen, 'The rise and fall of the Danish nobility, 1600–1800', in *European nobilities*, ed. Scott, vol. 2, pp. 56–7; M. Raeff, 'Home, school, and service in the life of the 18th-century Russian nobleman', *Slavonic and East European Review*, 40 (1961–2),

pp. 297–307, p. 299; Esper, 'The *odnodvortsy* and the Russian nobility', pp. 124–34; J. V. Beckett, *A history of Laxton: England's last open-field village* (Oxford: Blackwell, 1989), pp. 16–18, 29, 35, 36.

68.   Toth, 'Le monde de la petite noblesse hongroise', p. 175.

Chapter 6: Inheritance

1.   Quoted in Mousnier, *The institutions of France*, vol. 1, p. 51; H. A. Ellis, 'Genealogy, history and aristocratic reaction in early eighteenth-century France: the case of Henri de Boulainvilliers', *Journal of Modern History*, 58/2 (1985), pp. 414–51.

2.   For an entertaining account of this seemingly dry subject, see V. Stater, *High life, low morals: the duel that shook Stuart society* (London: Murray, 1999), esp. pp. 113–17.

3.   G. Tyack, *Warwickshire country houses* (Chichester: Phillimore, 1994), pp. 48–9.

4.   S. Staves, 'Resentment or resignation? Dividing the spoils among daughters and younger sons', in *Early modern conceptions of property*, ed. Brewer and Staves, p. 207.

5.   Cited in J. P. Cooper, 'Patterns of inheritance and settlement by great landowners', in *Family and inheritance*, ed. J. Goody, J. Thirsk and E. P. Thompson (Cambridge: Cambridge University Press, 1976), pp. 192–327, p. 237. The essay is an excellent starting-point for any discussion of noble inheritance.

6.   J. M. Hartley, *A social history of the Russian empire, 1650–1825* (Harlow: Longman, 1999), pp. 218–20; V. Kamendrowsky and D. M. Griffiths, 'The fate of the trading nobility controversy in Russia: a chapter in the relationship between Catherine II and the Russian nobility', *Jahrbücher für Geschichte Osteuropas*, NF, 26 (1978), pp. 203–4; Le Donne, *Absolutism and ruling class*, p. 227; J. Tovrov, *The Russian noble family: structure and change* (New York: Garland, 1987), p. 105.

7.   W. R. Augustine, 'Notes toward a portrait of the eighteenth-century Russian nobility', *Canadian–American Slavic Studies*, 4 (1970), pp. 395–402.

8.   Le Donne, *Absolutism and ruling class*, p. 227.

9.   Cooper, 'Patterns of inheritance', pp. 284–5.

10.   There was some dispute as to whether the 1747 Daguesseau ordinance referred to generations or successive holders: ibid., pp. 267, 270, 275.

11.   J. Van Horn Melton, 'The nobility in the Bohemian and Austrian lands, 1620–1780', in *European nobilities*, ed. Scott, vol. 2, pp. 126–8; P. Schimert, 'The Hungarian nobility in the seventeenth and eighteenth centuries', in ibid., pp. 173–4; T. M. Barker, 'Military nobility: the Daun family and the evolution of the Austrian officer corps', in *Army, aristocracy, monarchy: essays on war, society, and government in Austria, 1618–1780* (New York: Columbia University, 1982), p. 134.

12. A. Goodwin, 'Prussia', in *The European nobility in the eighteenth century*, ed. Goodwin, p. 94; Berdahl, *The politics of the Prussian nobility*, pp. 23–4; Hagen, 'The Junkers' faithless servants', pp. 77–81.

13. There is a huge literature on the subject. See, among others, Stone and Stone, *An open elite?*, pp. 69–79; E. Spring, 'The family, strict settlement and historians', *Canadian Journal of History*, 18/3 (1983), pp. 379–98.

14. Stone and Stone, *An open elite?*, p. 76.

15. J. Habakkuk, *Marriage, debt, and the estates system: English landownership, 1650–1950* (Oxford: Clarendon, 1994), pp. 49–51; Cooper, 'Patterns of inheritance', p. 231; L. Bonfield, 'Marriage settlements, 1660–1740: the adoption of the strict settlement in Kent and Northamptonshire', in *Marriage and society: studies in the social history of marriage*, ed. R. B. Outhwaite (London: Europa, 1981), pp. 104–5.

16. Cannon, *Aristocratic century*, pp. 74–5.

17. Stone and Stone, *An open elite?*, p. 110; Cannon, *Aristocratic century*, p. 82.

18. R. Pillorget, *Le tige et le rameau: familles anglaises et françaises, XVIe–XVIIIe siècles* (Paris: Calmann-Lévy, 1979), p. 181; I. Grundy, *Lady Mary Wortley Montagu: comet of the Enlightenment* (Oxford: Oxford University Press, 1999), pp. 600–9.

19. J. Goody, 'Strategies of heirship', *Comparative Studies in Society & History*, 15 (1973), pp. 3–20; Cannon, *Aristocratic century*, pp. 71–84; Spring, 'The family, strict settlement and historians', pp. 385–6.

20. Habakkuk, *Marriage, debt, and the estates system*, pp. 79–86; Spring, 'The family, strict settlement and historians', p. 391; C. Clay, 'Property settlements, financial provision for the family and sale of land by the greater landowners, 1660–1790', *Journal of British Studies*, 21/1 (1981), p. 31.

21. Cubells, *Provence*, pp. 74–8; Forster, *Merchants, landlords, magistrates*, pp. 14–15, 71, 118, 159–61.

22. Habakkuk, *Marriage, debt, and the estates system*, pp. 79–86; Spring, 'The family, strict settlement and historians', p. 391; D. Rapp, 'Social mobility in the eighteenth century: the Whitbreads of Bedfordshire, 1720–1815', *Economic History Review*, 2nd ser., 27 (1974), p. 388; R. Trumbach, *The rise of the egalitarian family: aristocratic kinship and domestic relations in eighteenth-century England* (New York: Academic Press, 1978), p. 93.

23. T. Astarita, *The continuity of feudal power: the Caracciolo di Brienza in Spanish Naples* (Cambridge: Cambridge University Press, 1992), p. 187.

24. Forster, *Merchants, landlords, magistrates*, p. 123.

25. Forster, *The nobility of Toulouse*, pp. 131–6; Carré, *La noblesse de France*, p. 97; R. B. Litchfield, 'Demographic characteristics of Florentine patrician families, sixteenth to the nineteenth centuries', *Journal of Economic History*, 29 (1969), p. 203.

26. Casey, *Early modern Spain*, p. 147; R. A. C. Parker, *Coke of Norfolk: a financial and agricultural study, 1707–1842* (Oxford: Clarendon, 1975), pp. 94, 130.

27. Clay, 'Property settlements', p. 32.

28. Astarita, *The continuity of feudal power*, pp. 182–9.

29. C. Lévy and L. Henry, 'Ducs et pairs sous l'ancien régime: caractéristique démographique d'une caste', *Population*, 15 (1960), pp. 822–6.

30. Blakiston, *Woburn and the Russells*, pp. 84, 99–102, 141–5, 169; Trumbach, *The rise of the egalitarian family*, p. 96.
31. Cannon, *Aristocratic century*, pp. 104–14.
32. Stone and Stone, *An open elite?*, pp. 214–17.
33. Wordie, *Estate management*, pp. 24–38.
34. Habakkuk, *Marriage, debt, and the estates system*, pp. 108–17.
35. H. Rosenberg, *Bureaucracy, aristocracy and autocracy: the Prussian experience, 1660–1815* (Boston: Beacon, 1966 edn), pp. 76–7; H. C. Johnson, *Frederick the Great and his officials* (New Haven, CN: Yale University Press, 1975), pp. 216–23; I. de Madariaga, *Russia in the age of Catherine the Great* (London: Weidenfeld, 1991), pp. 287–91.
36. Richard, *Noblesse d'affaires*, pp. 54–70.
37. J. Shovlin, 'Toward a reinterpretation of revolutionary antinobilism: the political economy of honor in the Old Regime', *Journal of Modern History*, 72/1 (2000), pp. 35–66.
38. W. H. Whelan, *Adapting to modernity: family, caste and capitalism among the Baltic German nobility* (Cologne: Böhlau, 1999), pp. 41, 151–2.
39. Meyer, 'La noblesse française au XVIIIe siècle', pp. 7–45.
40. Butler, *Choiseul*, vol. 1, p. 895.
41. O. Hufton, *The prospect before her: a history of women in western Europe* (London: HarperCollins, 1995), vol. 1, p. 85.
42. R. Oer, 'Estates and diets in ecclesiastical principalities of the Holy Roman Empire, 18th century', in *Liber memorialis Georges de Lagarde* (Louvain: Nauwelaerts, 1970), pp. 261–81.
43. Pelzer, *Der elsässische Adel*, pp. 181–5; T. C. W. Blanning, *Reform and revolution in Mainz, 1743–1803* (Cambridge: Cambridge University Press, 1974), pp. 52–6, 60; Oer, 'Estates and diets', pp. 261–72; J. Gagliardo, *Reich and nation: the Holy Roman Empire as idea and reality, 1763–1806* (Bloomington: Indiana University Press, 1980), pp. 5–6, 12–15.
44. Berdahl, *The politics of the Prussian nobility*, p. 25; P. Roosevelt, *Life on the Russian country estate: a social and cultural history* (New Haven, CN: Yale University Press, 1995), p. 273.
45. Grundy, *Lady Mary Wortley Montagu*, p. 32.
46. Blanning, *Reform and revolution*, pp. 58–9; Gagliardo, *Reich and nation*, pp. 35–9.
47. G. Hanlon, *The twilight of a military tradition: Italian aristocrats and European conflicts, 1560–1800* (London: UCL, 1998), pp. 209–19, 264–309.
48. Davis, *Venetian nobility*, pp. 47–72; Georgelin, *Venise au siècle des Lumières*, pp. 651–66.
49. R. Ago, 'Ecclesiastical careers and the destiny of cadets', *Continuity and Change*, 7/3 (1992), pp. 271–82.
50. Hufton, *Prospect*, p. 68; Astarita, *The continuity of feudal power*, pp. 182–9.
51. Pillorget, *Le tige et le rameau*, pp. 182–3.
52. Quoted in Davis, *Venetian nobility*, p. 69. On this (in the Anglo-Saxon world) too little known reformer, see M. Maestro, 'Gaetano Filangieri and his science of legislation', *Transactions of the American Philosophical Society*, n.s., 66/6 (1976), pp. 7–71.

53. Quoted in L. R. Farrell, 'Peter the Great's Law of Single Inheritance: state imperatives and noble resistance', *Russian Review*, 55 (1996), p. 442.

Chapter 7: Lifestyles

1. Mousnier, *The institutions of France*, vol. 1, p. 49.
2. First published in 1680, with numerous subsequent editions, including 1693, 1709, 1719, 1728, 1732, 1735, 1784.
3. Forster, *The nobility of Toulouse*, pp. 161–5; Brown, 'Reassessing the influence', p. 187.
4. Stone and Stone, *An open elite?*, p. 69.
5. Brown, 'Reassessing the influence', pp. 182–95; Blakiston, *Woburn and the Russells*, pp. 147–69.
6. C. Jones, 'James Brydges, earl of Carnarvon and the 1717 Hereford by-election: a case study in aristocratic electoral management', *Huntington Library Quarterly*, 46/4 (1983), pp. 310–20; Wordie, *Estate management*, pp. 227–71.
7. Carré, *La noblesse de France*, pp. 73, 80–3.
8. Ingrao, *The Hessian mercenary state*, pp. 112–15; A. Hunt, *Governance of the consuming passions: a history of sumptuary law* (Basingstoke: Macmillan – now Palgrave Macmillan, 1998), pp. 25–37, 341, 350–1; M. Stürmer, 'An economy of delight: court artisans of the eighteenth century', *Business History Review*, 53/4 (1979), pp. 502–3, 505, 512; Chaussinand-Nogaret, *The French nobility in the eighteenth century*, p. 92.
9. Beckett, *The aristocracy in England*, pp. 341–4.
10. Richard, *Noblesse d'affaires*, pp. 27–8.
11. J. Summerson, 'The classical country house in 18th-century England', *Journal of the Royal Society of Arts*, 107 (1958–9), pp. 543–5, 550–1.
12. Roosevelt, *Life on the Russian country estate*, pp. xii, 3.
13. Quoted in ibid., p. 34.
14. Tyack, *Warwickshire country houses*, p. xxiii.
15. J. S. Ackerman, *The villa: form and ideology of country houses* (London: Thames & Hudson, 1990), pp. 157–8; Stone and Stone, *An open elite?*, pp. 329–30; M. Girouard, *Life in the English country house* (Harmondsworth: Penguin, 1980), p. 151.
16. Girouard, *Life in the English country house*, pp. 138–41.
17. Ibid., p. 145.
18. Ibid., pp. 145, 149.
19. Whelan, *Adapting to modernity*, pp. 54–5.
20. Mercier's *Tableau de Paris*, 1780, quoted in Stürmer, 'An economy of delight', p. 497.
21. K. J. Allison, ' "Hull Gent. seeks a country residence", 1750–1850', *East Yorkshire Local History Society*, 36 (1981), pp. 3–6; C. Jones, 'The London life of a peer in the reign of Anne', *London Journal*, 16 (1991), pp. 149, 151.

22. Roosevelt, *Life on the Russian country estate*, pp. 18, 29.
23. Stürmer, 'An economy of delight', p. 496.
24. Roosevelt, *Life on the Russian country estate*, p. 53.
25. Ibid., pp. 246–67.
26. H. W. Eckardt, *Herrschaftliche Jagd, bauerliche Not und bürgerliche Kritik* (Göttingen: Vandenhoeck & Ruprecht, 1976), p. 40.
27. F. Rieupeyroux, 'Le droit de chasse en France de la fin du Moyen Age à la Révolution', *Information Historique*, 46/1 (1984), pp. 9–17.
28. Eckardt, *Herrschaftliche Jagd*, pp. 50–7, 76–89, 139.
29. Roosevelt, *Life on the Russian country estate*, pp. 122–4.
30. Quoted in D. C. Itzkowitz, *Peculiar privilege: a social history of English foxhunting, 1753–1885* (Hassocks: Harvester, 1977), p. 12.
31. Colonel John Cooke, *Observations on fox-hunting*, 1826, quoted in ibid., p. 70; cf. pp. 68–71, 74–7, 84–5, 100.
32. Whelan, *Adapting to modernity*, pp. 60–1.
33. Quoted in A. Ribeiro, *Dress in eighteenth-century Europe, 1715–1789* (London: Batsford, 1984), p. 17. Cf. p. 43.
34. Ibid., p. 48; Forster, *The house of Saulx-Tavanes*, p. 127.
35. Grundy, *Lady Mary Wortley Montagu*, p. 26.
36. W. Coxe, *Travels in Poland and Russia* (repr. of 5th, 1802 edn) (New York: Arno Press, 1970), pp. 167–8.
37. P. Camporesi, *Exotic brew: hedonism and exoticism in the eighteenth century* (Oxford: Polity, 1992), pp. 1–9, 29–30, 33.
38. Carré, *La noblesse de France*, pp. 95–103.
39. R. Porter and G. S. Rousseau, *Gout: the patrician malady* (New Haven, CN: Yale University Press, 2000), pp. 101–24; B. Rizzo, 'Decorums', in *The secret malady: venereal disease in eighteenth-century Britain and France*, ed. L. E. Merians (Lexington: University Press of Kentucky, 1996), p. 149.
40. Tobias Smollett, *The expedition of Humphrey Clinker*, ed. A. Ross (Harmondsworth: Penguin, 1982), p. 66.
41. R. S. Neale, *Bath, 1680–1850: a social history* (London: Routledge, 1981), pp. 25–8.
42. A. Foreman, *Georgiana, duchess of Devonshire* (London: HarperCollins, 1999), pp. 89, 126–7, 161–2, 168, 188–90, 241–2, 253.
43. Roosevelt, *Life on the Russian country estate*, pp. 175–6.
44. Astarita, *The continuity of feudal power*, pp. 47–50; Wordie, *Estate management*, pp. 80–1.
45 McGrew, *Paul I of Russia*, pp. 245–57.
46. M. Andrieux, *Daily life in Venice in the time of Casanova* (London: Allen & Unwin, 1972), p. 70.
47. A. Vickery, *The gentleman's daughter: women's lives in Georgian England* (New Haven, CN: Yale University Press, 1999), pp. 149–50.
48. *Letters of Lord Chesterfield to his son*, p. 302.
49. Ibid., p. 82.
50. Ibid., pp. 72, 73, 93, 122.
51. Ibid., pp. 97, 123, 165.
52. K. Pomian, *Collectors and curiosities: Paris and Venice, 1500–1800* (Oxford: Polity, 1990), pp. 96–7, 227.

53. S. West, 'Introduction: visual culture, performance culture and the Italian diaspora in the long eighteenth century', in *Italian culture in northern Europe in the eighteenth century*, ed. S. West (Cambridge: Cambridge University Press, 1999), p. 9
54. Quoted in Casey, *Early modern Spain*, p. 7.
55. Smollett, *Humphrey Clinker*, p. 364.
56. Pelzer, *Der elsässische Adel*, pp. 120–8.

Chapter 8: Authority

1. Beckett, 'Landownership and estate management', pp. 576–8; Cannadine, *Lords and landlords*, p. 92. The Arnold quotation is from T. Tanner's 'Introduction' to his edition of Jane Austen's *Mansfield Park* (Harmondsworth: Penguin, 1983), p. 12.
2. W. Daniel, 'Conflict between economic vision and economic reality: the case of M. M. Shcherbatov', *Slavonic and East European Review*, 67/1 (1989), pp. 42–67.
3. Cannadine, *Lords and landlords*, p. 27.
4. R. Porter, *English society in the eighteenth century* (Harmondsworth: Penguin, 1983), pp. 143–5; D. Eastwood, *Governing rural England: tradition and transformation in local government, 1780–1840* (Oxford: Clarendon, 1994), pp. 25–8.
5. Soame Jenyns, *Free enquiry into the nature and origin of evil*, 1757, quoted in Cannon, *Aristocratic century*, p. 36. For the wider debate on education, see H. Chisick, *The limits of reform in the Enlightenment: attitudes towards the education of the lower orders in eighteenth-century France* (Princeton, NJ: Princeton University Press, 1981).
6. David Hume, *Of the first principles of government*, 1741, quoted in Cannon, *Aristocratic century*, p. 149.
7. Voltaire, 'Equality', in *Philosophical dictionary* (first published 1764; Harmondsworth: Penguin, 1979), pp. 182–4.
8. Quoted in D. Moon, *The Russian peasantry, 1600–1930: the world the peasants made* (Harlow: Longman, 1999), p. 249.
9. See the observations of L. Weatherill, 'Consumer behaviour and social status in England, 1660–1750', *Continuity and Change*, 1/2 (1986), pp. 191–216, esp. pp. 191–3.
10. J. Money, *Experience and identity: Birmingham and the West Midlands, 1760–1800* (Manchester: Manchester University Press, 1977), pp. 107–8, 168–9; J. Cannon, *Samuel Johnson and the politics of Hanoverian England* (Oxford: Clarendon, 1994), p. 295.
11. Blakiston, *Woburn and the Russells*, p. 106; Wordie, *Estate management*, pp. 240–1.
12. J. M. Neeson, 'The opponents of enclosure in eighteenth-century Northamptonshire', *Past & Present*, 105 (1984), pp. 114–39; Brown, 'Reassessing the influence', pp. 189–91.
13. Porter, *English society*, p. 116; F. O'Gorman, *The long eighteenth century: British political and social history, 1688–1832* (London: Arnold, 1997), p. 229.

14. See Landau, *Justices of the Peace*, pp. 20, 47–8, 143, 202–8, 263–4, 293–4 and *passim*.

15. Whelan, *Adapting to modernity*, p. 54.

16. Stater, *High life, low morals*, pp. 108–9.

17. Alexander Engel'gardt, quoted in Moon, *The Russian peasantry*, p. 274.

18. Jones, *The emancipation of the Russian nobility*, pp. 133–5.

19. J. Held, 'The Horea-Closca revolt of 1784–85: some observations', in *Transylvania: the roots of ethnic conflict*, ed. J. F. Cadzow, A. Ludanyi and L. J. Elteto (Kent, OH: Kent State University Press, 1983), pp. 93–107.

20. P. M. Jones, *The peasantry in the French Revolution* (Cambridge: Cambridge University Press, 1988), p. 66.

21. Jones, *The emancipation of the Russian nobility*, p. 135; I. de Madariaga, 'Catherine II and the serfs: a reconsideration of the problems', *Slavonic and East European Review*, 52 (1974), pp. 48–9.

22. Landau, *Justices of the Peace*, pp. 291–2.

23. H. D. Hudson, *The rise of the Demidov family and the Russian iron industry in the eighteenth century* (Newtonville, MA: ORP, 1996), p. 98.

24. Blum, *The end of the Old Order*, pp. 221–6; H. Liebel-Weckowicz and F. J. Szabo, 'Modernization forces in Maria Theresa's peasant policies, 1740–1780', *Social History/Histoire Sociale*, 15 (1982), pp. 301–31.

25. Hagen, 'The Junkers' faithless servants', pp. 71–101; *idem*, 'Seventeenth-century crisis', pp. 302–35.

26. J. F. Noel, 'Une justice seigneuriale de Haute Bretagne à la fin de l'Ancien Régime', *Annales de Bretagne*, 83/1 (1976), pp. 127–66; O. Hufton, 'The seigneur and the rural community in eighteenth-century France: the seigneurial reaction: a reappraisal', *Transactions of the Royal Historical Society*, 5th ser., 29 (1979), pp. 21–39.

27. Hufton, 'The seigneur and the rural community', pp. 31–2; *idem*, 'Attitudes towards authority in eighteenth-century Languedoc', *Social History*, 3 (1978), pp. 287–92.

28. Butler, *Choiseul*, vol. 1, pp. 772–8.

29. E. Bruley, 'Nobles et paysans picards à la fin de l'Ancien Régime: le marquis de Mailly et son receveur', *Revue d'Histoire Moderne et Contemporaine*, 16 (1969), pp. 606–10.

30. Hufton, 'Attitudes towards authority', pp. 285–6.

31. H. L. Root, 'Challenging the seigneurie: community and contention on the eve of the French Revolution', *Journal of Modern History*, 57/4 (1985), pp. 652–81; A. Barruol and V. Sottocasa, 'Contestation et vie sociale en Basse Provence au XVIIIe siècle', *Provence Historique*, 36 (1986), pp. 277–307; Jones, *The peasantry in the French Revolution*, pp. 67–8.

32. Jones, *The peasantry in the French Revolution*, pp. 67–81.

33. J. Peleński, 'The Cossack insurrections in Jewish–Ukrainian relations', in *Ukrainian–Jewish relations in historical perspective*, ed. H. Aster and P. J. Potichnyi (Edmonton: Canadian Institute of Ukrainian Studies, 1990), pp. 31–42.

34. A. Wilson, 'Diderot in Russia, 1773–1774', in *The eighteenth century in Russia*, ed. J. G. Garrard (Oxford: Clarendon, 1973), pp. 189–90.

35. Held, 'The Horea-Closca revolt of 1784–85', pp. 93–107.

36. J. Topolski, 'Grand domaine et petites exploitations, seigneurs et paysans en Pologne au moyen age et dans les temps modernes', in *Grand domaine et petites exploitations en Europe au moyen age et dans les temps modernes (Large estates and small holdings in Europe in the Middle Ages and modern times)*, ed. P. Gunst and T. Hoffmann (Budapest: Akadémiai Kiádo, 1982), pp. 215–16.

37. E. P. Thompson, *The making of the English working class* (Harmondsworth: Penguin, 1968), pp. 95–125; Cannon, *Samuel Johnson*, p. 154.

Chapter 9: Noblewomen

1. Hannah Woolley, *The gentlewomans companion*, 1675, quoted in L. Vallone, *Disciplines of virtue: girls' culture in the eighteenth and nineteenth centuries* (New Haven, CN: Yale University Press, 1995), p. 30.

2. Montesquieu, *The spirit of the laws*, Book XXVI, ch. 8, p. 502.

3. J.-J. Rousseau, *Émile ou de l'éducation* (Paris: Flammarion, 1966), pp. 470–1. All references to this edition.

4. A. Rogers, 'Women and the law', in *French women and the age of the Enlightenment*, ed. S. I. Spencer (Bloomington: Indiana University Press, 1984), pp. 27–8.

5. N. Pushkareva, *Women in Russian history from the tenth to the twentieth century* (Stroud: Sutton, 1997), p. 177; L. Hughes, *Russia in the age of Peter the Great* (New Haven, CN: Yale University Press, 1998), p. 201.

6. Quoted in R. Weil, *Political passions: gender, the family and political argument in England, 1680–1714* (Manchester: Manchester University Press, 1999), p. 58.

7. Andrieux, *Daily life in Venice*, p. 68.

8. Wordie, *Estate management*, pp. 84, 88–91.

9. Trumbach, *The rise of the egalitarian family*, pp. 80–1; D. Thomas, 'The social origins of marriage partners of the British peerage', *Population Studies*, 26 (1972), pp. 99–111.

10. Pelzer, *Der elsässische Adel*, pp. 108–12; Chaussinand-Nogaret, *The French nobility in the eighteenth century*, pp. 123–7; Roberts, 'Lombardy', p. 102; Georgelin, *Venise au siècle des Lumières*, p. 664.

11. Pillorget, *Le tige et le rameau*, pp. 284–90.

12. Ellis, 'Genealogy, history and aristocratic reaction', pp. 435–6; Pelzer, *Der elsässische Adel*, pp. 108–9; Cannon, *Aristocratic century*, pp. 73–8.

13. Roosevelt, *Life on the Russian country estate*, pp. 107–8.

14. Quoted in Whelan, *Adapting to modernity*, p. 150.

15. Carlsson, 'The dissolution of the Swedish estates', esp. pp. 599–602.

16. Berdahl, *The politics of the Prussian nobility*, p. 25. But cf. E. Melton, 'The Prussian Junkers, 1600–1786', in *European nobilities*, ed. Scott, vol. 2, p. 90; T. Schieder, *Frederick the Great* (Harlow: Longman, 2000), p. 45.

17. D. Roche, *Les Républicains des lettres: gens de culture et lumières au XVIIIe siècle* (Paris: Fayard, 1988), pp. 350–69.

18. I. de Madariaga, 'The foundation of the Russian educational system by Catherine II', *Slavonic and East European Review*, 57/3 (1979), p. 379; Nash, 'Students and nobles', pp. 258–72.

19. Rousseau, *Émile*, pp. 506–7.

20. D. Goodman, *The Republic of Letters: a cultural history of the French Enlightenment* (Ithaca, NY: Cornell University Press, 1994), pp. 91–2, 74–7.

21. Roche, *Les Républicains des lettres*, p. 89; Goodman, *The Republic of Letters*, pp. 104–5, 118–19; J. I. Israel, *Radical Enlightenment: philosophy and the making of modernity, 1650–1750* (Oxford: Oxford University Press, 2001), pp. 82–96; Foreman, *Georgiana*, p. 14.

22. Rousseau, *Émile*, pp. 482–3, 490–1, 507, 512, 515.

23. F. Barrême, *L'Aritmétique de Barrême, ou le livre facile pour apprendre l'aritmétique de soy-même et sans maître*, enlarged 1706 edition, with numerous reprints into the nineteenth century.

24. Rousseau's views are found most clearly in Book V of *Émile*.

25. Quoted in Vickery, *The gentleman's daughter*, p. 221.

26. Quoted in Roosevelt, *Life on the Russian country estate*, p. 138.

27. J. Lewis, ' "'Tis a misfortune to be a great ladie": maternal mortality in the British aristocracy, 1558–1959', *Journal of British Studies*, 37 (1998), pp. 26–53. For a brilliant account of the work and abilities of a magnificent early modern midwife, see S. Schama, *The embarrassment of riches: an interpretation of Dutch culture in the Golden Age* (London: Collins, 1987), pp. 525–35.

28. Porter and Rousseau, *Gout*, p. 102; V. Fildes, *Wet nursing: a history from antiquity to the present* (Oxford: Blackwell, 1987), pp. 79–92, 111–26; C. Fairchilds, 'Women and family', in *French women and the age of the Enlightenment*, ed. Spencer, pp. 100–2.

29. Foreman, *Georgiana*, pp. 122–3, 251.

30. H. Wunder, *He is the sun, she is the moon: women in early modern Germany* (Cambridge, MA: Harvard University Press, 1998), p. 19; Foreman, *Georgiana*, p. 123.

31. Vickery, *The gentleman's daughter*, pp. 132–4; Tovrov, *The Russian noble family*, pp. 115–22; Pushkareva, *Women in Russian history*, pp. 96–7, 110, 147.

32. Vickery, *The gentleman's daughter*, pp. 159–60, 218–19.

33. Quoted in S. Staves, *Married women's separate property in England, 1660–1833* (Cambridge, MA: Harvard University Press, 1990), pp. 39, 27–54.

34. Habakkuk, *Marriage, debt, and the estates system*, p. 8.

35. Ibid., pp. 83–9; Staves, *Married women's separate property*, pp. 95–105.

36. Foreman, *Georgiana*, p. 42.

37. Staves, *Married women's separate property*, pp. 49–54.

38. Rizzo, 'Decorums', pp. 156–63.

39. B. Meehan-Waters, 'The development and the limits of security of noble status, person and property in eighteenth-century Russia', in *Russia and the West in the eighteenth century*, ed. A. G. Cross (Newtonville, MA: ORP, 1983), pp. 294–305.

40. M. L. Marrese, 'The enigma of married women's control of property in eighteenth-century Russia', *Russian Review*, 58/3 (1999), pp. 380–95; also J. M. Hartley, *A social history of the Russian empire, 1650–1825* (Harlow: Longman, 1999), pp. 213–14, 218–20; Foreman, *Georgiana*, p. 88.

41. Astarita, *The continuity of feudal power*, pp. 54–5, 193–9.

42. Grundy, *Lady Mary Wortley Montagu*, p. 25.

43. Astarita, *The continuity of feudal power*, pp. 172–3.

44. Grundy, *Lady Mary Wortley Montagu*, p. 48.
45. Vickery, *The gentleman's daughter*, pp. 20, 73–9.
46. Casey, *Early modern Spain*, pp. 200–1.
47. Vickery, *The gentleman's daughter*, p. 82.
48. J. Brewer, *The pleasures of the imagination: English culture in the eighteenth century* (New York: Farrar, Straus, Giroux, 1997), pp. xxii–xxiii, 179, 193–7.
49. B. Meehan-Waters, *Autocracy & aristocracy: the Russian service elite of 1730* (New Brunswick, NJ: Rutgers University Press, 1982), pp. 106–14; Tovrov, *The Russian noble family*, pp. 237–50, 290.
50. Fairchilds, 'Women and family', p. 99.
51. Rogers, 'Women and the law', p. 40. See also D. Andrew, ' "Adultery à-la-mode": privilege, the law and attitudes to adultery, 1770–1809', *History*, 82/265 (1997), pp. 5–23.
52. Davis, *Venetian nobility*, pp. 63–4, 68–70.
53. K. Norberg, 'From courtesan to prostitute: mercenary sex and venereal disease, 1730–1820', in *The secret malady*, ed. Merians, pp. 42–3.
54. Andrieux, *Daily life in Venice*, pp. 136–7, 148–52. On the cicisbeo in England, see Foreman, *Georgiana*, p. 54.
55. Habakkuk, *Marriage, debt, and the estates system*, pp. 117–26, 139.
56. Vickery, *The gentleman's daughter*, p. 14.
57. Astarita, *The continuity of feudal power*, pp. 173, 176–7, 181–7.
58. Davis, *Venetian nobility*, pp. 62–3; Andrieux, *Daily life in Venice*, pp. 168–70.
59. Meyer, 'La noblesse française au XVIIIe siècle', pp. 34–5. Admittedly, Meyer himself is the first to concede the speculative nature of these figures.
60. Roosevelt, *Life on the Russian country estate*, p. 179.
61. J. V. Beckett, 'Elizabeth Montagu: bluestocking turned landlady', *Huntington Library Quarterly*, 49 (1986), pp. 149–64; Pushkareva, *Women in Russian history*, pp. 146–50.
62. Brewer, *Pleasures of the imgination*, pp. 397–400; Foreman, *Georgiana*, p. 37.
63. W. Konopczyński, *Kiedy nami rządziły kobiety* (London, 1960) (published posthumously).
64. L. Colley, *Britons: forging the nation, 1707–1837* (New Haven, CN: Yale University Press, 1992), pp. 242–50. For a less than satisfactory introduction to the role of women in Polish politics, see M. Bogucka, 'Women in politics: the case of Poland in the 16th–18th centuries', *Acta Poloniae Historica*, 83 (2001), pp. 79–93.

Epilogue: The European Nobility and the French Revolution

1. Jones, *The emancipation of the Russian nobility*, pp. 275–6.
2. Translated from *Select documents illustrative of the French Revolution*, ed. L. G. Wickham Legg (Oxford: Clarendon, 1905), pp. 19–20.
3. J. M. Thompson, *The French Revolution* (Oxford: Blackwell, 1943), pp. 17–25; *The French Revolution: voices from a momentous epoch, 1789–1795*, ed. R. Cobb and C. Jones (London: Guild Publishing, 1988), pp. 60–3.
4. *The French Revolution*, ed. Cobb and Jones, pp. 77–84.

5. Jones, *The peasantry in the French Revolution*, pp. 67–85; *idem, Reform and Revolution in France*, pp. 180–6.
6. Gagliardo, *Reich and nation*, pp. 125–9.
7. *The French Revolution*, ed. Cobb and Jones, p. 80.
8. Higonnet, *Class, ideology and the rights of nobles*.
9. Ibid., pp. 58, 267; R. Forster, 'The survival of the French nobility during the French Revolution', *Past & Present*, 36 (1967), pp. 74–5. The actual percentages will vary, depending on the estimate of the size of the French pre-revolutionary nobility.
10. Doyle, *Venality*, pp. 275–308.
11. Higonnet, *Class, ideology and the rights of nobles*, p. 45.
12. Ibid., pp. 138–9.
13. See the entries for the two Chérins in *Dictionnaire de biographie française*, vol. 8, ed. M. Prevost and R. D'Amrat (Paris: Letouzey, 1959), cols. 1012–1014.
14. J.-D. Bredin, *Sieyès: la clé de la révolution française* (Paris: Fallois, 1988), pp. 678–82.
15. W. H. Zawadzki, *A man of honour: Adam Czartoryski as a statesman of Russia and Poland, 1795–1831* (Oxford: Clarendon, 1993), pp. 99–101.
16. The estimates vary. Behrens, *Society, government and the Enlightenment*, p. 14; J.-F. Zieseniss, 'Napoléon et la noblesse impériale', *Revue du Souvenir Napoléonien*, 313 (1980), pp. 3–24 (also available on line at http://www.napoleon. org/fr/salle_lecture/articles/files/Napoleon_noblesse2.asp); D. M. G. Sutherland, *France, 1789–1815: revolution and counterrevolution* (London: Fontana, 1985), pp. 366–9.
17. Louis-Gustave Doulcet de Pontécoulant, quoted by Higonnet, *Class, ideology and the rights of nobles*, p. 262.
18. Behrens, *Society, government and the Enlightenment*, p. 14.
19. Higonnet, *Class, ideology and the rights of nobles*, pp. 70–2.
20. A. L. Cardoza, *Aristocrats in bourgeois Italy: the Piedmontese nobility, 1861–1930* (Cambridge: Cambridge University Press, 1997), pp. 26–32.
21. Thompson, *The making of the English working class*, pp. 155–8; G. Woodcock, 'The meaning of revolution in Britain, 1770–1800', in *The French Revolution and British culture*, ed. C. Crossley and I. Small (Oxford: Oxford University Press, 1989), pp. 1–30.
22. Quoted in Behrens, *Society, government and the Enlightenment*, p. 45.
23. D. Lieven, *The aristocracy in Europe, 1815–1914* (Basingstoke: Macmillan – now Palgrave Macmillan, 1992), p. 2.
24. Beckett, 'Landownership and estate management', pp. 546–7; Lieven, *The aristocracy in Europe*, p. 23.
25. For a striking account of this in Britain, see D. Cannadine, *The decline and fall of the British aristocracy* (New Haven, CN: Yale University Press, 1990). At a wider European level, see Lieven, *The aristocracy in Europe*.

A SELECT BIBLIOGRAPHY OF
WORKS IN ENGLISH

Many of the non-English-language works consulted can be found in the notes; references to some of the primary sources used can also be found there.

Ackerman, J. S., *The villa: form and ideology of country houses* (London: Thames & Hudson, 1990).

Adamson, J., 'The making of the Ancien-Régime court, 1500–1700', in *The princely courts of Europe: ritual, politics and culture under the Ancien Régime, 1500–1700*, ed. J. Adamson (London: Weidenfeld & Nicolson, 1999).

Adamson, J. (ed.), *The princely courts of Europe: ritual, politics and culture under the Ancien Régime, 1500–1700* (London: Weidenfeld & Nicolson, 1999).

Ago, R., 'Ecclesiastical careers and the destiny of cadets', *Continuity and Change*, 7/3 (1992), pp. 271–82.

Allison, K. J., ' "Hull Gent. seeks a country residence", 1750–1850', *East Yorkshire Local History Society*, 36 (1981).

Allmayer-Beck, J. C., 'The establishment of the Theresian Military Academy in Wiener Neustadt', in *Essays on pre-revolutionary eighteenth-century east central European society and war*, ed. B. K. Király, G. E. Rothenberg and P. Sugar (New York: Columbia University Press, 1982).

Andrew, D. T., ' "Adultery à-la-mode": privilege, the law and attitudes to adultery, 1770–1809', *History*, 82/265 (1997), pp. 5–23.

Andrew, D. T., 'The code of honour and its critics: the opposition to duelling in England, 1700–1850', *Social History*, 5/3 (1980), pp. 409–34.

Andrieux, M., *Daily life in Venice in the time of Casanova* (London: Allen & Unwin, 1972).

Arriaza, A., 'Mousnier and Barber: the theoretical underpinning of the "Society of Orders" in early modern Europe', *Past & Present*, 89 (1980), pp. 39–57.

Astarita, T., *The continuity of feudal power: the Caracciolo di Brienza in Spanish Naples* (Cambridge: Cambridge University Press, 1992).

Augustine, W. R., 'Notes toward a portrait of the eighteenth-century Russian nobility', *Canadian–American Slavic Studies*, 4 (1970), pp. 373–425.

Bamford, P. W., *Privilege and profit: a business family in eighteenth-century France* (Philadelphia: University of Pennsylvania Press, 1988).

215

Barker, T. M., 'Armed service and nobility: general features', in *idem, Army, aristocracy, monarchy: essays on war, society, and government in Austria, 1618–1780* (New York: Columbia University Press, 1982), pp. 22–36.

Barker, T. M., 'Military nobility: the Daun family and the evolution of the Austrian officer corps', in *idem, Army, aristocracy, monarchy: essays on war, society, and government in Austria, 1618–1780* (New York: Columbia University Press, 1982), pp. 128–46.

Bartlett, R. P., 'J. J. Sievers and the Russian peasantry under Catherine II', *Jahrbücher für Geschichte Osteuropas*, 32 (1984), pp. 16–33.

Baugh, D. A. (ed.), *Aristocratic government and society in eighteenth-century England* (New York: New Viewpoints, 1975).

Becker, S., *Nobility and privilege in late imperial Russia* (Dekalb: Illinois University Press, 1985).

Beckett, J. V., *The aristocracy in England, 1660–1914* (Oxford: Blackwell, 1986).

Beckett, J. V., *Coal and tobacco: the Lowthers and the economic development of West Cumberland, 1660–1760* (Cambridge: Cambridge University Press, 1981).

Beckett, J. V., 'Elizabeth Montagu: bluestocking turned landlady', *Huntington Library Quarterly*, 49 (1986), pp. 149–64.

Beckett, J. V., 'The English aristocracy', *Parliamentary History*, 5 (1986), pp. 133–42.

Beckett, J. V., 'English landownership in the later seventeenth and eighteenth centuries: the debate and the problems', *Economic History Review*, 2nd ser., 30 (1977), pp. 567–81.

Beckett, J. V., *A history of Laxton: England's last open-field village* (Oxford: Blackwell, 1989).

Beckett, J. V., 'Landownership and estate management', in *The agrarian history of England and Wales*, vol. 6 (1750–1850), ed. J. Thirsk (Cambridge: Cambridge University Press, 1989), pp. 545–640.

Beckett, J. V., *The rise and fall of the Grenvilles: dukes of Buckingham and Chandos, 1710 to 1921* (Manchester: Manchester University Press, 1994).

Behrens, C. B. A., 'Government and society', in *Cambridge economic history of Europe*, vol. 5, ed. E. E. Rich & C. H. Wilson (Cambridge: Cambridge University Press, 1977), pp. 549–620.

Behrens, C. B. A., 'Nobles, privileges and taxes in France at the end of the Ancien Régime', *Economic History Review*, 2nd ser., 15 (1962–3), pp. 451–75.

Behrens, C. B. A., *Society, government and the Enlightenment: the experiences of eighteenth-century France and Prussia* (London: Thames & Hudson, 1985).

Berdahl, R. M., *The politics of the Prussian nobility: the development of a conservative ideology, 1770–1848* (Princeton, NJ: Princeton University Press, 1988).

Bien, D., 'The army in the French Enlightenment: reform, reaction and revolution', *Past & Present*, 85 (1979), pp. 68–98.

Bien, D., 'Manufacturing nobles: the chancelleries in France to 1789', *Journal of Modern History*, 61 (1981), pp. 445–86.

Bien, D., 'The secrétaires du roi: absolutism, corps and privilege under the Ancien Régime', in *Vom Ancien Régime zur Französischen Revolution*, ed. E. Hinrichs and others (Göttingen: Vandenhoeck & Ruprecht, 1978), pp. 153–69.

Billacois, F., *The duel: its rise and fall in early modern France* (New Haven, CN: Yale University Press, 1990).

Black, J., *The British and the Grand Tour* (London: Croom Helm, 1985).

Blakiston, G., *Woburn and the Russells* (London: Constable, 1980).

Blanning, T. C. W., *Reform and revolution in Mainz, 1743–1803* (Cambridge: Cambridge University Press, 1974).

Blum, J., *The end of the Old Order in rural Europe* (Princeton, NJ: Princeton University Press, 1978).

Blum, J., *Lord and peasant in Russia from the ninth to the nineteenth century* (Princeton, NJ: Princeton University Press, 1971).

Bonfield, L., ' "Affective families", "open elites" and family settlements in early modern England', *Economic History Review*, 2nd ser., 39/3 (1986), pp. 341–54.

Bonfield, L. 'Marriage settlements and the "rise of great estates": the demographic aspect', *Economic History Review*, 2nd ser., 22 (1979), pp. 483–93.

Bonfield, L., 'Marriage settlements, 1660–1740: the adoption of the strict settlement in Kent and Northamptonshire', in *Marriage and society: studies in the social history of marriage*, ed. R. B. Outhwaite (London: Europa, 1981), pp. 101–16.

Bonney, R., ' "Le secret de leurs familles": the fiscal and social limits of Louis XIV's *Dixième*', *French History*, 7/4 (1993), pp. 383–416.

Brewer, J., *The pleasures of the imagination: English culture in the eighteenth century* (New York: Farrar, Straus, Giroux, 1997).

Brooks, C., 'Public finances and political stability: the administration of the Land Tax, 1688–1720', *Historical Journal*, 17 (1974), pp. 281–300.

Brown, D. 'Reassessing the influence of the aristocratic improver: the example of the fifth duke of Bedford (1765–1802)', *Agricultural History Review*, 47/2 (1999), pp. 182–95.

Brown, J. H., 'The free economic society and the nobility, 1765–96: some observations', *Canadian–American Slavic Studies*, 14/3 (1980), pp. 427–35.

Burke, P., 'The language of orders in early modern Europe', in *Social classes & social orders in Europe since 1500: studies in social stratification*, ed. M. L. Bush (Harlow: Longman, 1992), pp. 1–12.

Büsch, O., *Military system and social life in Old Regime Prussia* (Atlantic Highlands, NJ: Humanities Press, 1996).

Bush, M. L., 'An anatomy of nobility', in *Social classes & social orders in Europe since 1500: studies in social stratification*, ed. M. L. Bush (Harlow: Longman, 1992), pp. 26–46.

Bush, M. L., *The English aristocracy: a comparative synthesis* (Manchester: Manchester University Press, 1984).

Bush, M. L., *Noble privilege* (Manchester: Manchester University Press, 1983).

Bush, M. L., *Rich noble, poor noble* (Manchester: Manchester University Press, 1988).

Bush, M. L. (ed.), *Social classes & social orders in Europe since 1500: studies in social stratification* (Harlow: Longman, 1992).

Butler, R., *Choiseul* (Oxford: Clarendon, 1980), vol. 1.

Butterwick, R., *Poland's last king and English culture: Stanisław August Poniatowski, 1732–1798* (Oxford: Clarendon, 1998).

Callahan, W. J., *Honor, commerce and industry in eighteenth-century Spain* (Clifton, NJ: A. M. Kelley, 1972).

Camporesi, P., *Exotic brew: hedonism and exoticism in the eighteenth century* (Oxford: Polity, 1992).

Cannadine, D., *The decline and fall of the British aristocracy* (New Haven: Yale University Press, 1990).

Cannadine, D., *Lords and landlords: the aristocracy and the towns, 1774–1967* (Leicester: Leicester University Press, 1980).

Cannon, J., *Aristocratic century: the peerage of eighteenth-century England* (Cambridge: Cambridge University Press, 1984).

Cannon, J., 'The British nobility, 1660–1800', in *The European nobilities in the seventeenth and eighteenth centuries*, ed. H. M. Scott (Harlow: Longman, 1995), vol. 1, pp. 53–81.

Cannon, J., 'The isthmus repaired: the resurgence of the English aristocracy, 1660–1760', *Proceedings of the British Academy*, 68 (1982), pp. 431–53.

Cannon, J., *Samuel Johnson and the politics of Hanoverian England* (Oxford: Clarendon, 1994).

Cardoza, A., *Aristocrats in bourgeois Italy: the Piedmontese nobility, 1861–1930* (Cambridge: Cambridge University Press, 1997).

Carlsson, S., 'The dissolution of the Swedish estates (1700–1865)', *Journal of European Economic History*, 1/3 (1972), pp. 574–624.

Carr, R., 'Spain', in *The European nobility in the eighteenth century*, ed. A. Goodwin (London: Black, 1967), pp. 43–59.

Carsten, F. L., *A history of the Prussian Junkers* (Aldershot: Scolar Press, 1989).

Casey, J., *Early modern Spain: a social history* (London: Routledge, 1999).

Cavallo, S., *Charity and power in early modern Italy: benefactors and their motives in Turin, 1541–1789* (Cambridge: Cambridge University Press, 1995).

Chaney, E., *The evolution of the Grand Tour* (London: Cass, 1998).

Chaussinand-Nogaret, G., *The French nobility in the eighteenth century*, trans. W. Doyle (Cambridge: Cambridge University Press), 1985.

Clark, S., *State and status: the rise of the state and aristocratic power in western Europe* (Cardiff: University of Wales Press, 1995).

Clay, C., 'English landlords and estate management', in *The agrarian history of England and Wales*, vol. 5 (1640–1750), pt 2, ed. J. Thirsk (Cambridge: Cambridge University Press, 1982), pp. 119–251; also in *Chapters from The agrarian history of England and Wales, vol. 2, Rural society: landowners, peasants and labourers*, ed. C. Clay (Cambridge: Cambridge University Press, 1982), pp. 246–378.

Clay, C., 'Marriage, inheritance and the rise of large estates in England, 1660–1815', *Economic History Review*, 2nd ser., 21 (1968), pp. 503–18.

Clay, C., 'Property settlements, financial provision for the family and sale of land by the greater landowners, 1660–1790', *Journal of British Studies*, 21/1 (1981), pp. 18–38.

Cobban, A., 'The *parlements* of France in the eighteenth century', *History*, 35 (1950), pp. 64–80.

Coley, L., *Britons: forging the nation, 1707–1837* (New Haven, CN: Yale University Press, 1992).

Collins, J. B., *The state in early modern France* (Cambridge: Cambridge University Press, 1995).

Confino, M., 'The limits of autocracy: Russia's economy and society in the age of Enlightenment', *Peasant Studies*, 13/3 (1986), pp. 149–70.

Cooper, J. P., 'Patterns of inheritance and settlement by great landowners', in *Family and inheritance*, ed. J. Goody, J. Thirsk and E. P. Thompson (Cambridge: Cambridge University Press, 1976), pp. 192–327.

Corfield, P. J., 'Class by name and number in eighteenth-century Britain', *History*, 72/234 (1987), pp. 38–61.

Cracraft, J., *The Church reform of Peter the Great* (London: Macmillan – now Palgrave Macmillan, 1971).

Cracraft, J., 'The succession crisis of 1730: a view from the inside', *Canadian–American Slavic Studies*, 12/1 (1978), pp. 60–85.

Crummey, R. O., 'Peter and the boiar aristocracy, 1689–1700', *Canadian–American Slavic Studies*, 8/2 (1974), pp. 274–87.

Crummey, R. O., 'Russian absolutism and the nobility', *Journal of Modern History*, 49 (1977), pp. 456–67.

Daniel, W., 'Conflict between economic vision and economic reality: the case of MM Shcherbatov', *Slavonic and East European Review*, 67/1 (1989), pp. 42–67.

Daniels, R. L., 'V. N. Tatishchev and the succession crisis of 1730', *Slavonic and East European Review*, 49 (1971), pp. 550–9.

Daniels, S., *Humphry Repton: landscape gardening and the geography of Georgian England* (New Haven, CN: Yale University Press, 1999).

Davis, J. C., *The decline of the Venetian nobility as a ruling class* (Baltimore: Johns Hopkins Press, 1962).

De Madariaga, I., 'The foundation of the Russian educational system by Catherine II', *Slavonic and East European Review*, 57/3 (1979), pp. 369–95.

De Madariaga, I., *Russia in the age of Catherine the Great* (London: Weidenfeld, 1991).

De Madariaga, I., 'The Russian nobility in the seventeenth and eighteenth centuries', in *The European nobilities in the seventeenth and eighteenth centuries*, ed. H. M. Scott (Harlow: Longman, 1995), vol. 1, pp. 223–73.

Desan, S., ' "War between brothers and sisters": inheritance law and gender politics in revolutionary France', *French Historical Studies*, 20/4 (1997), pp. 597–634.

Devine, T. M., 'Glasgow colonial merchants and land, 1770–1815', in *Land and industry*, ed. J. T. Ward and R. G. Wilson (Newton Abbot: David & Charles, 1971), pp. 203–65.

Devine, T. M., *The transformation of rural Scotland: social change and the agrarian economy, 1660–1815* (Edinburgh: John Donald, 1994).

Devine, T. M. and Young, J. R. (eds.), *Eighteenth-century Scotland: new perspectives* (East Linton: Tuckwell Press, 1999).

Dewald, J., *Aristocratic experience and the origins of modern culture: France, 1570–1715* (Berkeley: University of California Press, 1993).

Dewald, J., *The European nobility, 1400–1800* (Cambridge: Cambridge University Press, 1996).

Dewald, J., *Pont-St-Pierre, 1398–1789: lordship, community, and capitalism in early modern France* (Berkeley: University of California Press, 1987).

Dickens, A. G. (ed.), *The courts of Europe: politics, patronage and royalty, 1400–1800* (London: Thames & Hudson), 1977.

Dickson, P. G. M., *Finance and government under Maria Theresa, 1740–1780*, 2 vols. (Oxford: Clarendon, 1987).

Di Corcia, J., 'Bourg, Bourgeois, Bourgeois de Paris from the eleventh to the eighteenth century', *Journal of Modern History*, 50 (1978), pp. 207–331.

Donati, C., 'The Italian nobilities in the seventeenth and eighteenth centuries', in *The European nobilities in the seventeenth and eighteenth centuries*, ed. H. M. Scott (Harlow: Longman, 1995), vol. 1, pp. 237–68.

Donovan, A., *Antoine Lavoisier: science, administration, and revolution* (Oxford: Blackwell, 1993).

Doyle, W., 'Myths of order and ordering myths', in *Social classes & social orders in Europe since 1500: studies in social stratification*, ed. M. L. Bush (Harlow: Longman, 1992), pp. 218–29.

Doyle, W., *The parlement of Bordeaux and the end of the Old Regime, 1771–1790* (London: Benn, 1974).

Doyle, W., 'The price of offices in eighteenth-century France', *Historical Journal*, 27/4 (1984), pp. 831–60.

Doyle, W., *Venality: the sale of offices in eighteenth-century France* (Oxford: Clarendon, 1996).

Duffy, C., *The army of Frederick the Great* (Newton Abbot: David & Charles, 1974).

Dunkley, J., *Gambling: a social and moral problem in France, 1685–1792* (Studies on Voltaire and the Eighteenth Century, vol. 235) (Oxford: Taylor Foundation, 1985).

Eastwood, D., *Governing rural England: tradition and transformation in local government, 1780–1840* (Oxford: Clarendon, 1994).

Ellis, H. A., *Boulainvilliers and the French monarchy: aristocratic politics in early eighteenth-century France* (Ithaca, NY: Cornell University Press, 1988).

Ellis, H. A., 'Genealogy, history and aristocratic reaction in early eighteenth-century France: the case of Henri de Boulainvilliers', *Journal of Modern History*, 58/2 (1985), pp. 414–51.

English, B., *The great landowners of East Yorkshire, 1530–1910* (Hemel Hempstead: Harvester, 1990).

Esper, T., 'The *odnodvortsy* and the Russian nobility', *Slavonic and East European Review*, 45 (1967), pp. 124–34.

Fairchilds, C., 'Women and family', in *French women and the age of the Enlightenment*, ed. S. I. Spencer (Bloomington: Indiana University Press, 1984), pp. 97–110.

Farrell, L. R., 'Peter the Great's Law of Single Inheritance: state imperatives and noble resistance', *Russian Review*, 55 (1996), pp. 430–47.

Fawcett, T., *Bath entertain'd: amusements, recreations and gambling at the 18th-century spa* (Bath: Ruton, 1998).

Fildes, V., *Wet nursing: a history from antiquity to the present* (Oxford: Blackwell, 1987).

Firth, G., 'The roles of a West Riding land steward, 1773–1803', *Yorkshire Archaeological Journal*, 56 (1979), pp. 105–15.

Fitzsimmons, M. P., 'Privilege and the polity in France, 1786–1791', *American Historical Review*, 92/2 (1987), pp. 269–95.

Ford, F. L., *Robe and sword: the regrouping of the French aristocracy after Louis XIV* (Cambridge, MA: Harvard University Press, 1953).

Ford, G. S., 'The Prussian peasantry before 1807', *American Historical Review*, 24/3 (1919), pp. 358–78.

Foreman, A., *Georgiana, duchess of Devonshire* (London: Harper Collins, 1998).

Forster, R., 'The French provincial noble: a reappraisal', *American Historical Review*, 68 (1963), pp. 681–91.

Forster, R., *The house of Saulx-Tavanes: Versailles and Burgundy* (Baltimore: Johns Hopkins, 1971).

Forster, R., *Merchants, landlords, magistrates: the Depont family in eighteenth-century France* (Baltimore: Johns Hopkins, 1980).

Forster, R., *The nobility of Toulouse in the eighteenth century: a social and economic study* (Baltimore: Johns Hopkins, 1960).

Forster, R., 'The noble wine producers of the Bordelais in the eighteenth century', *Economic History Review*, 2nd ser., 14 (1961), pp. 18–33.

Forster, R., 'Obstacles to agricultural growth in eighteenth-century France', *American Historical Review*, 75 (1975), pp. 1600–15.

Forster, R., 'Seigneurs and their agents', in *Vom Ancien Régime zur Französischen Revolution*, ed. E. Hinrichs and others (Göttingen: Vandenhoeck & Ruprecht, 1978), pp. 169–87.

Forster, R., 'The survival of the French nobility during the French Revolution', *Past & Present*, 36 (1967), pp. 71–86.

Frevert, U., *Men of honour: a social and cultural history of the duel* (Cambridge: Polity, 1995).

Frost, R. I., 'The nobility of Poland–Lithuania, 1569–1795', in *The European nobilities in the seventeenth and eighteenth centuries*, ed. H. M. Scott (Harlow: Longman, 1995), vol. 1, pp. 183–222.

Gagliardo, J., *Reich and nation: the Holy Roman Empire as idea and reality, 1763–1806* (Bloomington: Indiana University Press, 1980).

Gates-Coon, R., *The landed estate of the Esterházy princes: Hungary during the reforms of Maria Theresa and Joseph II* (Baltimore: Johns Hopkins, 1994).

Giesey, R. E., 'Rules of inheritance and strategies of mobility in prerevolutionary France', *American Historical Review*, 82 (1977), pp. 271–89.

Ginter, D. E., *A measure of wealth: the English land tax in historical analysis* (London: Hambledon, 1992).

Girouard, M., *Life in the English country house* (Harmondsworth: Penguin, 1980).

Girouard, M., *Life in the French country house* (London: Cassell, 2000).

Givens, R. D., 'Eighteenth-century nobiliary career patterns and provincial government', in *Russian officialdom: the bureaucratization of Russian society from the seventeenth to the twentieth century*, ed. W. M. Pintner and D. K. Rowney (London: Macmillan – now Palgrave Macmillan, 1980), pp. 106–29.

Givens, R. D., 'Supplication and reform in the instructions of the nobility', *Canadian–American Slavic Studies*, 11/4 (1977), pp. 483–502.

Goodman, D., *The Republic of Letters: a cultural history of the French Enlightenment* (Ithaca, NY: Cornell University Press, 1994).

Goodwin, A., 'Prussia', in *The European nobility in the eighteenth century*, ed. A. Goodwin (London: Black, 1967), pp. 83–101.

Goodwin, A., 'The social origins and privileged status of the French eighteenth-century nobility', *Bulletin of the John Rylands Library*, 47 (1964–5), pp. 382–403.

Goodwin, A., 'The social structure and economic and political attitudes of the French nobility in the eighteenth century', *XIIe Congrès International des Sciences Historiques, 1965. Rapports*, vol. 1 (Horn, Vienna: F. Burger, 1966), pp. 356–68.

Goodwin, A. (ed.), *The European nobility in the eighteenth century* (London: Black, 1953; 2nd edn, 1967).

Goody, J., 'Strategies of heirship', *Comparative Studies in Society & History*, 15 (1973), pp. 3–20.

Goubert, P., *The Ancien Régime: French society, 1600–1750* (London: Weidenfeld, 1973).

Griffiths, D., 'Catherine's charters: a question of motivation', *Canadian–American Slavic Studies*, 23/1 (1989), pp. 58–82.

Gruder, V. R., *The royal provincial intendants: a governing elite in eighteenth-century France* (Ithaca, NY: Cornell University Press, 1968).

Gruder, V. R., 'The society of orders at its demise: the vision of the élite at the end of the *Ancien Régime*', *French History*, 1/2 (1987), pp. 210–37.

Grundy, I., *Lady Mary Wortley Montagu: comet of the Enlightenment* (Oxford: Oxford University Press, 1999).

Gunn, J. A. W., 'Eighteenth-century Britain: in search of the state and finding the quarter session', *Re-thinking Leviathan: the eighteenth-century state in Britain and Germany*, ed. J. Brewer and E. Hellmuth (Oxford: Oxford University Press, 1999), pp. 99–125.

Habakkuk, J., 'England', in *The European nobility in the eighteenth century*, ed. A. Goodwin (London: Black, 1967), pp. 1–21.

Habakkuk, J., 'English landownership, 1680–1740', *Economic History Review*, 1st ser., 10 (1940), pp. 2–17.

Habakkuk, J., *Marriage, debt, and the estates system: English landownership, 1650–1950* (Oxford: Clarendon, 1994).

Habakkuk, J., 'The rise and fall of English landed families, 1600–1800', pts. 1, 2, *Transactions of the Royal Historical Society*, 5th ser., 29 (1979), pp. 187–207; 30 (1980), pp. 199–221.

Hagen, W. W., 'The Junkers' faithless servants: peasant insubordination and the breakdown of serfdom in Brandenburg–Prussia, 1763–1811', in *The German peasantry: conflict and community in rural society from the eighteenth to the twentieth centuries*, ed. R. J. Evans and W. R. Lee (London: Croom Helm, 1986), pp. 71–101.

Hagen, W. W., 'Seventeenth-century crisis in Brandenburg: the Thirty Years' War, the destabilization of serfdom, and the rise of absolutism', *American Historical Review*, 94/2 (1989), pp. 302–35.

Hagen, W. W., 'Working for the Junker: the standard of living of manorial laborers in Brandenburg, 1384–1810', *Journal of Modern History*, 58 (1986), pp. 143–58.

Hajnal, H., 'European marriage patterns in perspective', in *Population in history: essays in historical demography*, ed. D. V. Glass and D. E. C. Eversley (London: Arnold, 1965), pp. 101–34.

Hammond, J. L., *The village labourer, 1760–1832: a study in the government of England before the Reform Bill* (Gloucester: Sutton, 1987).

Hanlon, G., *The twilight of a military tradition: Italian aristocrats and European conflicts, 1560–1800* (London: UCL, 1998).

Harnisch, H., 'Peasants and markets: the background to the agrarian reforms in feudal Prussia east of the Elbe, 1760–1807', in *The German peasantry: conflict and community in rural society from the eighteenth to the twentieth centuries*, ed. R. J. Evans and W. R. Lee (London: Croom Helm, 1986), pp. 37–70.

Hartley, J. M., *A social history of the Russian empire, 1650–1825* (Harlow: Longman, 1999).

Hayter, T., *The army and the crowd in mid-Georgian England* (London: Macmillan – now Palgrave Macmillan, 1978).

Held, J., 'The Horea-Cloşca revolt of 1784–85: some observations', in *Transylvania: the roots of ethnic conflict*, ed. J. F. Cadzow, A. Ludanyi and L. J. Elteto (Kent, OH: Kent State University Press, 1983), pp. 93–107.

Herr, R., *Rural change and royal finances in Spain at the end of the Old Regime* (Berkeley: University of California Press, 1989).

Hexter, J. H., 'The education of the aristocracy in the Renaissance', in *idem, Reappraisals in history* (Harlow: Longman, 1961), pp. 45–70.

Hibberd, C., *The Grand Tour* (London: Weidenfeld, 1969).

Higonnet, P., ' "Aristocrate", "Aristocratie": language and politics in the French Revolution', in *The French Revolution, 1789–1989: two hundred years of rethinking*, ed. S. Peluy (Special Issue, *The Eighteenth Century: theory & interpretation*, 1989), pp. 47–66.

Higonnet, P. *Class, ideology and the rights of nobles during the French Revolution* (Oxford: Clarendon, 1981).

Hintze, O., 'The Hohenzollern and the nobility', in *The historical essays of Otto Hintze*, ed. F. Gilbert (New York: Oxford University Press, 1975), pp. 35–63.

Holderness, B. A., 'Landlords' capital formation in East Anglia', *Economic History Review*, 2nd ser., 25 (1972), pp. 434–47.

Hollingsworth, T. H., 'The demography of the British peerage', supplement to *Population Studies*, 18 (1964).

Horn, P., 'An eighteenth-century land agent: the career of Nathaniel Kent (1737–1810)', *Agricultural History Review*, 30/1 (1982), pp. 1–16.

Horwitz, H., ' "The mess of the middle class" revisited', *Continuity and Change*, 2/2 (1987), pp. 263–96.

Houston, R. A., 'Coal, class and culture: labour relations in a Scottish mining community, 1650–1750', *Social History*, 8 (1983), pp. 1–18.

Hudson, H. D., *The rise of the Demidov family and the Russian iron industry in the eighteenth century* (Newtonville, MA: ORP, 1996).

Hudson, H. D., 'Urban estate engineering in eighteenth-century Russia: Catherine the Great and the elusive *Meshchanstvo*', *Canadian–American Slavic Studies*, 18/1 (1984), pp. 393–410.

Hufton, O., 'Attitudes towards authority in eighteenth-century Languedoc', *Social History*, 3 (1978), pp. 281–302.

Hufton, O., *The prospect before her: a history of women in western Europe*, vol. 1, *1500–1800* (London: Harper Collins, 1995).

Hufton, O., 'The seigneur and the rural community in eighteenth-century France. The seigneurial reaction: a reappraisal', *Transactions of the Royal Historical Society*, 5th ser., 29 (1979), pp. 21–39.

Hughes, E., 'The eighteenth-century estate agent', in *Essays in British and Irish history*, ed. H. A. Cronne, T. W. Moody and D. B. Quinn (London: Muller, 1949), pp. 185–99.

Hughes, L., *Russia in the age of Peter the Great* (New Haven, CN: Yale University Press, 1998).

Hunt, A., *Governance of the consuming passions: a history of sumptuary law* (Basingstoke: Macmillan – now Palgrave Macmillan, 1998).

Ingamells, J. (ed.), *A dictionary of British and Irish travellers in Italy, 1701–1800* (New Haven, CN: Yale University Press, 1997).

Ingrao, C. W., *The Hessian mercenary state: ideas, institutions, and reform under Frederick II, 1760–1785* (Cambridge: Cambridge University Press, 1987).

Israel, J. I., *Radical Enlightenment: philosophy and the making of modernity, 1650–1750* (Oxford: Oxford University Press, 2001).

Itzkowitz, D. C., *Peculiar privilege: a social history of English foxhunting, 1753–1885* (Hassocks: Harvester, 1977).

James, F., *Lords of the ascendancy, 1600–1800* (Dublin: IAP, 1995).

Jenkins, P., *The making of a ruling class: the Glamorgan gentry, 1640–1790* (Cambridge: Cambridge University Press, 1983).

Jespersen, K. J. V., 'The rise and fall of the Danish nobility, 1600–1800', in *The European nobilities in the seventeenth and eighteenth centuries*, ed. H. M. Scott (Harlow: Longman, 1995), vol. 2, pp. 41–70.

Johnson, H. C., *Frederick the Great and his officials* (New Haven, CN: Yale University Press, 1975).

Jones, C., 'The London life of a peer in the reign of Anne', *London Journal*, 16 (1991), pp. 140–55.

Jones, C., ' "Venice Preserv'd; or A Plot Discovered": the political and social context of the Peerage Bill of 1719', in *A pillar of the constitution: the House of Lords in British politics, 1640–1784*, ed. C. Jones (London: Hambledon, 1989), pp. 79–112.

Jones, P. M., *The peasantry in the French Revolution* (Cambridge: Cambridge University Press, 1988).

Jones, P. M., *Politics and rural society: the southern Massif Central, c. 1750–1880* (Cambridge: Cambridge University Press, 1985).

Jones, P. M., *Reform and revolution in France: the politics of transition, 1774–1791* (Cambridge: Cambridge University Press, 1995).

Jones, R. E., 'The Charter to the Nobility: a legislative landmark?', *Canadian–American Slavic Studies*, 23/1 (1989), pp. 1–16.

Jones, R. E., *The emancipation of the Russian nobility, 1762–1785* (Princeton, NJ: Princeton University Press, 1973).

Kahan, A., 'The costs of "westernization" in Russia: the gentry and the economy in the eighteenth century', *Slavic Review*, 25 (1966), pp. 40–66.

Kahan, A., *The plow, the hammer and the knout: an economic history of eighteenth-century Russia* (Chicago: Chicago University Press, 1985).

Kahk, J. and Tarvel, E., 'Large estates and small holdings in Estonia from the 16th to the 19th centuries', in *Grand domaine et petites exploitations en Europe au moyen age et dans les temps modernes (Large estates and small holdings in Europe in the*

Middle Ages and modern times), ed. P. Gunst and T. Hoffmann (Budapest: Akadémiai Kiádo, 1982), pp. 361–77.

Kamendrowsky, V. & Griffiths, D. M., 'The fate of the trading nobility controversy in Russia: a chapter in the relationship between Catherine II and the Russian nobility', *Jahrbücher für Geschichte Osteuropas*, NF, 26 (1978), pp. 198–221.

Kann, R. A., 'The social prestige of the officer corps in the Habsburg empire from the eighteenth century to 1918', in *War and society in east central Europe*, ed. B. K. Király and G. E. Rothenberg (New York: Columbia University Press, 1979), pp. 113–37.

Keep, J. H. L., *Soldiers of the tsar: army and society in Russia, 1462–1874* (Oxford: Clarendon, 1985).

Kelly, G. A., 'Duelling in eighteenth-century France: archaeology, rationale, implications', in *The Eighteenth Century: Theory & Interpretation*, 21/3 (1980), pp. 236–54.

Kiernan, V. E., *The duel in European history: honour and the reign of aristocracy* (Oxford: Oxford University Press, 1988).

Klein, L. E., 'The third earl of Shaftesbury and the progress of politeness', *Eighteenth-Century Studies*, 18 (1984–5), pp. 186–214.

Klingensmith, S. J., *The utility of splendor: ceremony, social life, and architecture at the court of Bavaria, 1600–1800* (Chicago: Chicago University Press, 1993).

Kohut, Z., 'The Ukrainian elite in the eighteenth century and its integration into the Russian nobility', in *The nobility in Russia and eastern Europe*, ed. I. Banac and P. Bushkovitch (New Haven, CN: Yale University Press, 1983), pp. 65–97.

Kopczyński, M., 'The nobility and the state in the 16th–18th centuries: the Swedish model', *Acta Poloniae Historica*, 77 (1998), pp. 111–26.

Kramar, Z., 'The military ethos of the Hungarian nobility, 1700–1848', in *War and society in east central Europe*, ed. B. K. Király and G. E. Rothenberg (New York: Columbia University Press, 1979), pp. 67–79.

Kula, W., *An economic theory of the feudal system* (London: NLB, 1976).

Kula, W., 'The seigneury and the peasant family in eighteenth-century Poland', in *Family and society: selections from the Annales E.S.C.*, ed. R. Forster and O. Ranum (Baltimore: Johns Hopkins, 1976), pp. 192–203.

Kwass, M., 'A kingdom of taxpayers: state formation, privilege, and political culture in eighteenth-century France', *Journal of Modern History*, 70/2 (1998), pp. 295–339.

Landau, N., *The Justices of the Peace, 1679–1760* (Berkeley: University of California Press, 1984).

Langford, P., *Public life and the propertied Englishman, 1689–1798* (Oxford: Clarendon, 1991).

Le Donne, J. P., *Absolutism and ruling class: the formation of the Russian political order, 1700–1825* (New York: Oxford University Press, 1991).

Le Donne, J. P., *Ruling Russia: politics and administration in the age of absolutism, 1762–1796* (Princeton, NJ: Princeton University Press, 1984).

Levron, J., *Daily life at Versailles in the seventeenth and eighteenth centuries* (London: Allen & Unwin, 1968).

Lewis, J., ' " 'Tis a misfortune to be a great ladie": maternal mortality in the British aristocracy, 1558–1959', *Journal of British Studies*, 37 (1998), pp. 26–53.

Liebel-Weckowicz, H. and Szabo, F. J., 'Modernization forces in Maria Theresa's peasant policies, 1740–1780', *Social History/Histoire Sociale*, 15 (1982), pp. 301–31.

Lieven, D., *The aristocracy in Europe, 1815–1914* (Basingstoke: Macmillan – now Palgrave Macmillan, 1992).

Link, E. M., *The emancipation of the Austrian peasantry, 1740–1789* (New York: Columbia University Press, 1949).

Litchfield, R. B., 'Demographic characteristics of Florentine patrician families, sixteenth to the nineteenth centuries', *Journal of Economic History*, 29 (1969), pp. 191–205.

Lowe, W. C., 'George III, peerage creations and politics, 1760–1784', *Historical Journal*, 35 (1992), pp. 587–609.

Lucas, C., 'Nobles, bourgeois and the origins of the French Revolution', *Past & Present*, 60 (1973), pp. 84–126.

Lucas, P., 'A collective biography of students and barristers of Lincoln's Inn, 1680–1804: a study of the "aristocratic resurgence" in the eighteenth century', *Journal of Modern History*, 46 (1974), pp. 227–61.

Luebke, D. M., 'Serfdom and honour in eighteenth-century Germany', *Social History*, 18/2 (1993), pp. 143–61.

Lukowski, J. T., *Liberty's folly: the Polish–Lithuanian Commonwealth in the eighteenth century, 1697–1795* (London: Routledge, 1991).

MaCartney, C. A., 'Austria', in *The European nobility in the eighteenth century*, ed. A. Goodwin (London: Black, 1967), pp. 118–34.

MaCartney, C. A., *The Habsburg empire, 1790–1918* (London: Weidenfeld, 1968).

McCahill, M. W., 'Open elites: recruitment to the French *noblesse* and the English aristocracy in the eighteenth century', *Albion*, 30/4 (1998), pp. 599–629.

McCahill, M. W., 'Peerage creations and the changing character of the British nobility, 1750–1850', *English Historical Review*, 96/379 (1981), pp. 259–84.

McCahill, M. W., 'Peers, patronage and the industrial revolution, 1760–1800', *Journal of British Studies*, 16/1 (1976), pp. 84–107.

McCahill, M. W., 'The Scottish peerage and the House of Lords in the late eighteenth century', *Scottish Historical Review*, 51 (1972), pp. 172–96.

McClelland, C., 'The aristocracy and university reform in eighteenth-century Germany', in *Schooling and society: studies in the history of education*, ed. L. Stone (Baltimore: Johns Hopkins University Press, 1978), pp. 146–73.

McClelland, C., *State, society and university in Germany, 1700–1914* (Cambridge: Cambridge University Press, 1980).

McGrew, R. E., *Paul I of Russia, 1754–1801* (Oxford: Clarendon, 1992).

McGrew, R. E., 'The politics of absolutism: Paul I and the Bank of Assistance for the Nobility', in *Paul I: a reassessment of his life and reign*, ed. H. Ragsdale (Pittsburgh, PA: Pittsburgh University Press, 1979), pp. 104–24.

McManners, J., 'France', in *The European nobility in the eighteenth century*, ed. A. Goodwin (London: Black, 1967), pp. 22–42.

Malcomson, A. P. W., *The pursuit of the heiress: aristocratic marriage in Ireland, 1750–1820* (Antrim: Ulster Historical Foundation, 1982).

Malet, H., *Bridgewater: the canal duke* (Manchester: Manchester University Press, 1977).

Mansel, P., *The court of France, 1789–1830* (Cambridge: Cambridge University Press, 1988).

Marrese, M. L., 'The enigma of married women's control of property in eighteenth-century Russia', *Russian Review*, 58/3 (1999), pp. 380–95.

Maxwell, K., *Pombal: paradox of the Enlightenment* (Cambridge: Cambridge University Press, 1995).

Mayer, A. J., *The persistence of the Old Regime: Europe to the Great War* (London: Croom Helm, 1981).

Maza, S., 'Luxury, morality and social change: why there was no middle-class consciousness in pre-revolutionary France', *Journal of Modern History*, 69 (1997), pp. 199–229.

Meehan-Waters, B., *Autocracy & aristocracy: the Russian service elite of 1730* (New Brunswick, NJ: Rutgers University Press, 1982).

Meehan-Waters, B., 'The development and the limits of security of noble status, person and property in eighteenth-century Russia', in *Russia and the West in the eighteenth century*, ed. A. G. Cross (Newtonville, MA: ORP, 1983), pp. 294–305.

Meehan-Waters, B., 'Elite politics and autocratic power', in *Great Britain and Russia in the eighteenth century: contacts and comparisons*, ed. A. G. Cross (Newtonville, MA: ORP, 1979), pp. 229–46.

Meehan-Waters, B., 'The Muscovite noble origins of the Russians in the Generalitet of 1730', *Cahiers du Monde Russe et Soviétique*, 12 (1971), pp. 28–75.

Meehan-Waters, B., 'The Russian aristocracy and the reforms of Peter the Great', *Canadian–American Slavic Studies*, 8/3 (1974), pp. 288–302.

Meehan-Waters, B., 'Social and career characteristics of the administrative elite, 1689–1761', in *Russian officialdom: the bureaucratization of Russian society from the seventeenth to the twentieth century*, ed. W. M. Pintner and D. K. Rowney (London: Macmillan – now Palgrave Macmillan, 1980), pp. 76–105.

Melton, E., 'The decline of Prussian *Gutsherrschaft* and the rise of the Junker as rural patron, 1750–1806', *German History*, 12 (1994), pp. 334–50.

Melton, E. 'The Prussian Junkers, 1600–1786', in *The European nobilities in the seventeenth and eighteenth centuries*, ed. H. M. Scott (Harlow: Longman, 1995), vol. 2, pp. 71–109.

Merians, L. E. (ed.), *The secret malady: venereal disease in eighteenth-century Britain and France* (Lexington: University Press of Kentucky, 1996).

Mettam, R. 'The French nobility, 1610–1715', in *The European nobilities in the seventeenth and eighteenth centuries*, ed. H. M. Scott (Harlow: Longman, 1995), vol. 1, pp. 114–41.

Mingay, G. E., *English landed society in the eighteenth century* (London: Routledge & Kegan Paul, 1970).

Mingay, G. E., 'Thrumpton: a Nottinghamshire estate in the eighteenth century', *Transactions of the Thoroton Society*, 61 (1957), pp. 50–6.

Money, J., *Experience and identity: Birmingham and the West Midlands, 1760–1800* (Manchester: Manchester University Press, 1977).

Moon, D., *The Russian peasantry, 1600–1930: the world the peasants made* (Harlow: Longman, 1999).

Motley, M., *Becoming a French aristocrat: the education of the court nobility, 1580–1715* (Princeton, NJ: Princeton University Press, 1990).

Mousnier, R., *The institutions of France under the absolute monarchy*, 2 vols. (Chicago: Chicago University Press, 1979–84).

Mousnier, R., *Social hierarchies* (London: Croom Helm, 1973).

Musgrave, A., *Land and economy in baroque Italy: Valpolicella, 1630–1797* (Leicester: Leicester University Press, 1992).

Namier, L., *The structure of politics at the accession of George III* (London: Macmillan – now Palgrave Macmillan, 1973).

Nash, C. S., 'Students and nobles: the Society for the Education of Noble Girls as a charitable institution', in *Russia and the world of the eighteenth century*, ed. R. P. Bartlett, A. G. Cross and K. Rasmussen (Columbus, OH: Slavica, 1988), pp. 258–72.

Neale, R. S., *Bath, 1680–1850: a social history* (London: Routledge, 1981).

Neeson, J. M., *Commoners: common right, enclosure and social change in England, 1700–1820* (Cambridge: Cambridge University Press, 1993).

Neeson, J. M., 'The opponents of enclosure in eighteenth-century Northamptonshire', *Past & Present*, 105 (1984), pp. 114–39.

Norberg, K., 'From courtesan to prostitute: mercenary sex and venereal disease, 1730–1820', in *The secret malady: venereal disease in eighteenth-century Britain and France*, ed. L. E. Merians (Lexington: University of Kentucky Press, 1996), pp. 34–50.

Oer, R., 'Estates and diets in ecclesiastical principalities of the Holy Roman Empire, 18th century', *Liber Memorialis Georges de Lagarde* (Louvain: Nauwelaerts, 1970), pp. 261–81.

Okenfuss, M. J., *The rise and fall of Latin humanism in early-modern Russia: pagan authors, Ukrainians, and the resiliency of Muscovy* (Leiden: Brill, 1995).

Pach, Z. P., 'Labour control on the Hungarian landlords' demesnes in the 16th and 17th centuries', in *Grand domaine et petites exploitations en Europe au moyen age et dans les temps modernes (Large estates and small holdings in Europe in the Middle Ages and modern times)*, ed. P. Gunst and T. Hoffmann (Budapest: Akadémiai Kiádo, 1982), pp. 157–73.

Palmer, R. R., *The age of the democratic revolution*, vol. 1, *The challenge* (Princeton, NJ: Princeton University Press, 1969).

Parker, R. A. C., *Coke of Norfolk: a financial and agricultural study, 1701–1842* (Oxford: Clarendon, 1975).

Parker, R. A. C., 'Coke of Norfolk and the agrarian revolution', *Economic History Review*, 2nd ser., 8 (1955–6), pp. 156–66.

Parker, R. A. C., 'Direct taxation on the Coke estates in the eighteenth century', *English Historical Review*, 71 (1956), pp. 247–8.

Pedlow, G. W., *The survival of the Hessian nobility, 1770–1870* (Princeton, NJ: Princeton University Press, 1987).

Peleński, J., 'The Cossack insurrections in Jewish–Ukrainian relations', in *Ukrainian–Jewish relations in historical perspective*, ed. H. Aster and P. J. Potichnyi (Edmonton: Canadian Institute of Ukrainian Studies, 1990), pp. 31–42.

Peller, S., 'Births and deaths among Europe's ruling families since 1500', in *Population in history: essays in historical demography*, ed. D. V. Glass and D. E. C. Eversley (London: Arnold, 1965), pp. 87–100.

Pintner, W. M., 'The evolution of civil officialdom, 1755–1855', in *Russian officialdom: the bureaucratization of Russian society from the seventeenth to the twentieth century*, ed. W. M. Pintner and D. K. Rowney (London: Macmillan – now Palgrave Macmillan, 1980), pp. 190–226.

Plakans, A., 'Seigneurial authority and peasant family life: the Baltic area in the 18th century', *Journal of Interdisciplinary History*, 5/4 (1974–5), pp. 629–54.

Plumb, J. H., 'The Walpoles: father and son', in *Studies in social history*, ed. J. H. Plumb (London: Longmans, 1955), pp. 179–207.

Pomian, K., *Collectors and curiosities: Paris and Venice, 1500–1800* (Oxford: Polity, 1990).

Port, M. H., 'West End palaces: the aristocratic town house in London, 1739–1830', *London Journal*, 20 (1995), pp. 17–46.

Porter, R. *English society in the eighteenth century* (Harmondsworth: Penguin, 1983).

Porter, R. and Rousseau, G. S., *Gout: the patrician malady* (New Haven, CN: Yale University Press, 2000).

Powis, J., *Aristocracy* (Oxford: Blackwell, 1984).

Price, J. L., 'The Dutch nobility in the seventeenth and eighteenth centuries', in *The European nobilities in the seventeenth and eighteenth centuries*, ed. H. M. Scott (Harlow: Longman, 1995), vol. 1, pp. 82–113.

Pushkareva, N., *Women in Russian history from the tenth to the twentieth century* (Stroud: Sutton, 1997).

Raeff, M., 'Home, school, and service in the life of the 18th-century Russian nobleman', *Slavonic and East European Review*, 40 (1961–2), pp. 297–307.

Raeff, M., 'The Russian nobility in the eighteenth and nineteenth centuries: trends and comparisons', in *The nobility in Russia and eastern Europe*, ed. I. Banac and P. Bushkovitch (New Haven, CN: Yale University Press, 1983), pp. 99–121.

Raeff, M., 'State and nobility in the ideology of M. M. Shcherbatov', *American Slavic and East European Review*, 19 (1960), pp. 363–79.

Rapp, D., 'Social mobility in the eighteenth century: the Whitbreads of Bedfordshire, 1720–1815', *Economic History Review*, 2nd ser., 27 (1974), pp. 380–94.

Ravitch, N., 'The social origins of French and English bishops in the eighteenth century', *Historical Journal*, 8 (1965), pp. 309–25.

Raybould, T. J., 'Aristocratic landowners and the industrial revolution: the Black Country experience, c. 1760–c. 1840', *Midland History*, 9 (1984), pp. 59–86.

Raybould, T. J., 'The development and organization of Lord Dudley's mineral estates, 1774–1845', *Economic History Review*, 2nd ser., 21 (1968), pp. 529–44.

Reden-Dohna, A. von, 'Problems of small estates of the empire: the example of the Swabian imperial prelates', *Journal of Modern History*, Supplement (1986), pp. S76–S87.

Redford, B., *Venice and the Grand Tour* (New Haven, CN: Yale University Press, 1996).

Ribeiro, A., *Dress in eighteenth-century Europe, 1715–1789* (London: Batsford, 1984).

Richards, E., 'The industrial face of a great estate: Trentham and Lilleshall, 1780–1860', *Economic History Review*, 2nd ser., 27 (1974), pp. 414–30.

Roberts, J. M., 'Lombardy', in *The European nobility in the eighteenth century*, ed. A. Goodwin (London: Black, 1967).

Roberts, M., 'Sweden', in *The European nobility in the eighteenth century*, ed. A. Goodwin (London: Black, 1967), pp. 136–53.

Rogers, A., 'Women and the law', in *French women and the age of the Enlightenment*, ed. S. I. Spencer (Bloomington: Indiana University Press, 1984), pp. 33–48.

Roosevelt, P., *Life on the Russian country estate: a social and cultural history* (New Haven, CN: Yale University Press, 1995).

Root, H. L., 'Challenging the seigneurie: community and contention on the eve of the French Revolution', *Journal of Modern History*, 57/4 (1985), pp. 652–81.

Rosenberg, H., *Bureaucracy, aristocracy and autocracy: the Prussian experience, 1660–1815* (Boston, MA: Beacon, 1966; first publ. Harvard University Press, 1958).

Rowlands, G., 'The ethos of blood and changing values? Robe, épée and the French armies, 1661 to 1715', *Seventeenth-century French Studies*, 19 (1997), pp. 95–108.

Rowlands, G., 'Louis XIV, aristocratic power and the elite units of the French army', *French History*, 13/3 (1999), pp. 303–31.

Sagarra, E., *A social history of Germany, 1648–1914* (London: Methuen, 1977).

Schenk, H. G., 'Austria', in *The European nobility in the eighteenth century*, ed. A. Goodwin (London: Black, 1967), pp. 102–17.

Schimert, P., 'The Hungarian nobility in the seventeenth and eighteenth centuries', in *The European nobilities in the seventeenth and eighteenth centuries*, ed. H. M. Scott (Harlow: Longman, 1995), vol. 2, pp. 144–82.

Scott, H. M. (ed.), *The European nobilities in the seventeenth and eighteenth centuries*, 2 vols. (Harlow: Longman, 1995).

Serna, P., 'The noble', in *Enlightenment portraits*, ed. M. Vovelle (Chicago: Chicago University Press, 1997), pp. 30–84.

Shackleton, R., 'The Grand Tour in the eighteenth century', in *The modernity of the eighteenth century*, ed. L. T. Milic (Cleveland, OH: Case Western Reserve University Press, 1971), pp. 127–42.

Shaw, J. S., *The management of Scottish society, 1707–1764: power, nobles, lawyers, Edinburgh agents and English influences* (Edinburgh: John Donald, 1983).

Shennan, J. H., *Philippe, duke of Orléans: regent of France, 1715–1723* (London: Thames & Hudson, 1979).

Sheppard, F., 'The Grosvenor estates, 1677–1977', *History Today* (Nov. 1977), pp. 726–33.

Shovlin, J., 'Toward a reinterpretation of revolutionary antinobilism: the political economy of honor in the Old Regime', *Journal of Modern History*, 72/1 (2000), pp. 35–66.

Sire, H. J. A., *The Knights of Malta* (New Haven, CN: Yale University Press, 1994).

Slicher van Bath, B. H., 'Eighteenth-century agriculture on the continent of Europe: evolution or revolution?', *Agricultural History*, 42 (1968), pp. 169–79.

Smith, J. M., *The culture of merit: nobility, royal service, and the making of absolute monarchy in France, 1600–1789* (Ann Arbor: Michigan University Press, 1996).

Smith, J. M., 'Social categories, the language of patriotism, and the origins of the French Revolution: the debate over *noblesse commerçante*', *Journal of Modern History*, 72/2 (2000), pp. 339–74.

Spencer, S. I., 'Women and education', in *French women and the age of the Enlightenment*, ed. S. I. Spencer (Bloomington: Indiana University Press, 1984), pp. 83–96.

Spring, E., 'The family, strict settlement and historians', *Canadian Journal of History*, 18/3 (1983), pp. 379–98.

Spring, E., *Law, land & family: aristocratic inheritance in England, 1300–1800* (Chapel Hill: University of North Carolina Press, 1994).

Spring, D. and Spring, E., 'Social mobility and the English landed elite', *Canadian Journal of History*, 26 (1986), pp. 333–51.

Stater, V., *High life, low morals: the duel that shook Stuart society* (London: Murray, 1999).

Staves, S., *Married women's separate property in England, 1660–1833* (Cambridge, MA: Harvard University Press, 1990).

Staves, S., 'Resentment or resignation? Dividing the spoils among daughters and younger sons', in *Early modern conceptions of property*, ed. J. Brewer and S. Staves (London: Routledge, 1995), pp. 194–218.

Stone, L. and Stone, J. C. F., *An open elite? England, 1540–1880* (Oxford: Clarendon, 1984; and 1995 abridged edn).

Storrs, C. and Scott, H. M., 'The military revolution and the European nobility, c. 1600–1800', *War in History*, 3/1 (1996), pp. 1–41.

Stürmer, M., 'An economy of delight: court artisans of the eighteenth century', *Business History Review*, 53/4 (1979), pp. 496–528.

Sugarman, D. and Warrington, R., 'Land law, citizenship, and the invention of "Englishness": the strange world of the equity of redemption', in *Early modern conceptions of property*, ed. J. Brewer and S. Staves (London: Routledge, 1995), pp. 111–43.

Summerson, J., 'The classical country house in 18th-century England', *Journal of the Royal Society of Arts*, 107 (1958–9), pp. 539–87.

Supple, J., 'François de la Noue and the education of the French "noblesse d'épée"', *French Studies*, 36 (1982), pp. 270–81.

Swann, J., 'The French nobility, 1715–1789', in *The European nobilities in the seventeenth and eighteenth centuries*, ed. H. M. Scott (Harlow: Longman, 1995), vol. 1, pp. 142–73.

Szabo, F. A. J., *Kaunitz and enlightened absolutism, 1753–1780* (Cambridge: Cambridge University Press, 1994).

Tackett, T., 'Nobles and Third Estate in the revolutionary dynamic of the National Assembly, 1789–1790', *American Historical Review*, 94/2 (1989), pp. 271–301.

Tadmore, N., *Family and friends in eighteenth-century England: household, kinship and patronage* (Cambridge: Cambridge University Press, 2000).

Taylor, G. V., 'Types of capitalism in eighteenth-century France', *English Historical Review*, 79 (1964), pp. 478–97.

Thomas, D., 'The social origins of marriage partners of the British peerage', *Population Studies*, 26 (1972), pp. 99–111.

Thompson, E. P., 'Eighteenth-century English society: class struggle without class?', *Social History*, 3 (1978), pp. 133–65.

Thompson, E. P., 'Patrician society, plebeian culture', *Journal of Social History*, 7 (1974), pp. 382–405.

Thompson, F. M. L., 'Landownership and economic growth in England in the eighteenth century', in *Agrarian change and economic development: the historical problems*, ed. E. L. Jones and A. J. Woolf (London: Methuen, 1969), pp. 41–60.

Thompson, F. M. L., 'The social distribution of landed property in England since the sixteenth century', *Economic History Review*, 2nd ser., 19 (1966), pp. 505–17.

Thompson, I. A. A., 'The nobility in Spain, 1600–1800', in *The European nobilities in the seventeenth and eighteenth centuries*, ed. H. M. Scott (Harlow: Longman, 1995), vol. 1, pp. 174–236.

Tovrov, J., *The Russian noble family: structure and change* (New York: Garland, 1987).

Trumbach, R., *The rise of the egalitarian family: aristocratic kinship and domestic relations in eighteenth-century England* (New York: Academic Press, 1978).

Tyack, G., *Warwickshire country houses* (Chichester: Phillimore, 1994).

Tyack, G., *Warwickshire country houses in the age of classicism, 1650–1800* (Warwickshire Local History Society: Occasional Paper No. 3, 1980).

Upton, A., 'The Swedish nobility, 1600–1772', in *The European nobilities in the seventeenth and eighteenth centuries*, ed. H. M. Scott (Harlow: Longman, 1995), vol. 2, pp. 11–40.

Vallone, L., *Disciplines of virtue: girls' culture in the eighteenth and nineteenth centuries* (New Haven, CN: Yale University Press, 1995).

Van Horn Melton, J., 'The nobility in the Bohemian and Austrian lands, 1620–1780', in *The European nobilities in the seventeenth and eighteenth centuries*, ed. H. M. Scott (Harlow: Longman, 1995), vol. 2, pp. 110–43.

Vickery, A., *The gentleman's daughter: women's lives in Georgian England* (New Haven, CN: Yale University Press, 1999).

Wallbank, M. V., 'Eighteenth-century public schools and the education of the governing elite', *History of Education*, 8 (1979), pp. 1–19.

Wasson, E. A., 'The penetration of new wealth into the English governing class from the Middle Ages to the First World War', *Economic History Review*, 2nd ser., 51 (1998), pp. 25–48.

Weatherhill, L., 'Consumer behaviour and social status in England, 1660–1750', *Continuity and Change*, 1/2 (1986), pp. 191–216.

Webb, S. and Webb, B., *English local government*: vol. 2/1, *The manor and the borough* (London: Cass, 1963).

Welby, G., 'Rulers of the countryside: the Justice of the Peace in Nottinghamshire, 1775–1800', *Transactions of the Thoroton Society*, 78 (1974), pp. 75–87.

West, S. (ed.), *Italian culture in northern Europe in the eighteenth century* (Cambridge: Cambridge University Press, 1999).

Whatley, C. A., 'The dark side of the Enlightenment? Sorting out serfdom', in *Eighteenth-century Scotland: new perspectives*, ed. T. M. Devine and J. R. Young (East Linton: Tuckwell Press, 1999), pp. 259–74.

Whelan, H. W., *Adapting to modernity: family, caste and capitalism among the Baltic German nobility* (Cologne: Böhlau, 1999).

Wick, D. L., 'The court nobility and the French Revolution: the example of the Society of Thirty', *Eighteenth Century Studies*, 13 (1980), pp. 263–84; also in *The French Revolution in social and political perspective*, ed. P. M. Jones (London: Arnold, 1996), pp. 214–30.

Williams, J. D., 'The finances of an eighteenth-century Essex nobleman', *Transactions of the Essex Archaeological Society*, 9 (1977), pp. 113–28.

Williamson, T., *Polite landscapes: gardens and society in eighteenth-century England* (Stroud: Sutton, 1995).

Wilson, A., 'Diderot in Russia, 1773–1774', in *The eighteenth century in Russia*, ed. J. G. Garrard (Oxford: Clarendon, 1973), pp. 166–97.

Wilson, P. H., 'Social militarization in eighteenth-century Germany', *German History*, 18/1 (2000), pp. 1–39.

Wilson, R. G., 'Denisons and Milneses: eighteenth-century merchant landowners', in *Land and industry*, ed. J. T. Ward and R. G. Wilson (Newton Abbot: David & Charles, 1971), pp. 145–72.

Woolf, S. J., 'The aristocracy in transition: a continental comparison', *Economic History Review*, 2nd ser., 23 (1970), pp. 520–31.

Wordie, J. R., *Estate management in eighteenth-century England: the building of the Leveson-Gower fortune* (London: Royal Historical Society, 1982).

Wordie, J. R., 'Social change on the Leveson-Gower estates, 1714–1832', *Economic History Review*, 2nd ser., 27 (1974), pp. 593–609.

Wright, W. E., *Serf, seigneur and sovereign: agrarian reform in eighteenth-century Bohemia* (Minneapolis: University of Minnesota Press, 1961).

Wunder, H., *He is the sun, she is the moon: women in early modern Germany* (Cambridge, MA: Harvard University Press, 1998).

Zielińska, T., 'Noblewomen's property rights in 16th–18C. Polish–Lithuanian Commonwealth', *Acta Poloniae Historica*, 81 (2000), pp. 79–89.

Żytkowicz, L., 'Grain yields in Poland, Bohemia, Hungary and Slovakia in the 16th to 18th centuries', *Acta Poloniae Historica*, 24 (1971), pp. 51–72.

INDEX